T-LEVELS
THE NEXT LEVEL QUALIFICATION

AGRICULTURE, ENVIRONMENT AND ANIMAL CARE

CORE

Robin Jackson

Sally Green

HODDER
Education

'T-LEVELS' is a registered trade mark of the Department for Education.

'T Level' is a registered trade mark of the Institute for Apprenticeships and Technical Education. The T Level Technical Qualification is a qualification approved and managed by the Institute for Apprenticeships and Technical Education.

Although every effort has been made to ensure that website addresses are correct at time of going to press, Hodder Education cannot be held responsible for the content of any website mentioned in this book. It is sometimes possible to find a relocated web page by typing in the address of the home page for a website in the URL window of your browser.

Hachette UK's policy is to use papers that are natural, renewable and recyclable products and made from wood grown in well-managed forests and other controlled sources. The logging and manufacturing processes are expected to conform to the environmental regulations of the country of origin.

To order, please visit www.hoddereducation.com or contact Customer Service at education@hachette.co.uk / +44 (0)1235 827827.

ISBN: 978 1 0360 0717 1

© Robin Jackson and Sally Green, 2024

First published in 2024 by Hodder Education,
An Hachette UK Company
Carmelite House
50 Victoria Embankment
London EC4Y 0DZ

www.hoddereducation.com

The authorised representative in the EEA is Hachette Ireland, 8 Castlecourt Centre, Dublin 15, D15 XTP3, Ireland (email: info@hbgi.ie)

Impression number 10 9 8 7 6 5 4 3 2 1

Year   2028 2027 2026 2025 2024

Cover photo © Chanelle Malambo/peopleimages.com - stock Adobe.com

City & Guilds and the City & Guilds logo are trade marks of The City and Guilds of London Institute and used under licence. City & Guilds Logo © City & Guilds 2024.

Illustrations by Aptara, Inc.

Typeset in India by Aptara, Inc.

Printed and Bound in Great Britain by Bell & Bain Ltd, Glasgow

A catalogue record for this title is available from the British Library.

Contents

Answers can be found online at **www.hoddereducation.com/answers-and-extras**

Acknowledgements

I would like to thank my parents Frank and Mabel, my wife Denise and my neighbour Jim Paine for their support, interest and helpful discussions whilst writing this book. I'd also like to thank Sally for making the co-authoring of this book such a positive and enjoyable experience.

Robin Jackson

Firstly, I would like to thank my friends and family, especially my parents Liz and David, for their support and encouragement throughout the writing process of this book. Secondly, thanks to my co-author Robin – it has been such a pleasure working with you on this book. Let's hope it is the first of many.

Sally Green

Photo credits

About the authors

Robin has been passionate about trees and woodlands since he can remember. This led him to initially study forest management and agroforestry, before his vocational interest focused on application of remote sensing technology to forests, and ultimately led him into teaching. He has subsequently spent the past 25 years in land-based technical and professional education and training. This has included serving as an elected member on the Education and Training Committee of a professional membership organisation. Robin considers himself fortunate to have direct experience of the delivery and management of qualifications across the land-based sector, in addition to playing a key role in development and quality assurance of qualifications and apprenticeships.

Originally from Belfast, Robin is now based in Norfolk and works as an assessment specialist at an awarding organisation, supporting the development and delivery of qualifications and apprenticeship assessments with the aim of supporting individuals to achieve their aspirations. He continues to champion the land-based sector, promoting opportunities for new entrants and working to meet skills needs of employers.

Sally has had an interest in animals and conservation since a small child and grew up with lots of pets. This interest continued into her academic studies and industry experience in animal management, zoology, and conservation, and it drives her passion to support education to improve animal welfare and husbandry. She has been working in vocational education, developing qualifications in the land-based sector, for 20 years.

Based in Warwickshire, Sally now works as an education consultant supporting businesses in the development of vocational education programmes, including bespoke training for employers, and works on the apprenticeships for the animal management industries.

Guide to the book

Learning outcomes

Core knowledge outcomes presented at the start of every chapter that you must understand and learn.

Case study

Placing knowledge into a fictionalised, real-life context to introduce dilemmas and problem solving.

Key term

Definitions to help you understand important terms.

Improve your maths

Short activities that encourage you to apply and develop your functional maths skills in context.

Test yourself

A knowledge-consolidation feature containing short questions and tasks to aid understanding and guide you to think about a topic in detail.

Improve your English

Short activities that encourage you to apply and develop your functional English skills in context.

Research

Research-based activities: either stretch and challenge activities enabling you to go beyond the course, or industry placement based activities encouraging you to discover more about your placement.

Assessment practice

Core content containing knowledge-based practice questions at the end of each chapter.

Further reading

A list of useful sources and additional reading material at the end of each chapter.

Industry tip

Helpful tips and guidelines to help develop professional skills during your industry placement.

Answers can be found online at www.hoddereducation.com/answers-and-extras

1 Health and safety

Introduction

The land-based sector has disproportionately high numbers and rates of serious accidents and incidents, as well as minor injuries and health problems, in relation to the size of the workforce. Workers use or work with machinery, equipment, chemicals, livestock and vehicles that can present potential hazards. Activities may also be physically demanding and repetitive, and lone working is commonplace. This is particularly the case if the boundaries between work life and home life become blurred.

Historically, there has also been a problem of unwise risk-taking, making individuals more susceptible to injury or illness. In addition, health, safety and welfare have been mistakenly considered to be discrete concepts, rather than integrated within all work activities and associated decision-making. Therefore, it is important to understand the key requirements of current legislation and how individuals, organisations and businesses can implement and maintain good standards of health and safety in their work.

Learning outcomes

By the end of this chapter, you will understand:
▶ the health and safety legislation that applies to the workplace
▶ the statutory duties of employers, employees and the self-employed
▶ the techniques and methods used to comply with legislation and promote health and safety standards
▶ the benefits of compliance with health and safety legislation
▶ the powers of health and safety enforcement officers
▶ the direct and indirect consequences of poor standards of workplace health and safety practice on businesses

▶ the direct and indirect consequences of poor standards of workplace health and safety practice on individuals
▶ the purpose of a risk assessment and hierarchy of control measures to manage risk
▶ the typical structure/layout of a risk assessment
▶ the steps needed to manage risk
▶ how risks assessments are developed, used and dynamically updated
▶ how to read and interpret a risk assessment
▶ the implications of poor development and application of a risk assessment.

1.1 Key requirements of health and safety legislation

Legislation

The land-based sector commonly exposes workers to activities associated with a high risk of accidents, and everyone has a role to play in managing health, safety and welfare at work (Figure 1.1).

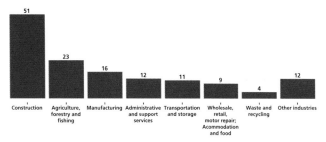

▲ Figure 1.1 Fatal injuries to workers in the agriculture, forestry and fishing sectors in comparison with other industries

Source: Health and Safety Executive, RIDDOR report 2023/24 (2024)
Work-related fatal injuries in Great Britain, 2024

However, workers have an expectation that their employer will ensure they are able to complete their work activities safely. To ensure employers take their role seriously, there is a legal framework they must work within. There is a hierarchy of importance, or legal weight, associated with this framework (and the guidance for employers), which is relied on by the UK court system in respect of health and safety in the workplace (Figure 1.2).

Primary legislation

Primary legislation is the highest form of law and is created by Acts of Parliament. These Acts are written rules that are passed by the UK Parliament as the legislative body and are binding on all individuals and organisations. Often these Acts only provide high-level obligations and might lack finer detail. The Health and Safety at Work etc. Act 1974 is the primary piece of legislation that sets out the framework for managing workplace health, safety and welfare in the UK. It is sometimes referred to as HSWA, the HSW Act, the 1974 Act or HASAWA.

Secondary legislation

Secondary legislation comprises sets of legally binding rules that are created by the government or other sanctioned bodies under the authority of an Act of Parliament. Often referred to as statutory instruments, these can be used to make changes or additions to primary legislation without the need for a new Act of Parliament. As a result, they may also be referred to as delegated legislation and may have the additional benefit of being able to be enacted relatively quickly.

There are three main types of secondary legislation, all of which have the same legislative importance: orders, regulations and rules. They are used to enforce the provisions of the relevant Act and contain more detailed information on the duties and responsibilities of individuals and organisations. For example, the Management of Health and Safety at Work Regulations 1999 require risk assessments to be carried out to

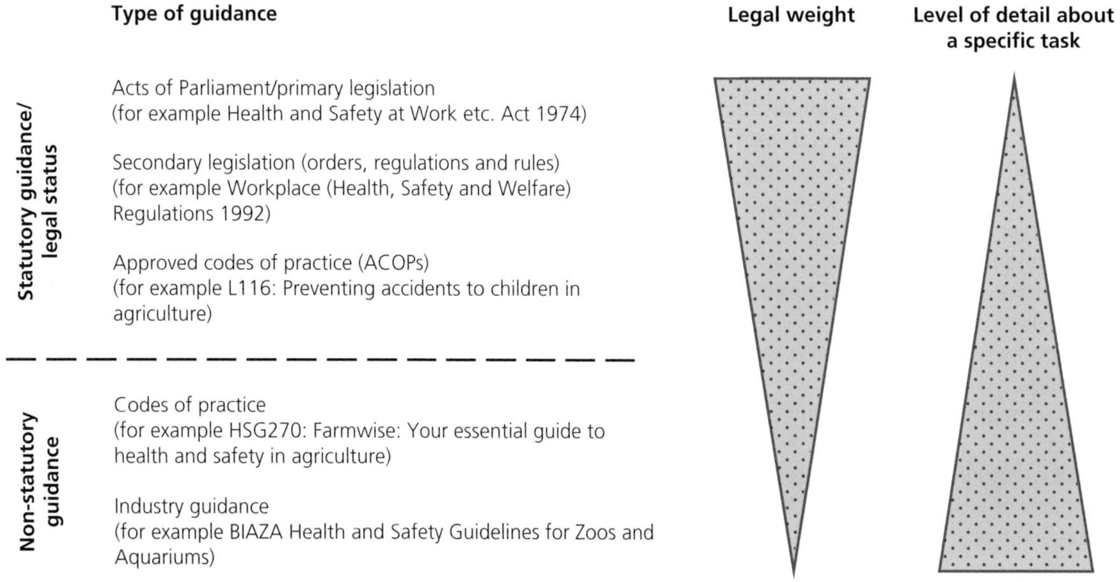

Type of guidance

Statutory guidance/legal status

Acts of Parliament/primary legislation
(for example Health and Safety at Work etc. Act 1974)

Secondary legislation (orders, regulations and rules)
(for example Workplace (Health, Safety and Welfare) Regulations 1992)

Approved codes of practice (ACOPs)
(for example L116: Preventing accidents to children in agriculture)

Non-statutory guidance

Codes of practice
(for example HSG270: Farmwise: Your essential guide to health and safety in agriculture)

Industry guidance
(for example BIAZA Health and Safety Guidelines for Zoos and Aquariums)

Legal weight

Level of detail about a specific task

▲ Figure 1.2 Employers must work within a legal framework

identify the measures that are required to comply with the Health and Safety at Work etc. Act 1974. The Acts that secondary legislation relate to are sometimes referred to as 'enabling Acts' or 'umbrella Acts'.

Byelaws are a special type of delegated legislation. Authority to make and enforce byelaws is delegated to local authorities (LAs) or other bodies. They are usually limited to the operations of a specific organisation/body or a particular geographical area and usually require something to be done, or not done. For example, the Forestry Commission Byelaws 1982 (Statutory Instrument 1982 No. 648) were made by the Forestry Commissioners under powers given to them under the Forestry Act 1967. One of the purposes of these byelaws is to prohibit specific acts that pose a risk of injury to members of the public visiting land under the management or control of the Forestry Commissioners. An example would be: 'Forestry Commission Byelaws 1982, 5 xxiv. Play or practise any game or sport in such a manner as to disturb the peaceful use of such lands or endanger the public or animals.

Approved codes of practice

Approved codes of practice (ACOPs) can accompany regulations and are practical guides that provide legal advice on how to comply with the regulations to which they relate. ACOPs have a special legal status and are approved by the Health and Safety Executive (HSE), with the consent of the Secretary of State. By following the advice given in an ACOP, an individual or organisation will be doing enough to comply with the law. However, it is not a legal requirement to comply with an ACOP. Failure to comply with an ACOP will not, in itself, result in an individual or organisation being prosecuted, but it may be used in evidence in any court proceedings to establish liability, unless they can show they used alternative methods to comply with the law.

An example of an ACOP and associated guidance is the *L117: Rider-operated lift trucks: Operator training and safe use,* which came into effect on 1 October 1999. It covers features, maintenance, inspection and thorough examination, as well as operator training requirements and safe use, of rider-operated lift trucks. These include rough-terrain telescopic forklift trucks, which are commonly used in the land-based sector for moving materials on pallets or in bulk, for example using a grain bucket.

The ACOP clearly states that children under 16 should never operate lift trucks. It also states that lift trucks are intended for lifting materials and not people. However, for planned work, lift trucks can be used with

integrated working platforms to allow people to work at height. **Integrated working platforms** have their own controls that are linked to and isolate the controls in the lift truck so that the height and movements of the lift truck and working platform can only be controlled by the individual in the working platform. They provide a higher level of safety than non-integrated working platforms. **Non-integrated working platforms** do not have separate controls so all lift truck and working platform movements are controlled by the lift truck operator, and therefore, should only be used in exceptional circumstances for 'occasional unplanned use'.

Other examples of ACOPs include those relating to the Control of Substances Hazardous to Health Regulations (2002) (L5), Provision and Use of Work Equipment Regulations 1998 (L22), Lifting Operations and Lifting Equipment Regulations 1998 (L113), and Workplace (Health, Safety and Welfare) Regulations 1992 (L24).

Codes of practice

Codes of practice (COPs) (including British Standards and guidance produced by regulators) are non-statutory documents that are widely accepted as providing practical guidance on how to comply with the law. They are not legally binding, but they can be used as evidence in court to show that a person has taken reasonable steps to comply with the law.

Industry guidance

Industry guidance is a broad term used to cover all non-statutory guidance produced by trade associations, professional bodies and other organisations. It provides detailed practical advice on how to comply with the law and is often tailored to specific industries or sectors.

For example, in 2015 the Arboricultural Association published the first edition of their *Industry Code of Practice for Arboriculture: Tree Work at Height (ICoP).* This was intended to provide best practice guidance on the principles of managing tree work at height and, in particular, to promote safe and efficient working practices. It was not intended to provide detailed guidance on how specific tasks should be undertaken or working techniques applied. This detail was subsequently provided within a range of technical guides.

Health and safety legislation that applies to the workplace

There are numerous pieces of legislation associated with health and safety of workers; their relevance and significance depends on the work activities being undertaken. In addition, the level of detail individuals are required to know depends on their role and occupational responsibilities. In general, most workers simply need to know what they have to do while at work to comply with the law.

Health and Safety at Work etc. Act 1974

This Act is the main piece of primary legislation covering health, safety and welfare in the workplace and is applicable to all industries. It places general duties on employers, self-employed workers and employees to ensure the health, safety and welfare of individuals at work and the protection of others who may be affected by work activities. The Act also requires employers to have a written health and safety policy if they employ five or more people. This policy should outline their general approach to health and safety at work and explain how they will manage safety within the business, as well as defining roles, responsibilities and procedures.

Management of Health and Safety at Work Regulations 1999

These regulations require risk assessments to be carried out to identify and implement the measures necessary to reduce risks to the health and safety of employees, self-employed workers and others who may be affected by work activities, as far as is **reasonably practicable**.

> ### Industry tip
>
> If an employer purchases a new item of machinery or equipment, or a new animal is introduced to the enterprise, the employer will need to review their existing risk assessment to identify whether workers need to be given specific new instructions or additional training.

Reporting of Injuries, Diseases and Dangerous Occurrences Regulations (RIDDOR) 2013

These regulations require employers or those in control of work premises to keep records of and report certain types of work-related accidents, incidents and ill health to the relevant enforcing authority (such as the HSE, local authority or Office for Rail Regulation). The following must be reported under RIDDOR: the death of any person; specified reportable injuries to workers; the incapacitation of workers for more than seven consecutive days; non-fatal accidents to people other than workers (for example members of the public).

There is also a requirement to report diagnoses of certain occupational diseases caused or made worse by work, as well as some **dangerous occurrences**.

With specific reference to injuries, the regulations require the enforcing authority to be notified if the following conditions are met:
- there has been an **accident** which caused the injury
- the accident was work-related
- the injury is of a type which is reportable.

Employers use accident books to help them meet their obligation to keep records and report details of work-related injuries and incidents. This record keeping is a requirement not only under RIDDOR but also under social security legislation (Social Security (Claims and Payments) Regulations 1979) if the business has ten or more employees. The following information must be recorded in an accident book:
- the date, time and place of the incident
- the injured person's full name, address and occupation
- a description of injury or illness
- any first aid given
- immediate actions after the incident.

These records must be retained for at least three years from the date the accident or incident was reported. Historically, accident books were paper-based documents and it was possible to see details about what had happened to individuals who had been injured. Many small- and medium-sized businesses and organisations still retain paper-based accident books, but these have been adapted to be compliant with data protection requirements (see Chapter 10, page 141). For example, they may have perforated pages which, once filled in, can be removed and filed securely to keep information confidential.

> ### Key terms
>
> **Reasonably practicable:** refers to employers exercising their judgement as to whether the time, money and trouble required to control workplace hazards is proportionate to the level of risk posed
>
> **Dangerous occurrence**: an incident which has the potential to cause death or serious injury, even though no one is harmed; the types of incident are listed in RIDDOR
>
> **Accident**: a distinct and identifiable unintended incident, associated with an external stimulus which causes physical injury; the term includes non-consensual violence to individuals at work

Given increasing concerns over unauthorised access to personal data, and an increasingly geographically diverse workforce (for instance remote workers), these paper-based documents have evolved, and many employers now use electronic accident recording systems. These electronic systems provide several advantages:

▶ the potential to restrict access to authorised individuals
▶ greater accessibility in order to reduce barriers to reporting
▶ the potential to provide automatic notifications for actions
▶ easier analysis of accident and incident statistics in order to identify possible trends.

Lifting Operations and Lifting Equipment Regulations (LOLER) 1998

These regulations require lifting operations to be appropriately planned and managed, lifting systems to be properly designed, and lifting equipment to be fit for purpose. The equipment should be uniquely identifiable and thoroughly examined by a **competent person** at prescribed intervals in order to reduce potential risks as far as is reasonably practicable.

Control of Substances Hazardous to Health (COSHH) Regulations 2002

These regulations require risk assessments to be carried out to identify and implement the measures necessary to reduce risks to the health of employees, self-employed people and others who may be affected by the storage, use and disposal of hazardous substances (as far as is reasonably practicable). This may include provision and use of respiratory protective equipment (RPE) that offers the wearer a degree of protection from airborne substances or particulates, depending on the specific equipment used. Where there is a risk to health, employers may need to carry out **health surveillance**.

Some hazardous substances can be readily identifiable by having one or more of the nine hazard pictograms (symbols) displayed on their packaging. These pictograms are in the shape of a diamond with a distinctive red border and white background and contain an image which provides information about the hazard (Figure 1.3). However, there are some substances to which COSHH applies where a hazard pictogram may not be present. These include hardwood and softwood dust arising from woodworking, grain dust or fumes resulting from welding.

Provision and Use of Work Equipment Regulations (PUWER) 1998

These regulations require employers to provide adequate instruction, training and supervision for individuals using work equipment and to ensure the equipment selected is suitable, fit for purpose and maintained to reduce potential risks to an acceptable level. In addition, when buying new equipment or machinery, it is a requirement to check it complies with the Supply of Machinery (Safety) Regulations 2008.

Manual Handling Operations Regulations 1992

These regulations require employers to assess and minimise the risks to health involved in manual handling activities. Manual handling should be avoided as far as is reasonably practicable, but if this is not possible, employers must identify and implement measures to reduce any risk of injury. See page 26 for more about manual handling risk assessments.

Work at Height Regulations 2005

These regulations require that all work at height is appropriately planned and managed, ensuring that the equipment and techniques selected are suitable and fit for purpose to reduce potential risks to an acceptable level. They cover work-related activities where there is the potential for someone to fall a distance and be injured.

▲ Figure 1.3 Hazard pictograms

This does not include falls on the level resulting from slips or trips. Work at height includes work:

▶ undertaken above the ground or floor level
▶ where there is the risk of falling from an edge or through an opening or fragile surface
▶ where there is the risk of falling from ground level into an opening in a floor or a hole in the ground.

Control of Noise at Work Regulations 2005

These regulations require employers to review work activities and take action to reduce risks from noise exposure as far as is reasonably practicable, and to ensure legal limits are not exceeded. Hearing protection must be supplied if noise exposure cannot be controlled by other means, and any protective equipment must be suitable, fit for purpose, worn/used properly when required and maintained, with appropriate training provided on how it should be used. Where there is a risk to health, employers may need to carry out health surveillance.

Personal Protective Equipment (PPE) at Work Regulations 2022

These regulations require employers to review work activities to determine whether PPE is required, and if so, ensure the equipment selected is suitable, fit for purpose, used/worn properly when required and maintained, with appropriate training provided on how it should be used, in order to reduce potential risks as far as is reasonably practicable. PPE is intended to be worn (or held) and offers the wearer a degree of protection depending on the specific equipment used.

Regulatory Reform (Fire Safety) Order 2005

This order consolidated all previous fire safety laws into a single piece of legislation. It covers fire safety for all non-domestic premises and requires anyone in control of those premises to take reasonable steps to reduce the risk of fire breaking out and to make sure people can escape safely if there is a fire. This normally involves an identified individual, known as the 'responsible person', undertaking a fire risk assessment and taking subsequent action to manage any identified risks. Compliance with the order is enforced by the relevant fire authority.

Fire Safety Act 2021

This Act was passed in response to the Grenfell Tower tragedy. It amends the Regulatory Reform (Fire Safety) Order by extending the responsible persons' scope of responsibilities to include buildings with two or more sets of domestic premises.

Workplace (Health, Safety and Welfare) Regulations 1992

These regulations cover a range of practical issues intended to make workplaces a healthy and safe environment for workers, for example workplace cleanliness, ventilation, temperature, lighting, pedestrian and traffic routes, sanitary conveniences and washing facilities, and equipment maintenance.

Working Time Regulations 1998

These regulations require employers to comply with specific rules associated with **working time**, including holiday entitlement, night work, rest during the working day, maximum weekly working hours, working arrangements for young workers and special arrangements during emergencies. They are in place to protect the health, safety and welfare of all workers.

Working Time (Amendment) Regulations 2003

The 2003 Amendment brought into scope certain sectors that had been excluded from the initial legislation, including the transport sectors, sea fishing, offshore work and the work of junior hospital doctors.

Supply of Machinery (Safety) Regulations 2008

These regulations implemented EU Directive 2006/42/EC on machinery and require manufacturers, or those marketing machinery intended for the Great Britain (GB) market and in scope of relevant UK product safety legislation, to ensure machinery is safe when supplied. Following the UK leaving the EU, the regulations have been amended through other legislation so the key requirements still apply to the GB market. The machinery should come with a declaration of conformity and user instructions in English and should be marked with the **UKCA** (United Kingdom Conformity Assessed) or **CE** (*Conformité Européenne* or European Conformity) marking when first sold or used.

The UKCA marking (Figure 1.4) has been used since 1 January 2021 and must be placed on certain products sold in the GB market. The technical requirements that allow the marking to be used depend on specific legislation associated with a product. In the UK, the CE marking is being replaced over time by the UKCA marking; however, the UKCA marking is not recognised in the EU. Transitional arrangements are in place to attach the UKCA marking via a label to the product or on a document which comes with the product until 11.00 p.m.

Key terms

Working time: when a worker is required to perform work activities, duties or training at their employer's instruction; it does not include a worker's routine travel between their home and their workplace or rest breaks during the working day

UKCA: certification marking used since 1 January 2021 that must be placed on certain products sold in the Great Britain marke; it is gradually replacing the CE marking in the UK

CE: certification marking required for certain products sold in the EU market which shows that the product meets relevant health, safety or environmental requirements

on 31 December 2027. From 1 January 2028, the UKCA marking is required to be attached to the product itself or its packaging.

0000

Where 0000 is the identification number of the UK approved body

▲ Figure 1.4 The UKCA conformity marking

The CE marking is required for certain products sold in the EU market. It shows that the product manufacturer has checked that the product meets relevant health, safety or environmental requirements.

> **Industry tip**
>
> Employers purchase equipment and machinery from reputable dealers and suppliers so they can be assured it meets relevant UK product safety legislation. They also keep records of any such purchases, as well as of subsequent inspections, maintenance and servicing, so they have an audit trail to show they are meeting their responsibilities (for example under PUWER 1998) in the event they need to prove this to an enforcement authority or a court.

Statutory duties of employers, employees and the self-employed

The Health and Safety at Work etc. Act 1974 defines the general duties of everyone in the workplace for maintaining health and safety, from employers (sections 2 and 3) and employees (sections 7 and 8) to managers of premises (sections 3 and 4). The duties and subsequent responsibilities of self-employed individuals are broadly the same as those of employers and employees.

Employers/self-employed responsibilities at work

▷ Provide a safe working environment.
▷ Provide safe equipment and systems of work.

▷ Provide information, instruction, training and supervision.
▷ Arrange for the safe storage, transport and use of articles and substances.
▷ Provide adequate welfare facilities for staff.
▷ Provide suitable personal protective equipment (PPE)/respiratory protective equipment (RPE) to all workers (including casual workers).
▷ Take responsibility for the maintenance, storage and replacement of all PPE/RPE.
▷ Ensure equipment is checked and regularly serviced.

> **Industry tip**
>
> The Health and Safety Information for Employees Regulations 1989 require employers to provide their employees with basic information on what employers must do for their workers and what workers must do. Employers usually meet this requirement by displaying the HSE-approved law poster (Figure 1.5) in a prominent position in the workplace or providing each worker with a copy of the equivalent leaflet.

▲ Figure 1.5 HSE-approved law poster

Employees/self-employed responsibilities at work

▷ Take reasonable care of their own health and safety.
▷ Take reasonable care of other people who may be affected by work activities.
▷ Co-operate with their employer on health and safety.
▷ Not interfere with or misuse anything provided for their health, safety or welfare.
▷ Use provided PPE/RPE (such as safety footwear, hearing protection or dust masks).
▷ Undertake training and instruction as required.

Test yourself

Look around your college or work experience premises to find the HSE-approved law poster. Who does the poster suggest you should talk to if you are worried about health and safety in your workplace?

Industry tip

Every employer must ensure their business has a policy for managing health and safety which clearly sets out duties and responsibilities. If the business employs five or more employees, this policy must be written. However, it is considered helpful to have a written policy even if there are fewer than five employees. For example, if a small landscaping contractor is tendering for work, it is sometimes a requirement to submit a health and safety policy as part of the tender process.

Techniques and methods used to comply with legislation and promote health and safety standards

Employers and businesses have a range of techniques and methods available to show they are compliant with their legal duties and responsibilities, as well as setting and promoting good health, safety and welfare standards. These include evidence of sufficient risk assessments and application of appropriate control methods, such as establishing systems for safe communication with workers who work by themselves (lone workers), provision of PPE/RPE, safety/warning signage and appropriate sanitary conveniences and washing facilities (such as toilet and washing facilities). Therefore, accurate health and safety records (for example thorough examination and inspection records, risk assessments and **method statements**) are an important consideration, as these may need to be produced if requested by an enforcement authority.

Key term

Method statements: documents that describe exactly how work tasks or activities are to be carried out and contain all the control measures identified in related risk assessments; sharing method statements with workers is an effective way to ensure they understand how they are expected to undertake an activity

Signage

Signage is a crucial part of communicating information to both employees and workers, as well as visitors and the general public who may be accessing a worksite (Figure 1.6). Signage has several advantages over more formal written notices. It communicates key safety information visually and is useful in noisy workplaces where auditory communication may be challenging. It also provides a regular reminder for workers and, importantly, can be interpreted by individuals who are unable to read or who have diverse English language fluency. There are five types of health and safety signs commonly found in the workplace:
▷ **Prohibition signs** provide an instruction NOT to do something and must be complied with.
▷ **Mandatory signs** provide an instruction to do something and must be complied with.
▷ **Warning signs** raise awareness about hazards but do not specify any actions.
▷ **Safe condition signs** indicate emergency exit routes or muster locations in the event of an emergency.
▷ **Fire equipment signs** indicate the location of fire safety equipment such as fire extinguishers.

▼ Table 1.1 Types of workplace safety sign

	Colour	Shape	Examples
Prohibition signs	Black symbol White background with a red crossed circle	Circular	No Entry Do not operate
Mandatory signs	White symbol Blue background	Circular	Keep clear Eye protection must be worn
Warning signs	Black symbol Yellow background	Triangular	Electrical hazard Fragile roof
Safe condition signs	White symbol Green background	Square or rectangular	First aid Emergency exit
Fire equipment signs	White symbol Red background	Square or rectangular	Fire alarm call point Fire extinguisher

▲ Figure 1.6 Safety signs

Training and certification

Employers have an overall responsibility to ensure their employees are trained and competent to undertake their roles. In meeting this responsibility, the employees should not be charged for this training and any time associated with the training counts as working time.

Most work activities do not require individuals to hold a formal qualification, so long as the employer can evidence the training is sufficient and fit for purpose. However, within the land-based sector there are a small number of proficiency/competency qualifications that are deemed to be licence-to-practise qualifications. These are directly or indirectly designated, either by legislation or an organisation undertaking a regulatory function (see Table 1.2 for examples), with demand for some other competency qualifications driven by employer expectations. The main exception to the need to hold one of these competency qualifications is where the individual is being trained by and is under the direct supervision of an appropriate person.

▼ Table 1.2 Activity for which a competency qualification is legally required

Activity	Designator
Application of pesticide products authorised for professional use (specified certificates)	Plant Protection Products (Sustainable Use) Regulations 2012
Buying or using sheep dip products	Medicines (Exemptions for Merchants in Veterinary Drugs) Order 1998
Professional chainsaw operators working in forestry and arboriculture	Section 9 of the approved code of practice (ACOP) associated with the Provision and Use of Work Equipment Regulations (PUWER) 1998
Practising as a veterinary nurse	Royal College of Veterinary Surgeons, as a statutory regulator under the Veterinary Surgeons Act 1966
Transporting livestock or poultry in connection with economic activity	Animal and Plant Health Agency (APHA), as the competent authority on behalf of the Secretary of State, as regulator for the Council Regulation (EC) No 1/2005 on the protection of animals during transport and the Welfare of Animals (Transport) Order 2006

First-aid arrangements

The Health and Safety (First-Aid) Regulations 1981 require all employers to have adequate and appropriate arrangements in place to get immediate help for employees who are injured or ill at work. They are required to provide employees with information about the first-aid arrangements, designate an **appointed person** to take control of first-aid arrangements and provide a suitably stocked first-aid kit. The specific arrangements should be based on an assessment of factors such as the type of work, employee working patterns, hazards and likely risks/severity of harm, size and location of the workforce and history of accidents and incidents, as well as how accessible the workplace is for emergency services. For example, following an assessment, an employer may decide they require an individual trained in first aid and, consequently, what level of training is adequate and, appropriate (such as emergency first aid at work (EFAW) or first aid at work (FAW)).

Although there is a British Standard (BS 8599-1:2019) which details the size and contents of a first-aid kit for different workplace environments, there is no legally mandated list of items that a first-aid kit should contain. Therefore, the contents should be based on an assessment of the work activities to be undertaken.

A first-aid kit for low-risk activities, such as in an office environment, might consist of a leaflet with general guidance on first aid, sterile plasters, bandages and wound dressings. However, for higher risk activities, such as those undertaken by chainsaw operators, a first-aid kit may also contain haemostatic and trauma dressings.

Fire equipment

Fire equipment is provided by employers to help individuals escape from a fire and reach a safe location or as initial tools to tackle small fires at an early stage. Because it is relied upon to work whenever it is required, it must never be tampered with, as this can have potentially serious consequences. Any accidental or deliberate use of, or damage to, fire equipment must be reported so that it can be replaced.

Fire equipment includes sprinkler systems, fire blankets (commonly found in kitchen facilities) and fire extinguishers. Fire extinguishers are the most commonly encountered equipment, so it is important to be able to recognise the different types available and what types of fire they can be used on. Fires are classified by the type of fuel that is burning (Table 1.3 and Figure 1.7).

▼ Table 1.3 Classes of fire

Class of fire	Type of fuel	Examples
Class A	Combustible materials	Wood, coal, paper, straw, textiles, plastics
Class B	Flammable liquids	Diesel, petrol, oils, paint, paraffin, ethanol
Class C	Flammable gases	Butane, propane, natural gas, hydrogen
Class D	Combustible metals	Magnesium, aluminium, lithium, potassium
Electrical fires	Electrical equipment	Faulty wiring, broken electrical machinery, overloaded plug sockets
Class F	Cooking oils	Cooking oils, grease, fats

Key term

Appointed person: someone in the workplace who is responsible for looking after first-aid equipment and facilities and calling the emergency services; the role includes responsibility for maintaining and replacing the contents of any first-aid kit(s)

All fire extinguishers have a red body. Their type is indicated by a coloured label at the top of the extinguisher that usually also carries a brief text description. Each extinguisher also has safe condition symbols to summarise the classes of fire it can safely be used for and prohibition symbols for situations when it must NOT be used. There is also normally a wall-mounted sign located beside the fire extinguisher which summarises this information (Figure 1.8).

Fire equipment should be located in obvious places close to fire exits or alarm points to encourage individuals to move away from a fire towards safe areas. In the event of a fire, the priority must be to raise the alarm, evacuate everyone (including livestock where possible) from the site of the fire in line with evacuation plans and call the emergency services. Fire extinguishers should not be used unless the alarm has already been raised, you have been trained to use them, the fire is small and you are confident you can put the fire out. However, even if these conditions are met, you must ensure you have a clear and safe exit route.

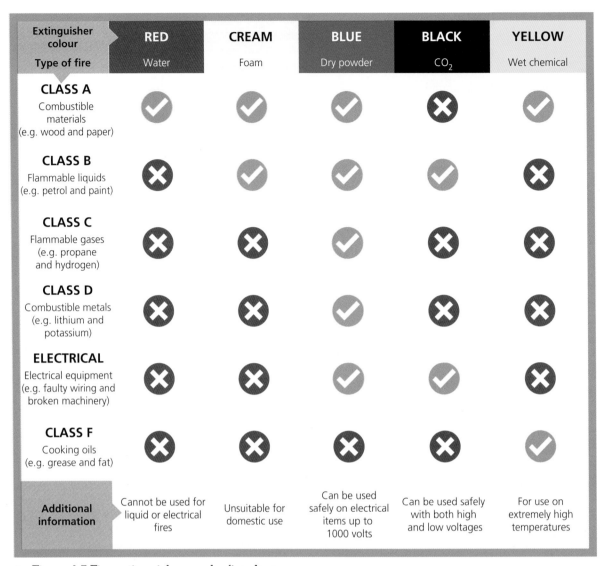

Extinguisher colour	RED	CREAM	BLUE	BLACK	YELLOW
Type of fire	Water	Foam	Dry powder	CO$_2$	Wet chemical
CLASS A Combustible materials (e.g. wood and paper)	✓	✓	✓	✗	✓
CLASS B Flammable liquids (e.g. petrol and paint)	✗	✓	✓	✓	✗
CLASS C Flammable gases (e.g. propane and hydrogen)	✗	✗	✓	✗	✗
CLASS D Combustible metals (e.g. lithium and potassium)	✗	✗	✓	✗	✗
ELECTRICAL Electrical equipment (e.g. faulty wiring and broken machinery)	✗	✗	✓	✓	✗
CLASS F Cooking oils (e.g. grease and fat)	✗	✗	✗	✗	✓
Additional information	Cannot be used for liquid or electrical fires	Unsuitable for domestic use	Can be used safely on electrical items up to 1000 volts	Can be used safely with both high and low voltages	For use on extremely high temperatures

▲ Figure 1.7 Fire extinguisher use by fire class

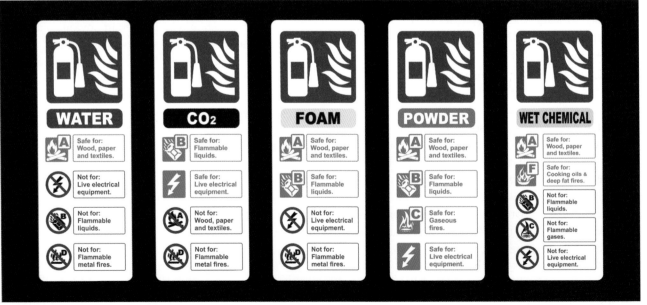

▲ Figure 1.8 Fire extinguisher labels showing fire classes

Benefits of compliance with health and safety legislation

Employers and businesses comply with health and safety legislation to protect their workforce and working environment for a wide variety of reasons, including the following:

Legal:
▶ to minimise intervention by an enforcement authority and avoid the consequences of non-compliance.

Financial:
▶ to reduce risk of compensation claims
▶ to minimise breakdowns and potentially reduce the frequency that equipment and machinery need to be replaced
▶ to potentially reduce insurance premiums through low accident rates
▶ to reduce risk of fines.

Reputation:
▶ it is easier to attract and retain customers due to positive reputation
▶ employer of choice as a result of positive reputation.

Employees:
▶ to increase staff morale and productivity
▶ to reduce staff turnover and sickness
▶ to reduce the number and severity of physical injuries to staff/number of deaths.

Powers of health and safety enforcement officers

The Health and Safety Executive (HSE) is the government-appointed body responsible for enforcing workplace health, safety and welfare legislation in the UK. The HSE also has responsibility to analyse data relating to health and safety and produce codes of practice and general guidance to promote health and safety. However, the HSE shares its enforcement duty with other organisations, such as local authorities (LAs). Which organisation has responsibility is based on the main activity carried out at the premises concerned. In general, LAs are the main enforcing authority for retail, wholesale distribution, warehousing, hotel and catering premises, offices and the consumer/leisure industries. The HSE is widely considered the enforcing authority for the land-based sector. However, there is no specific definition of the land-based sector within health and safety legislation. Instead, the HSE has allocated authority for **agricultural activities**, which are defined by the Health and Safety (Enforcing Authority) Regulations 1998.

> **Key term**
>
> **Agricultural activities**: defined by the HSE as including cultivation of ground, sowing and harvesting of crops, horticulture, fruit growing, seed growing, dairy farming, livestock breeding and keeping (including the management of livestock up to the point of slaughter or export from Great Britain, so covers livestock markets), forestry (and arboriculture), the use of land as grazing land, market gardens and nursery grounds, and the preparation of land for agricultural use

It is sometimes not immediately clear who has allocated responsibility for enforcing health and safety legislation. However, it is based on whether the activity to be enforced is the main activity on the premises or an incidental activity. For example, horticultural activities are not considered agricultural activities when they are carried out in a garden centre or other shop. The main activity in such premises will be retail and the LA will be the enforcing authority. However, a shop operated by a farmer on farm premises is allocated to the HSE, as the main activity remains agriculture. Where livestock breeding and keeping is considered incidental to the main activity, for example, a circus, zoo or 'open farm' (entertainment visited by the public) or a shop (retail sales), the LA will enforce legal requirements. The HSE has responsibility for fish breeding and fish farming, but recreational fishing activities on inland waters is allocated to the LA. The LA has responsibility for riding stables, but the HSE has responsibility where the main activity is horse breeding or training.

> **Test yourself**
>
> There are an increasing number of land-based employees who are considered 'homeworkers'. Research the legislation to identify who the allocated enforcement authority is for homeworkers.

To enable the HSE to carry out its work effectively, HSE inspectors are tasked with inspecting, investigating and providing support and guidance. To allow them to undertake their role, they have a number of wide-ranging powers which they can exercise at their discretion. These include:
▶ entering work premises at a reasonable time; they may enter at any time without prior warning if they believe there is imminent danger
▶ requiring those present to provide facilities and assistance, including answering questions to enable the inspector to undertake their work

▶ collecting photographs, recordings, samples or measurements, or taking possession of articles and substances, or inspecting and taking copies of documents.

Often inspectors arrive without warning. If they find dangerous activities taking place during the visit, they can require work activities to stop immediately (for example machinery being used in an unsafe manner by untrained workers).

Where an allocated enforcement authority such as the HSE has evidence of non-compliance with a legal requirement, the individual(s) concerned and potentially the organisation may be committing a criminal offence. This evidence may arise from, for example, a random or targeted inspection of a workplace, or an investigation following an incident. Depending on the seriousness and significance of the non-compliance, the consequences could include:

▶ receiving verbal or written advice (for example warning an employer why an inspector believes they are failing to comply with the law)
▶ being issued with a notification of contravention if there has been a **material breach** of a health and safety duty
▶ being issued with an improvement notice (for example requiring an employer to provide updated training for their employees within a specific period of time to ensure they have appropriate knowledge and skills to undertake an activity)
▶ being issued with a prohibition notice (for example a safety device on a piece of machinery is not working and because of the risk of serious injury to workers, the machinery must not be used until the safety device is fixed and working properly)
▶ being prosecuted.

> ### Key term
>
> **Material breach**: a contravention of health and safety law that an HSE inspector considers to be sufficiently serious that they need to write to the duty holder formally requiring them to take action to deal with it; the duty holder (the employer or self-employed person) is then required to pay the HSE for the time it has taken to identify the breach and support the duty holder to deal with the breach (known as the 'fee for intervention (FFI)')

Depending on the significance of the offence, the HSE may choose to prosecute the duty holder in either the Magistrates' Court or the Crown Court. In the event

of a successful prosecution, the possible penalties can include a fine or period of imprisonment. For offences committed after 12 March 2015, the maximum penalty in the Magistrates' Court is an unlimited fine or imprisonment for a term not exceeding six months, or both. In the Crown Court, the maximum penalty is an unlimited fine or imprisonment not exceeding two years, or both. Both courts also have the discretionary power to order the duty holder to take action to remedy matters associated with the offence and order compensation to be paid for loss, damage or injury resulting from the offence.

To ensure its enforcement activity is seen to be proportionate, consistent and transparent, the HSE provides information on enforcement notices and convictions on public registers accessible through its website.

> ### Test yourself
>
> Search the HSE public register of convictions and research one case. Identify what legislation (Acts or regulations) was breached and what the penalty was.

1.2 Consequences of non-compliance and poor standards of health and safety practice

There is a wide range of possible consequences for both businesses and individuals as a result of non-compliance with legal requirements or poor health and safety practices. In respect of the latter, this can include an indirect negative impact on friends and family of those affected, which may not be immediately realised but which can have a significant effect on life outside work and relationships.

Direct and indirect consequences on businesses

Financial:
▶ compensation claims
▶ repairs/replacement of damaged equipment
▶ recruitment and retention/retraining of staff
▶ loss of productivity
▶ increased insurance premiums
▶ fines by the HSE
▶ legal fees.

Emotional:
▶ mental health issues and stress.

Reputational:
▶ loss of reputation
▶ difficulty retaining customers
▶ difficulty attracting new staff
▶ negative publicity.

Employee:
▶ reduced staff morale and productivity
▶ increased staff turnover and sickness
▶ inability to continue in current role(s)/change careers
▶ physical injuries to staff, including disablement as well as death.

Direct and indirect consequences on individuals

Physical:
▶ temporary or chronic pain
▶ disablement
▶ death.

Financial:
▶ loss of income/financial stress
▶ compensation claims.

Emotional:
▶ mental health issues and stress.

Reputation:
▶ loss of reputation
▶ negative publicity.

Employee:
▶ reduced staff morale and productivity
▶ increased staff turnover and sickness
▶ physical injuries to staff/death.

Social:
▶ loss of independence
▶ imprisonment
▶ reduced social activity.

Test yourself

Imagine you have been injured in a work-related accident and are unable to work and earn an income for 12 months. Make a list of how this might impact your life and domestic situation, including the potential impacts on your friends or family.

1.3 Purpose of a risk assessment

The purpose of a risk assessment is to identify **hazards**, evaluate the **risks** associated with those

hazards, and put appropriate control measures in place to eliminate or reduce those risks, thereby creating as safe and healthy a workplace as possible. There are several pieces of secondary legislation in addition to the Management of Health and Safety at Work Regulations 1999 which may require a risk assessment to be undertaken. Although the purpose of each may be slightly different, the general principles applied are similar.

Key terms

Hazard: something which has the potential to cause harm or adversely affect the health of individuals

Risk: the likelihood of a hazard occurring and causing harm or adversely affecting the health of individuals

Typical structure/layout of a risk assessment

Any risk assessment should be completed by someone who is competent and familiar with the work activities to be undertaken. Although there is no prescribed format for a risk assessment, it is important that it is undertaken systematically and results in a reduction in the risk to workers as far as is reasonably practicable. However, most employers use a variation of the risk assessment template made available by the HSE (Figure 1.9).

Steps needed to manage risks

Management of risk within the workplace requires employers to adopt a systematic process.

Step 1: identify hazards

Review the workplace (both the premises themselves and the activities to be undertaken) and identify what has the potential to cause harm. Then for each hazard identify how employees, contractors, visitors or members of the public might be harmed.

Some of the common hazards that may be encountered include:
▶ lone working and remote locations
▶ spillages
▶ rough/steep/uneven terrain
▶ exposure to and use of chemicals and hazardous materials
▶ operation and maintenance of equipment, tools and machinery (hand-held, pedestrian, driven)
▶ transporting or supporting a load (i.e. manual handling)

Risk assessment						
Company:			Assessment carried out by:			
Date of assessment:			Date of next review:			
What are the hazards?	Who might be harmed and how?	What are you already doing to control the risks?	What further action do you need to take to control the risks?	Who needs to carry out the action?	When is the action needed by?	Done

▲ Figure 1.9 A risk assessment template based on an HSE example

- other people
- falling objects (for example, falling trees and branches)
- flora and fauna
- flying debris
- water and flooding
- bulk storage
- fire and explosion
- above-ground and underground services
- controlled atmospheres
- noise
- vibration.

Weather can be considered as a hazard but also as something that could influence the risk of a hazard causing harm. For example, felling trees on a windy day might increase the risk of the tree not falling where intended and cause the operator to be injured by falling objects in the canopy or struck by the tree as it falls.

Step 2: assess the risks (likelihood, severity, number of people affected)

Decide how likely it is that someone could be harmed and if so, how serious the harm could be. A simple risk assessment table can help with this (Figure 1.10).

Some of the potential consequences or harm caused by the hazards listed above include:
- fatality
- ill health
- electrocution
- cuts, amputations, sharp-edge related injuries

- being struck by a vehicle, impact injuries, crush injuries
- injuries from slips or falls, musculoskeletal disorders (MSDs)
- injury from falling objects
- hypothermia, heat exhaustion, physiological stress
- psychological trauma
- transmitted infections, poisoning and contamination, bites
- dermatitis
- hearing loss/damage
- hand–arm vibration syndrome (HAVS)/white finger
- drowning, suffocation.

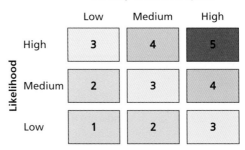

▲ Figure 1.10 A simple risk assessment matrix

In addition to the harm that might be caused to workers or others who are nearby, it is also important to consider the potential damage to equipment or services (for example to vehicles, tools or buildings), pollution and environmental damage.

Step 3: control the risks

Identify what controls you already have in place to manage or reduce the risk. Then consider the hierarchy of control measures (see page 18) to determine what more can be reasonably done to either remove the hazard or reduce the risk of it causing harm.

Step 4: record findings

It is a legal requirement for an employer to record their significant findings if they employ five or more people. However, it is considered best practice to record the findings irrespective of how many people are employed, so that there is evidence of risk management in the event of an accident. However, just having a written risk assessment does not itself prove an employer is complying with the law. The important consideration is what they do to manage and control risk in the workplace. It is also important to ensure the findings of the risk assessment are effectively communicated to everyone who needs to be aware, so they understand their role and responsibilities. The method(s) of communication used should meet the needs of those involved.

Step 5: review the controls

It is important to regularly review the controls in place to ensure they are still working. There may be workplace changes such as new staff, substances, equipment, machinery or processes, which mean the current controls are not as effective as they could be. It is also considered best practice to review the controls following any accident or near misses, or following feedback from workers.

Test yourself

Investigate the common hazards associated with the industry you are most familiar with. Make a list of the most common causes of fatal accidents and a list of the most common causes of non-fatal injuries. For each cause, identify one thing that could be done to potentially reduce the risk to a worker.

How risk assessments are developed, used and dynamically updated

As we have already learned, any risk assessment should be completed by someone who is competent and familiar with the work activities to be undertaken. Therefore, not all risk assessments may be undertaken by the same person. Indeed, an employer may involve and consult with their workers when developing a risk assessment.

Case study

An employer who offers a range of arboricultural and landscaping services may develop most of the risk assessments covering the services they offer. However, where a risk assessment is required for tractor-mounted equipment operations, they may ask their most competent and experienced operator to complete it. Likewise, where a risk assessment is required for aerial tree work operations, they may ask their most competent and experienced climber to complete it.

► What factors might an employer consider when deciding who is most appropriate to complete a risk assessment?
► How might the findings from the risk assessment be shared with those who might be affected?

There are generally considered to be two stages to risk assessment within the land-based sector. First, a formal risk assessment is carried out in advance of the work activities to be undertaken. While this is largely sufficient, the hazards, risks and subsequent necessary controls may need to be updated to reflect changes in circumstances, such as specific workers, animal behaviour, the worksite and weather conditions. For example, landscaping contractors may work on a range of different client worksites, each of which may have different constraints (such as the location of outbuildings, ditches and drains, or garden features). A change in weather conditions during the working day may impact on the risk to workers, for example an increase in wind speed may mean forestry work has to stop, or rain may make ground traction for machinery difficult resulting in agricultural fieldwork stopping. An animal collection worker may observe a change in the behaviour of the animals which means the planned activities may have to be stopped for the welfare both of the animals and the worker. This process of constantly keeping a risk assessment under review while the work is taking place is known as **dynamic risk assessment** and is common practice throughout the land-based sector.

Key terms

Dynamic risk assessment: continuously reviewing a risk assessment throughout the period of work in order to respond to changing circumstances and hazards

Vulnerable workers: a collective term used to refer to young workers under the age of 18 (who may need more supervision than adults), migrant workers (commonly working in agriculture and food-processing industries), new or expectant mothers and people with disabilities

Test yourself

Reflect on an industry-specific work activity you are familiar with. Make a list of factors that may result in you having to dynamically update a risk assessment.

When considering who might be harmed, it is important to consider **vulnerable workers**, as they may have specific requirements which need to be considered.

Young workers are considered vulnerable because they may:
▶ lack experience or maturity
▶ lack physical strength
▶ be eager to impress or please
▶ be unaware of how to raise concerns.

Migrant workers are considered vulnerable because they may:
▶ be new to or unfamiliar with the job
▶ have limited knowledge of the health and safety system, which may be different to the system in their home country
▶ have limited knowledge of their health and safety rights
▶ be eager to impress or please to ensure job security
▶ have limited ability to communicate effectively due to their English language proficiency.

Some working conditions and processes can potentially harm new or expectant mothers and/or their child. For example, people who are, or who may be, pregnant are advised to avoid close contact with livestock. This is because organisms that are infectious and dangerous for the foetus may be present in birth fluids of animals, particularly sheep, cattle and goats. Therefore, farmers and livestock keepers have a responsibility to minimise the risks to pregnant people, including members of their

family, the public and professional staff visiting farms or animal collections.

People with disabilities may have impairments which impact their working practices. Therefore, employers may need to make reasonable adjustments, such as provision of additional or extended rest breaks, or adapted equipment or machinery, to support them to be effective in the workplace while reducing any risk of harm.

It is common for land-based workers to work outdoors, moving across changing terrain and negotiating obstacles in changing weather conditions throughout the year. Therefore, there is always the potential for workers to suffer fatigue. Employers have a responsibility to ensure there are adequate rest breaks depending on the work being done (see Chapter 3, page 55). In particular, they should consider the needs of lone workers, who may be at a greater risk of stress and fatigue going unnoticed because of their working context. For example, this may mean employers should make additional first-aid arrangements or put in place specific communication measures and reporting procedures.

Hierarchy of control measures

A critical step in the risk assessment process is to consider the possible control measures to determine what more can be reasonably done to either remove a hazard or reduce the risk of it causing harm. There is an accepted hierarchy to these possible control measures (Figure 1.11); the measures at the top of the hierarchy are likely to reduce the risk more meaningfully than those measures towards the bottom of the hierarchy. Potentially, employers may need to put a number of different control measures in place in order to reduce the risk sufficiently.

It may not be necessary to work down through every level in the hierarchy above. For example, if the risk can be sufficiently managed or mitigated through isolation, further control measures may not be required.

It is important to consider PPE/RPE as the last line of defence, or last resort, and ideally the risk should be sufficiently reduced using other control measures so that it is not required. Therefore, if PPE/RPE is required, it is important that it is appropriate for the intended purpose. For example, with hearing protection, it is important to balance the noise reduction offered with the ability to communicate in the workplace. PPE/RPE should be suitable for, and fit, the individual concerned, and they must be trained in how to store, maintain and use it. It should

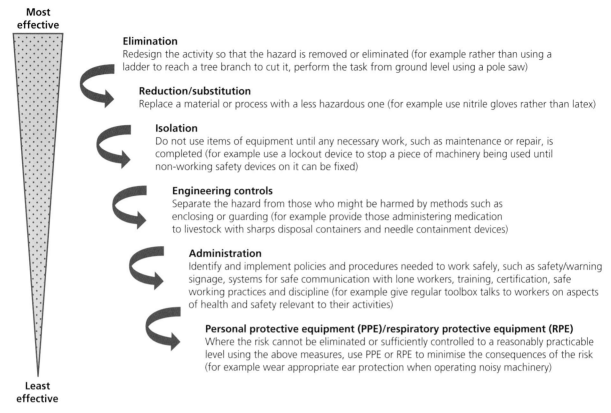

Most
effective

Elimination
Redesign the activity so that the hazard is removed or eliminated (for example rather than using a ladder to reach a tree branch to cut it, perform the task from ground level using a pole saw)

Reduction/substitution
Replace a material or process with a less hazardous one (for example use nitrile gloves rather than latex)

Isolation
Do not use items of equipment until any necessary work, such as maintenance or repair, is completed (for example use a lockout device to stop a piece of machinery being used until non-working safety devices on it can be fixed)

Engineering controls
Separate the hazard from those who might be harmed by methods such as enclosing or guarding (for example provide those administering medication to livestock with sharps disposal containers and needle containment devices)

Administration
Identify and implement policies and procedures needed to work safely, such as safety/warning signage, systems for safe communication with lone workers, training, certification, safe working practices and discipline (for example give regular toolbox talks to workers on aspects of health and safety relevant to their activities)

Personal protective equipment (PPE)/respiratory protective equipment (RPE)
Where the risk cannot be eliminated or sufficiently controlled to a reasonably practicable level using the above measures, use PPE or RPE to minimise the consequences of the risk (for example wear appropriate ear protection when operating noisy machinery)

Least
effective

▲ Figure 1.11 Hierarchy of control measures

be replaced when it is no longer fit for purpose. It is also important that employers are aware they should not charge individuals for any PPE/RPE required to perform a task and should check workers are using it when required. Different types of PPE/RPE are designed to protect specific parts of the body against relevant hazards:

▶ **Eyes (splashes, projectiles or radiation)**: safety glasses, goggles, face shields and welding masks
▶ **Ears (noise exposure)**: ear defenders and earplugs offering protection appropriate to the noise intensity
▶ **Head (hair entanglement in moving machinery, falling objects)**: bump caps and safety helmets
▶ **Hands (cuts, pesticides/chemicals, radiation)**: gloves and gauntlets
▶ **Body (temperature extremes, poor visibility or pesticides/chemicals)**: high-visibility clothing, flame-retardant clothing, spray suits, safety harnesses, waterproof clothing
▶ **Feet and legs (moving equipment, falling objects, moving heavy loads, slipping)**: chainsaw boots and trousers (types A and C), boots or shoes with protective toecaps.

RPE is a specialised type of protective equipment that is used to remove contaminants from the air before it is breathed in or to provide clean air. It includes powered and non-powered respirators and breathing apparatus. Particular attention must be given to choosing the most appropriate type for the hazard likely to be encountered during the work task, including the protection factor.

How to read and interpret a risk assessment

When risk assessments are undertaken thoroughly, and the control measures shared with those involved, they can make a positive contribution to reducing the risk of anyone being injured while at work. Therefore when reading and interpreting a risk assessment, it is important to understand the context within which it was developed, in order to make a decision as to whether it is fit for purpose. Risk assessment types are as follows:

▶ **Generic risk assessment**: this covers all eventualities. This means it may include hazards and consequences which are theoretically possible but may not be relevant or likely. These assessments may lack detail in relation to the control measures or may contain more detail than is relevant. They are intended as a starting point and subsequently adapted to accommodate the site, task and individuals involved.

▶ **Site-specific risk assessment**: this focuses on the worksite. This means it includes considerations such as access, terrain and infrastructure (for example structures, buildings and underground/overground services).

▶ **Task-specific risk assessment**: this focuses on the task or activity to be undertaken. This means it includes considerations such as tools, equipment or machinery to be used, individuals undertaking the task, or livestock/animals that individuals will interact with.

Risk assessments are normally formal written documents. Having them written down allows them to be referred to during work activities, as well as providing evidence that a risk assessment was undertaken in the event of an accident or incident. A business or organisation might have a range of risk assessments which cover different aspects of the work and activities it carries out.

It is common practice to start with a broad-based risk assessment that is then refined according to the work tasks or location. For example, a florist may have a site-specific risk assessment for working in their shop, which they then adapt on a daily basis depending on the tasks they are doing; a dog groomer may have a site-specific risk assessment for working in their salon, which they then adapt on a daily basis depending on the dogs they are grooming; a landscaping contractor may have a task-specific risk assessment, which they then adapt for the worksite they will be working on.

A credible risk assessment should always reflect the worksite, the task(s) being undertaken, the individuals involved and, because many land-based activities are undertaken outdoors, where appropriate it should reflect the weather conditions on the day the work is being done. It should also be easy to use and not complicated by unnecessary information.

It is important to be aware that risk assessments may be completed before the work is undertaken, such as the day before. Therefore, they should always be reviewed immediately before the work starts in case anything has changed, for example a different item of equipment is used or the individuals undertaking the work have changed. They should also be reviewed throughout the work activity in case anything changes (dynamic risk assessment), for example a change in the weather during the day which increases the risk of an accident happening, or individuals being injured and therefore the control measures needing to be amended.

It is difficult for any risk assessment to be considered comprehensive. Therefore, risk assessments normally focus on the most typical hazards associated with an activity that are likely to occur and have the most serious consequences, such as death, serious injury or damage to an individual's health. For example, in their risk assessments florists might expect to see harmful plants, cuts, or slips, trips and falls; dog groomers might expect to see bites, cuts, or slips, trips and falls; arborists might expect to see falls from height, flying debris or contact with moving machinery parts; agricultural machinery operators might expect to see contact with moving vehicles or contact with powerlines; and animal collection workers might expect to see zoonoses, bites, kicks or scratches.

Figure 1.12 is an example of a risk assessment produced by a landscaping contracting business for using pedestrian-operated machinery (lawnmowers, chainsaws, hedge cutters and brushcutters). This has been based on the HSE template and is likely a generic risk assessment because it is not contextualised to a specific worksite (such as a client's garden which may be on a slope or which might contain features such as a shed, greenhouse or garden ornaments which need to be considered) or a specific activity (such as trimming a boundary hedge between the client's garden and the neighbours' gardens). In this generic risk assessment, the contractor has existing controls already in place. However, they have identified some additional control measures that they still need to implement.

Risk assessment – Pedestrian-operated landscaping machinery

Company name: Felix Landscaping

Assessment carried out by: Amani Felix

Date assessment was carried out: 01/02/2025

Date of next review: In 12 months' time

What are the hazards?	Who might be harmed and how?	What are you already doing to control the risks?	What further action do you need to take to control the risks?	Who needs to carry out the action?	When is the action needed by?	Done
Slips and trips Slippery surfaces (e.g. from water mud, ice and snow), uneven surfaces and obstacles	• Workers • Injuries from slipping or from tripping over objects	• Safe systems of work in place • Suitable safety footwear (with slip-resistant soles providing good grip) worn and maintained by monitoring	Inspect worksite for objects before starting work	Workers	Before starting work	
Weather conditions e.g. snow, ice, wind, low temperatures	• Workers • Increased risk of injury, exposure	• Safe systems of work in place • Appropriate clothing for the weather conditions (e.g. waterproof/windproof clothing, warm clothing, hats) worn and maintained by monitoring • Supply of clean drinking water	• Check local weather forecast before starting work • Review conditions throughout the working day	Workers	Before starting work and during work	
Objects ejected Broken equipment (e.g. cutters breaking) or flying debris (e.g. stones)	• Workers and bystanders/public • If struck, bruising, abrasion, fractures and potentially serious injuries	• All guarding in place and checked before use • Machinery regularly maintained and records kept • Use of appropriate PPE (e.g. safety glasses, goggles, visors, faceshields) which is maintained by monitoring	Use of signage and establishment of safety zones	Workers	Before starting work	
Vibration	• Workers • Reduction in feeling, e.g. hand-arm vibration syndrome (white finger)	• Minimising amount of time machinery is used • Regular maintenance and checks on anti-vibration mounts • Reference made to manufacturers' vibration levels and exposure times	Workers to be regularly reminded to report maintenance concerns	Supervisor	Weekly team meetings	
Manual handling	• Workers • Injuries or back pain or pain elsewhere from handling machinery	• Manual handling avoided where possible • Workers trained in safe manual handling and monitored.	Replace petrol-powered machinery with battery-powered machinery through replacement programme	Supervisor	Ongoing	
Noise Exposure to levels in excess of statutory limits	• Workers • Reduction in hearing capacity, short-term or permanent hearing loss	• Hearing protection worn if indicated by mandatory signage • Minimising exposure time to levels in excess of statutory limits • Appropriate hearing protection provided and maintained by monitoring	Agree and use communication system to ensure all involved can communicate effectively	Workers and supervisor	Before starting work	

▲ Figure 1.12 Risk assessment for pedestrian-operated landscaping machinery (Cont.)

What are the hazards?	Who might be harmed and how?	What are you already doing to control the risks?	What further action do you need to take to control the risks?	Who needs to carry out the action?	When is the action needed by?	Done
Mechanical equipment Moving parts	• Workers • Serious injury from unguarded moving parts of machinery • Cuts from sharp edges • Scalds or burns from hot parts	• All equipment checked before use and faults reported • Equipment not left running unattended • Appropriate guarding provided in line with manufacturer's handbook • Ear defenders and safety goggles provided and worn and maintained through monitoring	None			
Hazardous substances Contact with substances during pre-start checks and field repairs as well as machinery operation (including biological hazards and animal waste)	• Workers • Skin contact can lead to severe dermatitis and skin cancer, burns, skin irritation • Ingestion of animal waste can lead to toxocariasis etc.	• All workers wear overalls at all times while undertaking pre-start checks and repairs which are maintained through monitoring • Regular cleaning of overalls undertaken for workers • Faceshields provided and worn and maintained through monitoring • Workers informed to clean hands thoroughly and use skin creams or protective gloves before/after contact with hazardous substances and monitored.	None			
Fumes and dust Engine running, toxic exhaust fumes (e.g. carbon monoxide)	• Workers • Fumes may cause eye irritation and breathing difficulties	• Running engines restricted to outside use only	None			
Fire Refuelling of machinery	• Workers • Serious or fatal injuries from smoke inhalation/ burns	• Safe refuelling of machinery • Fuel stored safely in appropriate containers • Extinguishers provided and inspected under contract • Spillages contained and cleared immediately using spill kit/appropriate absorbent materials • Workers use safe stop procedure before carrying out refuelling	Replace petrol-powered machinery with battery-powered machinery through replacement programme	Supervisor	Ongoing	

This generic risk assessment has a review date set for 12 months' time, which may be appropriate. However, it may need to be reviewed before then if necessary, for example if the tools, equipment or machinery are changed, or there are changes in the law which need to be considered. It is also good practice to review risk assessments following an accident or incident to reflect on whether they need to be updated.

To contextualise and make this risk assessment site and task specific, it would be necessary to walk around the worksite and consider the tasks to be undertaken and who is involved or might be impacted (such as clients, visitors or the general public), in order to identify if there are any additional hazards or the risks have changed for existing hazards. Based on this, the existing controls should be reviewed to decide whether they are sufficient, or whether there is anything else which could be done to reduce the risks. For example, the landscaping contractor might be able to move obstacles in the client's garden so that they do not impact the work.

Figure 1.13 is an example of a risk assessment produced by a farm manager. Unlike the generic one produced by the landscaping contractor, this livestock risk assessment has been completed for a specific site and task (moving livestock). This risk assessment contains more specific details, such as the date and location the work will be done and some information which may be helpful in the event of an emergency. It also has a space for those involved to sign and date the risk assessment, which may provide evidence that they are aware of the risk controls.

Risk assessment – Moving livestock

Company name	N Matthew Limited	Assessment carried out by	D O'Connor
Date of assessment	01/06/2025	Date of work activity	02/06/2025
Location of work activity (including postcode)	Matthews Farm Near Bournemouth BH1 VVV	Meeting point for emergency services	Farm office Access via The Bull pub
Details of nearest telephone/mobile	01201 000000	Nearest accident and emergency unit and telephone number	Bournemouth General Hospital 01201 999999
Description of task	Moving herd of 30 cows between shed and field; no vehicles being used to support movement but tractor being used in vicinity of sheds		

What are the hazards?	Who might be harmed and how?	What are you already doing to control the risks?	What further action do you need to take to control the risks?	Who needs to carry out the action?	When is the action needed by?	Done
Slips and trips Slippery surfaces (e.g. from water, mud, ice and snow), uneven surfaces and obstacles	• Workers • Injuries from slipping or from tripping over objects	• Suitable safety footwear (with slip-resistant soles providing good grip) worn and maintained by monitoring	• Inspect worksite for hazards before starting task	Workers	Before starting task	02/06/2025
Weather conditions (e.g. high temperatures)	• Workers • Increased risk of injury, sunstroke, sunburn	• Appropriate clothing worn (e.g. overalls, hats) • Supply of clean drinking water • Sunblock worn	• Check local weather forecast before starting task • Review conditions throughout the working day	Workers	Before starting and during task	02/06/2025
Animal contact	• Workers • Trampling, crush injuries, bites, scratches, gores	• Warning signs in place • Careful layout preventing access to unsafe livestock • Workers trained in animal handling and movement • Use of appropriate PPE	• Monitor animal behaviour • Tractor driver not to operate close to livestock shed when animals being moved	Workers	Before starting and during task	02/06/2025

▲ Figure 1.13 Risk assessment for moving livestock *(Cont.)*

What are the hazards?	Who might be harmed and how?	What are you already doing to control the risks?	What further action do you need to take to control the risks?	Who needs to carry out the action?	When is the action needed by?	Done
Ill health/ hazardous substances	• Workers • Infection or disease from animals/ zoonotic diseases	• Biosecurity arrangements in place • Workers aware of need to report illness and aware of possible symptoms of common zoonotic diseases • Hygiene facilities available • Daily checks to ensure washing resources are sufficient • Regular cleaning of overalls undertaken for workers • Workers informed to clean hands thoroughly and use skin creams or protective gloves before/after contact with hazardous substances • Workers informed no food or drink to be consumed in livestock contact areas	Monitor livestock daily for signs of ill health	Workers	Before starting task	02/06/2025
Manual handling	• Workers • Injuries or back pain or pain elsewhere from lifting, pushing or pulling	• Manual handling avoided where possible • Workers trained in safe manual handling	None			
Contact with moving vehicles/ machinery	• Workers • Struck by vehicles, crush injuries	All workers driving farm vehicles are trained	None			

Name	Signature	Date
D O'Connor	D O'Connor	02/06/2025
N Smith	N Smith	02/06/2025

As noted above, there is no single format that risk assessments must follow, so long as they are suitable and sufficient. However, they are frequently derived from the HSE template. Figure 1.14 is an example of a risk assessment used in a zoo. This is a different format to the HSE template and makes reference to a generic risk assessment. This is likely to have been produced by first considering the generic risk assessment and then identifying what further control measures are required for a specific task to be undertaken. This risk assessment requires those involved to be aware of the details in the generic risk assessment, including the control measures.

Risk assessment – Zoo

Location address (including postcode)	Cambridge Animal Collection Cambridge CBY ZZZ
Emergency services meeting point	Main car park, access via A12
Nearest A&E hospital	Cambridge General Hospital A&E 01223 999999
Location of nearest telephone landline	Telephone access in staff room or main reception

Hazards *Additional hazards **not covered** by the generic risk assessment* *Who might be harmed and how?*	Control measures/precautions *Measures in place to reduce risks to acceptable level for each day any activity is undertaken*
Animal bites/ scratches from handling/moving/ interaction Staff	• Use of appropriate PPE (e.g. gloves) and handling and restraint equipment appropriate to the species • Training in safe handling and restraint of animals • Second member of staff always available in case required • Only authorised staff allowed to handle animals; visitors not allowed to handle animals
Spread of zoonotic disease Staff	• Minimised direct contact with animals • Appropriate PPE or RPE worn if identified (e.g. by COSHH assessment) • Hygiene procedures in place, e.g. access to hand-washing facilities, hand sanitiser, foot/boot dip Warning signs in place • Regular health checks/vet assessments of animals to identify those that are high risk and health monitoring of staff (checks in line with COSHH assessment if identified) • Visitors not allowed direct contact with animals
Slips/trips/falls Staff/visitors	• High standard of cleaning procedures in place to deal with spillages etc. • Safety footwear (with slip-resistant soles providing good grip) worn • Removal of potential trip hazards and associated obstacles • Use of wet floor signs/hazard warning signs where required
Fire hazards Staff/visitors	• Fire detection alarm systems in place, appropriate fire equipment (e.g. fire extinguishers) in place, emergency evacuation and general training in place, fire policy in place • Smoking restricted to designated areas • Visitors notified of fire alarm testing and evacuation procedure
Use of hazardous chemicals (disinfectants) Staff	• COSHH training provided for all staff, all cleaning duties undertaken in accordance with good housekeeping practices, use of appropriate PPE or RPE (if identified by COSHH assessment), warning signage used • Chemicals clearly labelled and stored in secure area

Additional information	• First aiders and first-aid kit available onsite (staff room and main reception) • Refer to generic workplace risk assessment available in staff room • Formal accident reporting and investigation procedure in place

RA completed by:	S White	Date:	12/04/24

▲ Figure 1.14 Risk assessment for a zoo

When interpreting risk assessments, it is vital to implement both the pre-existing control measures (what should already be happening) as well as any additional control measures that have been identified. It is also appropriate, as noted above, to adapt control measures during the work activity. Finally, it is important to reflect on the work when it is completed and identify if anything has been learned which might impact on completion of the next risk assessment.

Test yourself

Review the three sample risk assessments provided in Figures 1.12, 1.13 and 1.14. What differences can you identify between them? What additional information or details might you add in?

Documents associated with risk assessments

Where a risk assessment identifies high-risk tasks (for example the severity and likelihood of harm are high), employers may decide to produce a method statement. Method statements expand on the control measures and provide more detailed information about how a task should be done in order to reduce the risk of accidents or incidents occurring. Method statements set out step by step how the task should be completed and are used to communicate information such as:
- roles and responsibilities of everyone involved
- details about the tools, equipment and machinery to be used
- what safety measures should be in place
- a step-by-step procedure of how the work must be done (including set up and tidy up at the end)
- PPE requirements
- first-aid and welfare provision and details of any emergency procedures.

Each method statement also contains information which sets out where and when it is relevant, for example location, date or timescale when it is valid and scope (what it covers and what it does not cover).

Risk assessments are required under the Management of Health and Safety at Work Regulations 1999, but method statements are normally only required for tasks considered to be high risk (for example, they are frequently produced for arboriculture work). Together they are referred to as RAMS (**R**isk **A**ssessments and **M**ethod **S**tatements). Method statements provide evidence that work activities have been properly planned and risk controlled. A requirement for RAMS

to be produced and made available may be written into work contracts or tenders.

Additionally, risk assessments can contribute to the development of a safe system of work (SSOW). An SSOW is perhaps best described as the business' or organisation's standard way of undertaking a work activity, which implements the outcome from a relevant risk assessment. It is similar to a method statement but can be broader in scope. For example, it may include additional information such as arrangements for monitoring compliance with work procedures, or competency requirements for individuals specific to their roles.

Manual handling risk assessments

Given the types of activities undertaken within the land-based sector, it is inevitable that workers are required to move tools, equipment and resources around the workplace. Under the Manual Handling Operations Regulations 1992 (see page 5), employers are required to risk assess manual handling tasks. The regulations require manual handling tasks to be avoided if reasonably practicable, for example by materials or products being delivered directly to the worksite by the supplier. Where manual handling cannot be avoided, employers should make the risk as low as reasonably practicable. This could involve organising tasks so that a mechanical aid (for example pallet truck, forklift, timber tongs, cylinder trolley, engine hoist) could be used to reduce the risk of harm. In addition, employers are required to provide workers with appropriate instruction and training to enable them to understand safe manual handling techniques as they relate to lifting/lowering and carrying loads.

There are four key variables to consider when risk assessing a manual handling activity:
1. Individual (the capabilities and limitations of the individual handling the load)
2. Task (the distance the load needs to be moved)
3. Load (the weight, stability and shape of the load to be handled)
4. Environment (potential obstacles and lighting).

In terms of the individual handling the load, employers should take into account vulnerable workers and others who may be at an increased risk, such as people with a disability, new or expectant mothers, inexperienced or young workers, lone workers or those for whom English is not their first language (see Chapter 6). In addition, these individuals might be at

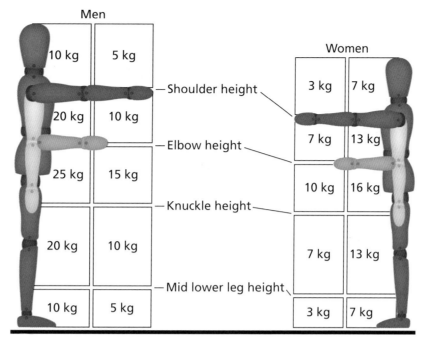

▲ Figure 1.15 Lifting and lowering risk filter

an increased risk when undertaking other types of work activities.

As a result of the four manual handling variables, there is not a safe weight limit associated with lifting/ lowering and carrying of loads. The regulations, therefore, do not set limits. However, the HSE has suggested what load weights might be reasonably handled for straightforward lifting/lowering activities (Figure 1.15). This is based on the assumption that the load is easily grasped with both hands, is handled in reasonable working conditions and the worker is in a stable body position.

The HSE suggests that these filter weights may be reasonably applied to carrying activities under certain conditions. For example, the individual is able to walk normally, the load is held against the body and the distance travelled is no further than approximately 10 m without resting.

However, where the handling is more complex (such as where the load exceeds the filter weight, the lift involves twisting of the torso, or more than one lift is undertaken every two minutes) then the employer must carry out a more detailed risk assessment. To support employers, the HSE has published manual handling assessment charts (known as 'the MAC tool') to undertake three types of assessment:

▶ lifting operations
▶ carrying operations
▶ team handling operations.

There can be significant health consequences for anyone undertaking unsafe manual handling activities. These include:

▶ short-term injuries, such as sprains and muscle strain
▶ long-term injuries and health conditions, such as musculoskeletal injuries.

In addition, there are other non-health-related consequences which can result from an injury caused or exacerbated by poor manual handling, including:

▶ absence from work
▶ loss of comfort and dignity
▶ investigation/action by an enforcement authority (for example HSE).

Implications of poor development and application of a risk assessment

It is important to consider the risk assessment process as a helpful activity that contributes to a positive working environment for everyone, rather than just an administrative task that must be performed.

The implications of poor development and application of a risk assessment are wide-ranging but potentially include:

▶ poor working practices (for example unmotivated workers and low productivity)
▶ higher risk of accidents resulting in long-term consequences (for example a high number of days lost through staff sickness/injury)

- risk of time lost in an emergency situation, call out or rescue (for example time spent liaising with the emergency services)
- financial impact in loss of working time, income or reputation (for example poor reputation with potential customers reducing the likelihood of gaining work).

Procedures to follow when dealing with emergency situations

The land-based sector is particularly vulnerable to the working environment changing unexpectedly (for example working with animals, changing weather conditions), hence the importance of dynamic risk assessment. However, despite prior planning of work activities, it is common practice for employers to produce emergency plans or take additional measures because of the risk of an emergency situation or accident occurring.

Case study

Forestry England expects first aiders working in core operations such as harvesting, fencing and pesticides application or lone workers on Forestry Commission managed land to hold either:

- First Aid at Work (FAW+F), based on a minimum three-day course
- Emergency First Aid at Work (EFAW+F), based on a minimum one-day course.

The term '+F' refers to additional training on topics such as hypothermia/exposure, Lyme's disease, catastrophic bleeding (application of haemostatic dressings etc.) and casualty evacuation.

What factors might make first aid in these situations more challenging?

Examples of emergency situations include:

- accidents causing injury
- falls from working at height
- accidents involving vehicles, tools, machinery and equipment
- spillage of hazardous substances
- flooding
- fire
- medical issues
- accidents in remote/restricted-access locations
- weather-related emergencies
- dangers posed by above-ground and underground services.

In the event of an emergency occurring, it is important to remain as calm as possible and take decisive action. Typical steps to take may include the following:

- **Assess the situation**: how serious is the emergency and is there a risk of it spreading or becoming more severe?
- **Ensure the safety of self and others in the area**: if possible, move away from any immediate danger to a safe location.
- **Seek assistance if required**: contact the emergency services or employer.
- **Administer first aid if required**
- **Evacuate the area and warn others**: by using signage or by telephone.

Given the potential remoteness of worksites, emergency communications are an important consideration for emergency planning. There are alternative ways to contact the emergency services (police, ambulance, fire and rescue or coastguard) in addition to calling 999. For example, 112 is the pan-European equivalent to 999 but can also be used in the UK. Alternatively, the emergency SMS service in the UK allows anyone to send an SMS text message from a mobile phone to the 999 services. However, the mobile phone must be registered before this service can be used. Although intended to support deaf, hearing-impaired and speech-impaired people, it can be used by anyone, particularly where a mobile phone signal is poor. Note that communications will take longer than the standard voice 999 service. For non-emergencies, the police can be contacted by calling 101, and the NHS can provide medical advice by calling 111.

Research

Figure 1.16 shows an emergency planning sheet for Crane Hill Farm, which includes contact details, worksite location and the nearest access point. Talk to your tutor or industry experience provider about how emergency planning can be applied to your chosen industry. Do they already use something similar? What additional or alternative information might be helpful to include?

Emergency contact details and information	
Worksite location	Crane Hill Farm
Grid reference	TL123456
Location	Hill Farm Estate
Nearest access point(s) (AP)	National Grid Reference (NGR), AP1: Crane Hill Farm TL789101
What3words location	
Type of access	AP1: Track suitable for emergency vehicles only
Nearest Accident & Emergency hospital:	Address: Telephone number (landline):
Emergency contact details	Address: Office telephone number (landline):
Emergency contact(s)	Name and job title: Telephone number (mobile):
Ancillary information	First aid kit located in the works vehicle
Date information last updated	21/08/2024

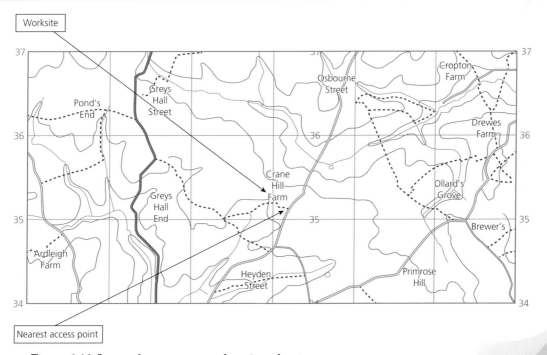

▲ Figure 1.16 A sample emergency planning sheet

Assessment practice

1 A worker has been asked to move 25 bags of animal feed from the load bay of a van into the feed store. What should be considered first? (2 marks)

2 When undertaking a risk assessment, certain groups of workers might be considered at greater risk than others and may need additional or different control measures. Identify three of these groups of workers. (3 marks)

3 Explain why dynamic risk assessments are essential in the workplace. (2 marks)

4 Explain why approved codes of practice (ACOPs) are helpful to employers. (2 marks)

5 Describe **two** advantages of signage for communicating information about health and safety in the workplace. (4 marks)

6 Explain **three** factors which should be considered when deciding if an item of personal protective equipment is appropriate. (6 marks)

7 Describe **four** legal responsibilities of an employee/worker while at work. (4 marks)

8 Explain the steps in the hierarchy of control measures. (6 marks)

9 Tilly manages a small forestry harvesting contracting business. One worker was seriously injured at work, and this was reportable under RIDDOR. As a result of the accident, the business is going to be visited by an inspector from the Health and Safety Executive.

Explain what the potential consequences might be for the business if the inspector finds evidence of non-compliance with health and safety requirements. (6 marks)

10 Marek is planning the induction programme for Jaime, a new employee who is about to start working at the zoo. Marek wants to make sure Jaime is informed of key health, safety and welfare information.

Explain what health, safety and welfare information relating to the workplace might be included within a new employee's induction programme. (6 marks)

Further reading

You may find some of the following helpful for keeping up to date with changes in health, safety and welfare legislation and guidance on how to comply with current legislation:

▶ Advisory, Conciliation and Arbitration Service (Acas)
▶ Farm Safety Foundation (FSF)
▶ Forestry Industry Safety Accord (FISA)
▶ Health and Safety Executive (HSE)
▶ British and Irish Association of Zoos and Aquariums (2020) *BIAZA Health and Safety Guidelines for Zoos and Aquariums.*
▶ Health and Safety Executive (HSE) (2013) *Preventing accidents to children on farms (INDG472),* HSE Books.
▶ Health and Safety Executive (HSE) (2013) *Rider-operated lift trucks: Operator training and safe use: Approved Code of Practice and guidance (L117),* 3rd edition, HSE Books.
▶ Health and Safety Executive (HSE) (2013) *Control of substances hazardous to health: The Control of Substances Hazardous to Health Regulations 2002: Approved Code of Practice and guidance (L5),* 6th edition, HSE Books.
▶ Health and Safety Executive (HSE) (2013) *Workplace health, safety and welfare: Workplace (Health, Safety and Welfare) Regulations 1992: Approved Code of Practice and guidance (L24),* 2nd edition, HSE Books.
▶ Health and Safety Executive (HSE) (2014) *Safe use of lifting equipment: Lifting Operations and Lifting Equipment Regulations 1998: Approved Code of Practice and guidance (L113),* 2nd edition, HSE Books.
▶ Health and Safety Executive (HSE) (2014) *Safe use of work equipment: Provision and Use of Work Equipment Regulations 1998: Approved Code of Practice and guidance (L22),* 4th edition, HSE Books.

▶ Health and Safety Executive (HSE) (2016) *Manual handling: Manual Handling Operations Regulations 1992: Guidance on Regulations (L23)*, 4th edition, HSE Books.

▶ Health and Safety Executive (HSE) (2017) *Farmwise: Your essential guide to health and safety in agriculture (HSG270)*, 3rd edition, HSE Books.

▶ Health and Safety Executive (HSE) (2019) *Manual handling assessment charts (the MAC tool) (INDG383)*, 3rd edition, HSE Books.

▶ Health and Safety Executive (HSE) (2021) *Controlling noise at work: The Control of Noise at Work Regulations 2005: Guidance on Regulations (L108)*, 3rd edition, HSE Books.

▶ Health and Safety Executive (HSE) (2022) *Personal protective equipment at work: The Personal Protective Equipment at Work Regulations 1992 (as amended): Guidance on Regulations (L25)*, 4th edition, HSE Books.

2 Sustainability

Introduction

The concept of sustainability has evolved over time to become an integral part of the activities undertaken by organisations and businesses across all sectors and industries. It encompasses the responsible use of natural and physical resources to avoid their depletion over time and without negatively impacting their accessibility for future generations.

Sustainability is about making choices to achieve a balance between economic, environmental and social demands. While there are potential opportunities for the land-based sector, sustainability is complex and open to challenges from stakeholders who believe not enough is being done, particularly to minimise the impact of development on climate change.

Learning outcomes

By the end of this chapter, you will understand:
- ▶ the purpose of legislation and associated obligations for businesses, employees and stakeholders
- ▶ the implications of not complying with legislation
- ▶ opportunities and risks that sustainability policies bring to the agriculture, environmental and animal care sector
- ▶ environmental performance measures, including water and energy use, carbon capture, species targets, water, soil and air quality and mandatory reporting
- ▶ the UK government definition and purpose of sustainable development
- ▶ types of sustainable solutions and improvements to meet development goals, including social, environmental, economic and human

- ▶ awareness of sustainable development goals nationally
- ▶ sustainable development goals at a macro (national and international) and micro (business) level
- ▶ concerns and expectations of key stakeholders (social, environmental, economic and human)
- ▶ the causes, impact and management of climate change
- ▶ the difference between weather and climate
- ▶ the meaning of climate change – long-term shifts in temperatures and weather patterns
- ▶ policies and initiatives to manage these changes at national and local level
- ▶ the Ten Point Plan for a Green Industrial Revolution.

2.1 Key requirements of environmental legislation and key government policies

Purpose of legislation and associated obligations for businesses, employees and stakeholders

Environmental legislation and government policies are the result of factors which include stakeholder pressure groups and campaigns, specific environmental incidents, outcomes from court cases and statutory reviews. They are also influenced by international agreements associated with nature and biodiversity, to which the UK is a signatory, or adopted legislation. These include:

▶ Convention on Biological Diversity
▶ Ramsar Convention on Wetlands
▶ Convention on International Trade in Endangered Species of Wild Fauna and Flora
▶ Bern Convention of the Conservation of European Wildlife and Natural Habitats
▶ Bonn Convention on Migratory Species of Wild Animals
▶ OSPAR Convention (for the Protection of the Marine Environment of the North-East Atlantic)
▶ Convention Concerning the Protection of the World Cultural and Natural Heritage (UNESCO World Heritage Convention)
▶ G7 2030 Nature Compact.

One of the consequences of the UK being a signatory to international agreements has been the creation of designated sites or protected areas, in addition to those that are nationally or locally designated. These sites or areas include:

▶ National Nature Reserves (NNRs)
▶ Sites of Special Scientific Interest (SSSIs)
▶ Marine Conservation Zones (MCZs)
▶ Special Protected Areas (SPAs) and Special Areas of Conservation (SACs) (designated under EU law)
▶ Sites designated under the Ramsar Convention
▶ National Landscapes (formerly known as Areas of Outstanding Natural Beauty (AONBs))
▶ National Parks.

This approach to protecting specific species or landscapes/habitats because of their importance places restrictions on certain developments and activities. It is, therefore, important for land-based managers to check for, and be aware of, any protected area restrictions that might apply, before starting any works.

Industry tip

When surveying land and planning work, land-based managers often use the UK government MAGIC (Multi-Agency Geographic Information for the Countryside) website, managed by the Department for Environment, Food and Rural Affairs (Defra). This website brings together information about the natural environment from a number of government departments. It is an interactive map which allows anyone to freely search and explore geographic information about designated areas, habitats and species etc.

25 Year Environment Plan (25 YEP)

Current UK government policy is based on the 25 Year Environment Plan (25 YEP). This was published by the government in 2018 and set out how it intended to work with businesses and communities to improve the environment within a generation. It set the following 25-year goals:

1 Clean air
2 Clean and plentiful water
3 Thriving plants and wildlife
4 A reduced risk of harm from environmental hazards such as flooding and drought
5 Using resources from nature more sustainably and efficiently
6 Enhanced beauty, heritage and engagement with the natural environment
7 Mitigating and adapting to climate change
8 Minimising waste
9 Managing exposure to chemicals
10 Enhancing biosecurity.

To support the government in monitoring the impact of the plan, the Outcome Indicator Framework was designed, based on the concept of a natural capital approach. This is defined within the 25 YEP as the sum of our ecosystems, species, freshwater, land, soils, minerals, air and seas, that either directly or indirectly bring value to people and the country (UK) at large. As a result, natural capital provides us with ecosystem services, climate regulation, genetic resources, soil fertility and production, clean air and water, biodiversity, recreation and protection from hazards.

Source: UK Government (2018) *A Green Future: Our 25 Year Plan to Improve the Environment*, Department for Environment, Food and Rural Affairs

The framework uses a set of indicators, arranged into ten broad themes:

A Air
B Water
C Seas and estuaries
D Wildlife
E Natural resources
F Resilience
G Natural beauty and engagement
H Biosecurity, chemical and noise
I Resource use and waste
J International

Each theme is then broken down into a series of individual indicators. Each indicator expresses one aspect of natural capital as numbers/statistics. By monitoring changes in these indicators over time, the government's stated intention is to monitor performance of natural capital and therefore assess progress towards the 25 YEP goals.

Case study

Wildlife D

▲ Figure 2.1 Wildlife indicator Theme D

One example of a 25 YEP indicator is *Wildlife – D5: Conservation status of our native species*. This indicator is used to track changes in the risk of extinction to our native terrestrial, freshwater and marine species, through a Red List index based on the International Union for Conservation of Nature's (IUCN) Red List categories. It uses the numbers of species in each Red List category to determine an index value for groups of species. This index value is subsequently intended to be used to monitor long-term improvement or deterioration in their risk of extinction.

▶ Why might indicators be a useful way of monitoring the impact of a plan?
▶ If the D5 indicator showed the conservation status of a specific species was becoming more vulnerable over time, what might be the potential responses?

Key term

Circular economy: system in which pollution and waste are eliminated as resources are kept in circulation through reuse or recycling, for example composting, refurbishment and remanufacture

Environment Act 2021

The Environment Act 2021 is the key strategic piece of legislation associated with how we sustainably manage our environment. It was intended to protect and enhance the environment for future generations by moving towards a **circular economy**. As a result, it set out governmental intentions, including:

▶ making better use of natural resources
▶ increasing biodiversity
▶ improving air and water quality
▶ reducing waste
▶ restoring natural habitats
▶ halting species decline by 2030 (for example reverse decline in water vole, hedgehog and red squirrel populations, including overseas).

Industry tip

It is important to be aware that some key legislation protects identified species wherever they exist. Therefore, individual species protection may not be tied to a specific location, but travels with the species concerned.

Test yourself

It is common for stakeholder groups such as conservation charities and environmental groups to take the position that environmental legislation is not sufficiently robust to deal with risks to our environment.

Investigate what aspects of the Environment Act 2021 stakeholder groups do not believe does enough to protect our environment. Explain whether you agree with them.

The Environment Act made it a requirement for the 25 YEP to be reviewed every five years. The plan was subsequently revised and published as the Environmental Improvement Plan (EIP) 2023 for England. This set thriving plants and wildlife as the apex goal, with eight other goals under its umbrella.

Connections between our environmental goals

Our apex goal
Goal 1:
Thriving plants and wildlife

Improving environmental quality

Goal 2:
Clean air

Goal 3:
Clean and plentiful water

Goal 4:
Managing exposure to chemicals and pesticides

Improving our use of resources

Goal 5:
Maximise our resources, minimise our waste

Goal 6:
Using resources from nature sustainably

Improving our mitigation of climate change

Goal 7:
Mitigating and adapting to climate change

Goal 8:
Reduced risk of harm from environmental hazards

Improving our biosecurity

Goal 9:
Enhancing biosecurity

Goal 10:
Enhanced beauty, heritage, and engagement with the natural environment

▲ Figure 2.2 Connections between environmental goals, Environmental Improvement Plan 2023

Source: UK Government (2023) *Environmental Improvement Plan 2023: First revision of the 25 Year Environment Plan*, Department for Environment, Food and Rural Affairs

It also amended 'managing exposure to chemicals' to 'managing exposure to chemicals and pesticides'.

The Act also allows the government to set legally binding long-term environmental targets (for example to reduce levels of fine particulate matter) and created the Office for Environmental Protection (OEP). This is an independent, non-departmental public body, sponsored by the Department for Environment, Food and Rural Affairs (Defra), with powers to hold the following to account on their environmental obligations:
▶ government ministers
▶ government departments
▶ regulators
▶ local authorities
▶ some private bodies with public duties (such as water companies).

Test yourself

Research the OEP. Identify the four types of activities it undertakes and what enforcement powers it has.

There are other key pieces of legislation which are narrower in scope but focus on, and play a critical role in, environmental, species and habitat protection:
▶ Control of Pollution Act 1974
▶ Environmental Protection Act 1990
▶ Wildlife and Countryside Act 1981
▶ Weeds Act 1959
▶ Protection of Badgers Act 1992
▶ National Parks and Access to the Countryside Act 1949
▶ Countryside and Rights of Way Act 2000
▶ Climate Change Act 2008
▶ Food and Environment Protection Act 1985

- Plant Protection Products (Sustainable Use) Regulations 2012
- Town and Country Planning Act 1990
- Conservation of Habitats and Species Regulations 2017.

Test yourself

Investigate how three of these pieces of legislation impact on working practices in your chosen land-based industry. What activities must you do or not do to ensure you are compliant with the law?

Purpose of legislation and associated obligations for businesses, employees and stakeholders

Collectively, current environmental legislation places a range of obligations on **public authorities**, **public bodies**, organisations, businesses, employees and stakeholders. These obligations may contribute to or involve:

- improving the natural environment (for example planning permission being subject to approval of a biodiversity gain plan)
- waste and resource efficiency (for example charging for single-use plastics and providing efficiency information such as product recyclability labelling)
- improving air quality (for example enforcement of smoke control areas)
- improving water quality (for example reduction in sewage discharges into waterways)
- enhancing nature and biodiversity (for example large businesses being prohibited from using resources associated with wide-scale deforestation, including overseas deforestation)
- reducing recurring noise and nuisance (ensuring noise does not reach specific levels or intensities)
- enhancing **conservation covenants** (for example inclusion on the Biodiversity Gain Site Register)
- regulation of chemicals (for example the use and disposal of veterinary medicines or plant protection products).

Test yourself

Research the Biodiversity Gain Site Register and identify what the purpose of the register is and who manages it.

Biodiversity net gain

The Environment Act 2021 made biodiversity net gain a legal requirement in England from 12 February

Key terms

Public authorities: organisations that perform a public function, which include ministerial departments and local authorities

Public bodies: publicly funded organisations that deliver a government or public service but are not ministerial departments, for example Animal and Plant Health Agency, British Wool, Environment Agency, Health and Safety Executive, Joint Nature Conservation Committee, Met Office and Veterinary Medicines Directorate; public bodies may also be partially or wholly funded through industry levies (payment demands) or customers directly paying for specific services

Conservation covenants: legally binding agreements between a landowner (such as a property developer) and a charity or public body (such as a local authority) to do (or not do) something to conserve the heritage or natural features of their land; these covenants must deliver a public good but do not have to allow public access onto the land

2024. Enforceable under the Town and Country Planning Act 1990, developers are required to ensure developments achieve a minimum biodiversity net gain of 10 percent which is then retained for at least 30 years. This means it is a planning condition and requirement of planning consent that all developments, with few exceptions, must provide 10 per cent more or better-quality biodiversity than was present before the development. Consequently, there is a formal requirement to measure biodiversity. To ensure consistent measurement, local planning authorities and other stakeholders base decisions on measurements made using the current version of the Department for Environment, Food and Rural Affairs (Defra) biodiversity metric.

Implications of not complying with legislation

Implications of not complying with environmental legislation include:

- adverse publicity
- expulsion from industry accreditation schemes or membership of trade organisations
- restoration costs
- increased insurance premiums
- increased regulatory scrutiny

- increased **pollution** (including air, water, soil/land, noise and light)
- local authority fines and enforcement notices
- regulatory action (specific options depend on the type of offence) including:
  - advice or guidance
  - warning
  - formal caution
  - fine/monetary penalty (fixed or variable)
  - enforcement notices (compliance notice, restoration notice, stop notice)
  - prosecution.

Improve your English

The word **adverse** is an adjective that is used in this context to refer to something that has a negative or harmful impact. What potential negative effects might pollution have for the long-term health of the UK's flora and fauna?

The word **diffuse** is an adjective that is used in this context to refer to something that is spread out over a large area or between a large number of people, which usually makes it weaker or less noticeable. What challenges might pollution described as diffuse present when trying to reduce the pollution?

Penalties

The penalties following successful prosecution are usually a fine and/or imprisonment. In the Magistrates' Court, the maximum penalty is usually a fine of up to £50,000 and/or six months' imprisonment. In the Crown Court, the maximum penalty is usually an unlimited fine and/or two years' imprisonment. The courts can also impose ancillary orders which can result in further penalties, such as seizure of vehicles. Following conviction for a serious environmental offence, there are potentially additional implications. For example, a prosecutor may request that:

- the Serious Organised Crime Agency (SOCA) confiscate assets from offenders equal to the financial benefit gained from the criminal activity
- the Crown Court make a serious crime prevention order (SCPO) which restricts the offender's ability to commit further serious crimes in the future.

There are a number of government departments and public bodies who have regulatory powers that allow them to enforce environmental laws:

- Forestry Commission (for example breaches of felling licences)
- Environment Agency (for example failure to register as a waste broker or dealer)
- Natural England (for example breaches of wildlife licences)
- Local authorities (for example breaches of tree preservation orders).

Case study

Local authority environmental health officers have the power to serve an **abatement notice** under the Environmental Protection Act to deal with a **statutory nuisance**. If the person named on the notice does not satisfactorily address the nuisance within 21 days (such as restrict when something happens), they can be fined for each day the nuisance continues, or the local authority can do whatever is necessary to abate the nuisance, such as confiscating equipment.
- What is considered a statutory nuisance?
- What might cause a statutory nuisance?

Improve your English

The word 'abatement' is a noun which refers to either reducing or ending something.

What do you think this means in the context of a pollution abatement notice?

Key terms

Pollution: the release or introduction of something into the environment that causes an *adverse* effect; it can take a variety of forms (for example gas, solid, energy) and arises from both natural and human activities; the origin of a pollutant is commonly categorised as either:
- point source, as it originates from a specific location (for example a fuel container leaking into a stream or river)
- *diffuse* source (or non-point source), as it originates from multiple locations (for example pesticide or fertiliser run-off from agricultural land)

Abatement notice: a legal enforcement notice that informs the recipient of actions they are required to take in relation to a statutory nuisance

Statutory nuisance: something that poses a public health risk (for example animal keeping, offensive smells, dust, noise or smoke) or substantially interferes with someone's reasonable enjoyment of their property, either regularly or for an unreasonable period of time

Opportunities and risks that sustainability policies bring to the land-based sector

Governmental sustainability policies can present both opportunities and risks to the agriculture, environmental and animal care sector.

Opportunities

Financial opportunities include the potential to:

▶ target new and emerging markets through sustainable practices, leading to sustainability branding
▶ expand goods and services into the sustainability agenda
▶ develop new products to serve the sustainability agenda
▶ take advantage of government initiatives and funding for environmental services
▶ use or repurpose waste products to generate additional income or increase profit
▶ increase customers because of a reputation for good waste management practices.

Environmental opportunities include the potential to utilise waste as a resource.

Risks

Financial risks include the potential for:

▶ additional business costs during a product recall
▶ loss of custom through reputation damage from non-compliance
▶ financial costs of repairing or restoring damage to ecosystems associated with poor waste management.

Environmental risks include the potential for environmental damage (for example due to poor waste management).

Legal risks include the potential for enforcement action (such as prosecution) for breaches of legislation.

However, it is important to consider that the outcome may be organisation or business specific and can be influenced by the mechanism used by the government to implement policy. 'Hard' implementation may be through legislation or regulation, which require compliance. 'Soft' implementation may be through financial incentives such as grants or tax breaks or disincentives (taxation) used to encourage desired behaviours.

Environmental performance measures

Some organisations and businesses publish information on their environmental performance because they believe this brings them, their investors or their shareholders direct or indirect benefits. For example, they use this information to promote their green credentials, which may provide them with a competitive advantage in the marketplace. It may also generate new business opportunities. These environmental performance measures include water and energy use, carbon capture, species targets, and water, soil and air quality targets.

Since 6 April 2022, some UK companies and limited liability partnerships have a legal requirement to include environmental and climate-related financial information, including what **key performance indicators (KPIs)** they use, as part of their annual report. This could include how much water they use or greenhouse gases or waste they produce when delivering their services or products. The information should include climate-related risks (both physical risks and transition risks) and opportunities as they relate to technology, policy, market and legal and reputational. The information should be sufficiently detailed to enable someone to understand the potential impact on the company, as well as what mitigation the company has put in place, or intends to put in place.

Waste management

Historically, the UK has managed waste through approaches such as unregulated landfill or disposing directly into waterways and the sea. However, it is accepted that inconsiderate and inappropriate disposal can have a significant negative impact on the environment and human health. With a move towards a circular economy, minimisation of waste and the potential to use waste as a resource are becoming increasingly important to organisations and businesses looking to increase profit, as well as reduce any environmental impact. Therefore, it is important to consider what waste might be produced and how it can be appropriately managed.

> **Key term**
>
> **Key performance indicators (KPIs)**: individual criteria which can be measured and quantified; this means that once each criterion has been measured or counted, it is expressed as a numerical value, which has meaning

Common waste materials include:
- metal
- wood
- arisings (left over materials, surplus products or by-products from work or industrial activities)
- glass
- plastics
- paper
- electronics
- fuels and oils
- chemicals and substrates
- asbestos
- crop residues
- bulky organic material.

The requirements of the EU Waste Framework Directive 2008, which sets out what is deemed waste and how it should be managed, has been incorporated into UK regulation of waste. The Environment Agency is the enforcement authority associated with discarded waste in England. In general, something is considered to be waste if it has been discarded by the **holder**. Therefore, what might be referred to as waste might not be legally considered to be waste. The Environment Agency considers factors such as potential for environmental harm, burden on the holder, value to the holder, certainty of use or management by the holder when determining whether materials are discarded waste.

Waste classification

Residues from work might not be considered discarded waste if they are clearly intended to be (re)used or recycled. If these residues are subsequently recovered or recycled, they are considered to be a useful material and classed as non-waste if they meet the following four conditions (referred to as the 'end of waste test'):
- Condition (a) – the substance or object is to be used for specific purposes
- Condition (b) – a market or demand exists for such a substance or object
- Condition (c) – the substance or object fulfils the technical requirements for the specific purposes and meets the existing legislation and standards applicable to products

> **Key term**
>
> **Holder**: defined by the Environment Agency as the legal entity or individual who has control over waste at the time it is discarded

- Condition (d) – the use of the substance or object will not lead to overall adverse environmental or human health impacts.

Alternatively, in specific circumstances the residues may be considered as by-product (non-waste) status if they meet the following four conditions (referred to as the 'by-product test'):
- Condition (a) – further use of the substance or object is certain
- Condition (b) – the substance or object can be used directly without any further processing other than normal industrial practice
- Condition (c) – the substance or object is produced as an integral part of the production process
- Condition (d) – further use is lawful, that is the substance or object fulfils all relevant product, environmental and health protection requirements for the specific use and will not lead to overall adverse environmental or human health impacts.

Source: Environment Agency (2024) *Guidance: Check if your material is waste*

Individuals or organisations can self-assess if a material meets the by-product test, the end of waste test or should be considered waste, or they can contact the Environment Agency's definition of waste service for an opinion. This is not a free service and costs £125 per hour, based on the time and materials involved in undertaking the review. It typically takes 3 to 18 months for the Environment Agency to form its opinion.

> **Test yourself**
>
> For your industry, consider what residues might be produced and identify if any might be considered by-product (non-waste) status.

There are a range of terms that are commonly applied to waste:
- **Controlled waste**: the Controlled Waste (England and Wales) Regulations 2012, enabled under the Environmental Protection Act 1990, classify waste into three main categories which set out expectations for management and disposal:
  - commercial waste
  - household waste
  - industrial waste.
- **Hazardous waste** contains substances or has properties with the potential to harm the environment or human health (for example pesticides).

- **POPs waste** contains a high level of persistent organic pollutants (POPs) with the potential to harm the environment or human health (for example a common source of POPs waste is waste electrical and electronic equipment (WEEE)).
- **Non-hazardous waste** does not have the potential to harm the environment or human health.
- **Recyclable waste** can be reused or transformed into new products such as glass jars and bottles.
- **Non-recyclable waste** cannot be reused or transformed into new products.

It is possible for more than one of these terms to be applied to a parcel of waste. For example, general household waste could be considered non-hazardous, non-recyclable, controlled waste.

Classifying something as waste has a specific legal meaning. Indeed, a by-product that might be described as waste does not have to be classified if it is non-waste or a type of waste excluded from classification. The Environment Agency has published detailed guidance (*Technical Guidance WM3: Waste Classification – Guidance on the classification and assessment of waste*) on what waste must be classified under the Waste Directive. However, this does not mean that waste that does not need to be classified is not covered by other legislation. The current classification system is set out in the List of Waste (LoW). Following consideration of the substances within the waste and the properties of the waste, the classification assigned is based on the principle of the worst-case substance (such as mixed waste). The classification system assigns the waste to one of three classes: physical hazard, human health hazard or environmental hazard (Figure 2.3). These classes have an associated hazard warning symbol (see Chapter 1, page 12).

The majority of wastes from agriculture, horticulture, aquaculture, forestry, hunting and fishing, and food preparation and processing are considered 'absolute non-hazardous' wastes and automatically not hazardous. One exception is agrochemical waste. However, it is important to carefully assess the contents of the waste and how it has been produced.

Waste management hierarchy

Organisations and businesses can use the waste management hierarchy to make decisions about waste (Figure 2.4). This consists of five levels and is similar to the hierarchy of control measures (see Chapter 1, page 18). Users should start at the top and work downwards. The aim is to minimise the waste that needs to be disposed of. The levels are as follows:

- **Prevention**: use resources and implement processes that minimise the production of waste.
- **Reuse**: reuse waste by repairing, repurposing or refurbishing.
- **Recycling**: process waste to produce new products, thereby conserving resources and reducing consumption of new raw materials.
- **Recovery**: recover energy from the waste (such as through anaerobic digestion or incineration).
- **Disposal**: as a last resort, dispose of the minimum amount of waste responsibly (via licensed landfill or waste treatment).

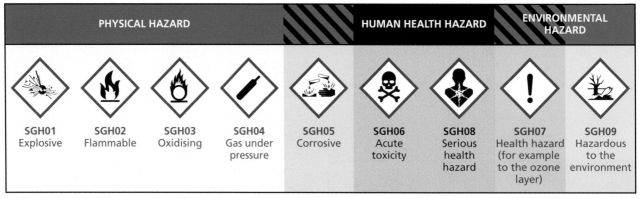

▲ Figure 2.3 Different types of hazards

Waste management hierarchy — 5 Rs of waste management

Most preferred → ... → Least preferred

Prevention — Refuse, Reduce
Reuse — Reuse, Repurpose
Recycling — Recycle
Recovery
Disposal

▲ Figure 2.4 Relationship between the waste management hierarchy and the five Rs of waste management

An alternative is for organisations and businesses to consider the '5 Rs' of waste management, which also sets out a hierarchical framework to support decision-making:

▶ **Refuse**: take opportunities to eliminate the potential to generate waste
▶ **Reduce**: find ways to minimise the waste produced
▶ **Reuse**
▶ **Repurpose**: find alternative uses for waste
▶ **Recycle**.

Waste duty of care

The Environmental Protection Act 1990 (as amended) established the duty of care for anyone that produces, carries or disposes of waste, as well as the requirement for a waste management licence to deposit, treat, keep or dispose of controlled waste. The current *Waste Duty of Care: Code of Practice* is issued under this Act and sets out practical guidance on how to comply with the waste duty of care requirements. The Act also allows for fixed penalty notices to be issued for certain waste deposit offences.

The waste duty of care requires reasonable steps to be taken to ensure waste is properly handled, so as to prevent harm to human health and the environment. In practical terms, this requires organisations and businesses to consider:

▶ segregating waste to support efficient recycling and disposal
▶ using licensed waste carriers (companies holding a **waste transfer licence**) to transport waste
▶ using authorised or appropriately licensed disposal sites
▶ maintenance of waste transfer records (such as **waste transfer notes** or hazardous **waste consignment notes**) to show how waste has been transported and disposed of.

UK government definition and purpose of sustainable development

The phrase **sustainable development** is commonly referenced by governments and organisations within their business plans and external communications. The first principles of sustainable development emerged at the 1972 United Nations (UN) Conference on the Human Environment (known as the Stockholm Conference). The next key event was the 1987 UN-sponsored World Commission on Environment and Development, which issued a report entitled 'Our Common Future' (also known as the Brundtland Report). This report introduced and defined the holistic concept of sustainable development, which recognised the importance of natural systems to current and future generations.

> ### Key terms
>
> **Waste transfer licence**: licence normally issued by the Environment Agency, which is required by any organisation that transports (carries) waste, irrespective of whether it owns or produced the waste
>
> **Waste transfer notes**: legal documents which are required when non-hazardous waste is passed on to others, so that there is an audit trail from the point at which the waste is produced through to disposal; these notes should be retained for at least two years; a waste transfer note is not required for the initial collection of household waste but is required if the waste is subsequently passed on
>
> **Waste consignment notes**: notes required every time hazardous waste (such as pesticides and oils) is moved, irrespective of whether it is passed on to someone else or not; they should be retained for at least three years
>
> **Sustainable development**: defined by the Brundtland Report as 'development that meets the needs of the present without compromising the ability of future generations to meet their own needs'; this definition is often interpreted and adapted to meet the circumstances of the environmental, social, economic and cultural context in which it is being used

Several years later at the 1992 UN Conference on Environment and Development (also known as the Rio Earth Summit), over 178 governments agreed 27 principles to guide nations to move towards environmentally sustainable development. These principles were outlined in the Rio Declaration on Environment and Development (also known as the Rio Principles). The other outcome from the summit was the global adoption of Agenda 21; the '21' referring to the twenty-first century as the target for governments to take action. This was a voluntary action plan that outlined global strategies for restoring the environment and encouraging environmentally sound development. The aim was for each government to take away the principles and develop their own local Agenda 21 plan.

In April 2013, the UK government published its 'Making sustainable development a part of all government policy and operations' policy. This defined sustainable development as 'making the necessary decisions now to realise our vision of stimulating economic growth and tackling the deficit, maximising wellbeing and protecting our environment, without affecting the ability of future generations to do the same'.

In 2015, all UN member nations adopted the 2030 Agenda for Sustainable Development, seen as a 'blueprint for peace and prosperity for people and the planet'. This agreement set out the aim to eradicate extreme poverty, fight inequality and injustice, and leave no one behind. Governments pledged over the following 15 years until 2030 to adhere to 17 Sustainable Development Goals (SDGs), each of which addressed a specific global challenge:
- Goal 1: No Poverty
- Goal 2: Zero Hunger
- Goal 3: Good Health and Wellbeing
- Goal 4: Quality Education
- Goal 5: Gender Equality
- Goal 6: Clean Water and Sanitation
- Goal 7: Affordable and Clean Energy
- Goal 8: Decent Work and Economic Growth
- Goal 9: Industry, Innovation and Infrastructure
- Goal 10: Reduced Inequalities
- Goal 11: Sustainable Cities and Communities
- Goal 12: Responsible Consumption and Production
- Goal 13: Climate Action
- Goal 14: Life Below Water
- Goal 15: Life on Land
- Goal 16: Peace, Justice and Strong Institutions
- Goal 17: Partnerships for the Goals.

Each country has taken different approaches to adopting the SDGs. This is largely the result of different political ideology and factors such as domestic priorities and elections. The UK set out its approach in 'Agenda 2030', which was published in 2017. Within this document, the UK government set out how it intended to deliver against its commitments both 'at home' and around the world through its actions and influence. It committed to embed the 17 SDGs and Agenda 21 principles within planned activities of each government department; each is required to report annually on its progress to deliver the goals. Specifically, they were embedded within policy and planning frameworks across the UK as a whole and within the devolved nations of Scotland, Wales and Northern Ireland.

Types of sustainable solutions and improvements to meet development goals

Through all the global agreements and initiatives, there have emerged three pillars of sustainability (Figure 2.5) which are seen as essential for future successful delivery of development:
- **Social sustainability** focuses on people and their wellbeing.
- **Economic sustainability** focuses on economic systems and how they impact society and the environment.
- **Environmental sustainability** focuses on the Earth and its ecosystems.

Critically, it is important to recognise that without all three pillars, any development is considered unsustainable.

There are a number of practical ways that land-based organisations and businesses can apply the three pillars to their operational activities to meet sustainability targets:
- **Social sustainability**: promote health, safety and welfare of their employees (see Chapter 1, page 8) as well as those in their supply chain; engage with local communities; challenge social exclusion; value diversity (see Chapter 6, page 100).
- **Economic sustainability**: consider social factors (such as fair wages) and environmental factors (such as waste minimisation) when making economic decisions; balance profit and financial performance with environmental and social impact of decisions.
- **Environmental sustainability**: comply with environmental legislation; maximise efficiency of resource use to minimise waste; prioritise use of renewable sources of energy.

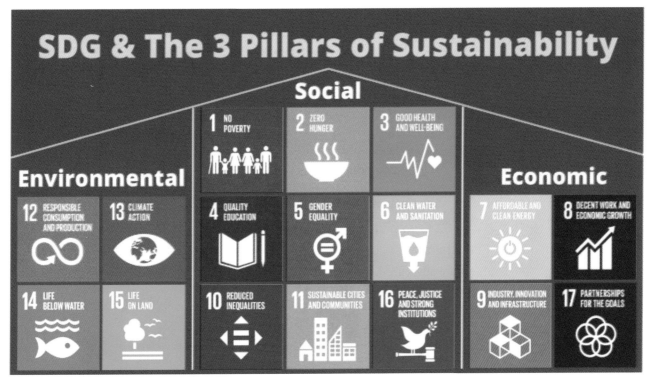

▲ Figure 2.5 SDGs and the three pillars of sustainability

Industry tip

Good health, safety and welfare practices contribute to sustainability by maximising the efficiency and effectiveness of the workforce and minimising waste associated with workplace accidents. In addition, integrating health and safety into organisational culture positively contributes to an organisation's corporate social responsibility.

Awareness of sustainable development goals nationally

As a requirement of the 2030 Agenda for Sustainable Development, all governments are required to undertake at least one voluntary national review (VNR). The UK government undertook its first VNR in 2019, which it presented that year to the UN High Level Political Forum. This review set out the government's assessment of national progress towards the SDGs at a macro (national and international) and micro (business) level.

Sustainable development goals at a macro and micro level

SDGs at a macro level are set by national governments and international organisations.

At the micro level, individual businesses and organisations can demonstrate their engagement with the SDGs through various approaches, for example:

▶ publishing corporate social responsibility (CSR) strategies which set out their aspirations, commitments and actions
▶ calculating their carbon footprint or using similar metrics to monitor progress against the SDG targets.

Concerns and expectations of key stakeholders

While the SDGs are viewed as a helpful framework, they are not without their critics. Some stakeholders have expressed concerns about the effectiveness and implementation of solutions and improvements to meet SDGs, such as **greenwashing**.

Key term

Greenwashing: a derogatory term used to describe an approach to marketing where an organisation or business presents its activities, products or services as environmentally sound, when this might not be true; critics suggest this misleads or deceives customers and the public, eroding trust and undermining genuine efforts towards sustainable goals

Some of the criticisms include the following:

▶ there are too many goals and they are too complex to be easily implemented and monitored
▶ there is insufficient funding to ensure the goals can be delivered
▶ the goals are not legally binding so are difficult to enforce
▶ there is a potential loss of competitive advantage unless there is universal adoption by everyone
▶ there are practical challenges in balancing economic growth with social and environmental goals
▶ global economic inequalities mean there is an uneven international playing field.

Misleading environmental claims

Where misleading or false claims are advertised, complaints can be made to the Advertising Standards Authority (ASA), the UK's independent advertising regulator. Claims are investigated and judgements made against the relevant advertising code:

▶ The UK Code of Non-broadcast Advertising and Direct & Promotional Marketing (CAP Code) covers sales promotions, direct marketing and non-broadcast advertisements.
▶ The UK Code of Broadcast Advertising (BCAP Code) covers advertising on radio and television services licensed by Ofcom.

The ASA has a range of sanctions, with Trading Standards able to support legal enforcement on non-broadcast advertising and Ofcom able to support legal enforcement on broadcast advertising.

> **Test yourself**
>
> Identify two actions you can take as an individual to contribute to sustainable development.

2.3 The causes, impact and management of climate change

The difference between weather and climate

The terms climate and weather are frequently used together, but often mistakenly referred to as the same thing. Weather relates to the atmospheric conditions in a specific location and can change over minutes, hours, days and weeks. For example, today it may be cold, wet and windy, but tomorrow it might be cold, dry and calm.

Meteorologists study weather by monitoring changes in atmospheric conditions (for example air pressure and air currents), to identify trends or patterns over time. This average weather pattern over a long period of time is referred to as climate; the World Meteorological Organisation uses a 30-year period when considering climate. The British Isles are considered to have a temperate maritime climate. This means they have mild winters, warm summers and high rainfall.

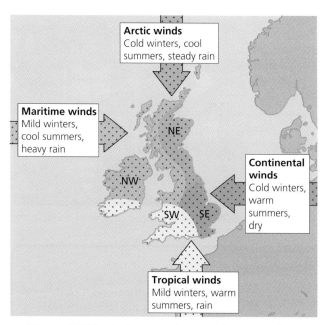

▲ Figure 2.6 The influence of atmospheric conditions on UK weather patterns

Climate is dynamic and normally considered on a regional scale/over a large area. This is because factors like latitude, altitude, topography, land surface and distance from the sea can affect local climate. This means that the climate across the British Isles varies.

Local climate, alongside factors such as topography, geology and soil, influences the **land cover** and wildlife distribution, and consequentially potential **land use**. Information about both land cover and land use can be obtained using remote sensing technologies or field surveying.

> **Key terms**
>
> *Land cover*: the physical type of land (vegetation type, water features or construction)
>
> *Land use*: the activity or purpose the land is used for (recreation, food production, housing)

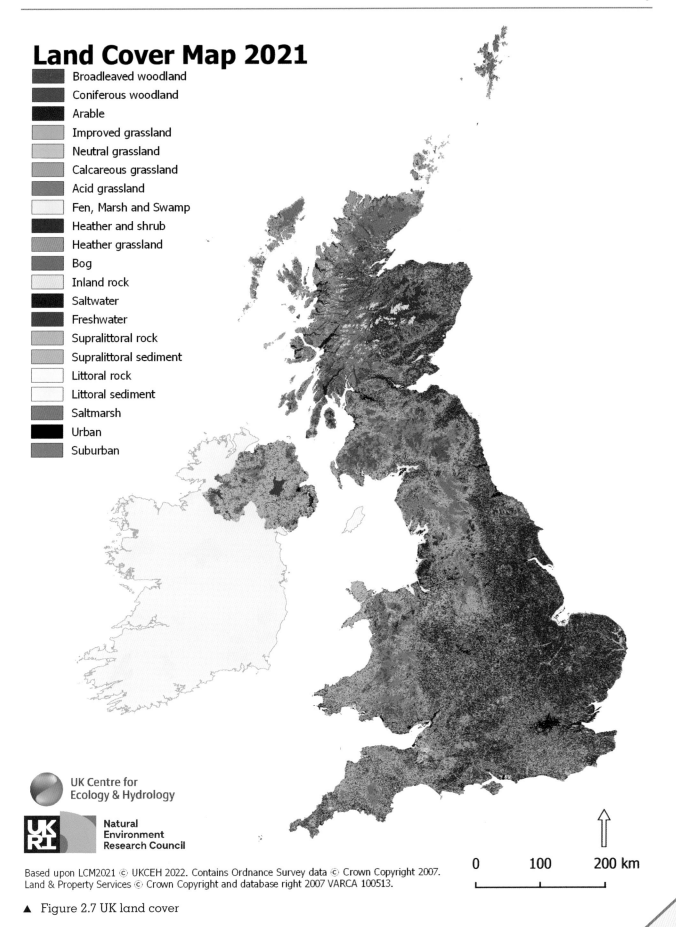

▲ Figure 2.7 UK land cover

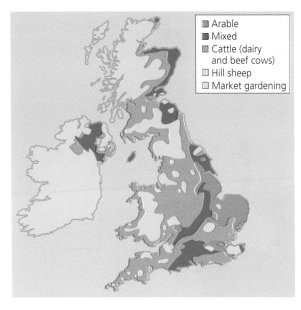

Legend:
- ▣ Arable
- ▣ Mixed
- ▣ Cattle (dairy and beef cows)
- ▢ Hill sheep
- ▢ Market gardening

▲ Figure 2.8 UK land use patterns

The meaning of climate change

Climate is powered by solar radiation, and over long periods of time it evolves because of **internal dynamics** and external **forcings**. Over time, the Earth's climate has changed in natural cycles, including:

▶ 10,000 to 100,000 year cycles associated with major glacial (cold) and interglacial (warm) periods, driven by changes in the Earth's orbit around the Sun

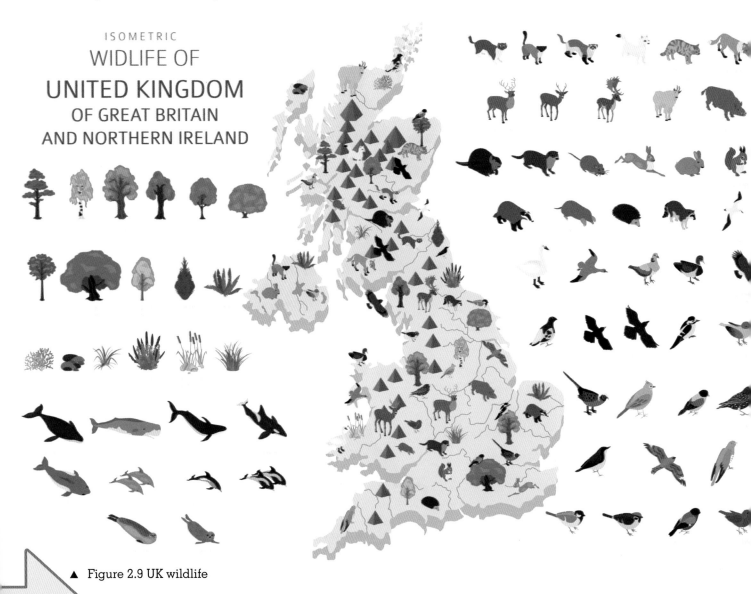

ISOMETRIC
WIDLIFE OF
UNITED KINGDOM
OF GREAT BRITAIN
AND NORTHERN IRELAND

▲ Figure 2.9 UK wildlife

- 200 to 1,500 year cycles associated with shorter cold and warm periods, likely driven by changes in the Sun
- months to years cycles (such as El Niño Southern Oscillation – ENSO) driven by oceanic–atmospheric interactions.

However, humans can influence the solar radiation that is reflected off the Earth's surface (termed albedo) by changing the land surface or particles in the atmosphere, or by altering longwave radiation leaving the atmosphere (by changing concentrations of **greenhouse gases**). The release of greenhouse gases into the atmosphere as a result of the everyday activities of an organisation or business is commonly referred to, or measured, as its **carbon footprint**.

Since the Industrial Revolution in the 1800s, the Earth's temperature has increased at a faster rate than scientific consensus can explain by natural climate cycles (i.e. **global warming**). A consequence of this increase in temperature has been a change in weather patterns and, hence, **climate change**.

Improve your English

The term 'carbon footprint' is considered a metaphor.

In the context of climate change, why might a metaphor be used to indicate an organisation's impact on climate?

Key terms

Internal dynamics: the ongoing interactions between the different interconnected systems which impact the global climate system; these include the atmosphere, hydrosphere, lithosphere, cryosphere and biosphere

Forcings: factors that affect climate which are not normally considered to be part of the global climate system; they can include natural phenomena such as volcanic eruptions or changes in the orbit of the Earth and the Earth's crust as well as changes in the composition of the atmosphere as a result of human activity

Greenhouse gases: gases that absorb infrared radiation emitted from the Earth's surface, rather than letting it travel into space, and re-emit it back to the Earth, causing the surface to heat up; key greenhouse gases associated with human activity include carbon dioxide (CO_2), methane (CH_4) and nitrous oxide (N_2O)

Carbon footprint: the amount of greenhouse gases released as a result of a business' or organisation's activities; the term includes all greenhouse gases but makes explicit reference to carbon because carbon dioxide (CO_2) is considered the main greenhouse gas and the impact of other greenhouse gases can be expressed as carbon dioxide equivalent

Global warming: the increase in the average surface temperature of the Earth as a consequence of greenhouse gas emissions

Climate change: a long-term shift in temperature and weather patterns

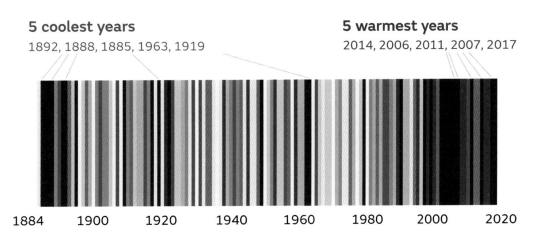

5 coolest years
1892, 1888, 1885, 1963, 1919

5 warmest years
2014, 2006, 2011, 2007, 2017

1884   1900   1920   1940   1960   1980   2000   2020

▲ Figure 2.10 UK annual temperature (Met Office)

There is a scientific and governmental consensus that climate change will affect Earth's biodiversity. Among the consequences and impacts are:

▶ increased risk of heatwaves and droughts (which present a serious health risk to vulnerable individuals)
▶ increased risk of cold weather
▶ displacement of human/wildlife/flora habitations
▶ increased risk of changes to habitats and species extinction (such as from changes to food chains)
▶ melting ice caps resulting in sea level rise and increased risk of coastal erosion/storm surges (causing damage to property and transport infrastructure)
▶ increased risk of flooding (leading to damage to property and livelihoods)
▶ increased risk of wildfires (causing damage to important habitats)
▶ risks to food security and food safety (disruption to growing seasons and pressure on water supplies for irrigation).

It is accepted that climate change is a long-term driver of change for the UK marine, freshwater and terrestrial ecosystems and associated species. For example, the State of Nature 2023 report notes that since 1970, the distributions of 54 per cent of flowering plant species have decreased across the UK. However, the report set out five mechanisms to anticipate and potentially mitigate these impacts:

▶ improved species status
▶ nature-friendly farming and sustainable fisheries and forestry
▶ protected areas
▶ ecosystem and habitat restoration
▶ nature, climate and people.

The Intergovernmental Panel on Climate Change (IPCC) has concluded that human activity is the leading cause of climate change. Some of the key activities responsible are the burning of fossil fuels, changing land use and the release of greenhouse gases. The burning of fossil fuels such as coal, oil and natural gas for electricity generation or to fuel manufacturing processes, transportation or heating systems releases carbon dioxide into the atmosphere. Human activities such as deforestation also release carbon dioxide into the atmosphere when the trees are burned and soil carbon is oxidised, and without reforestation, trees cannot be used as a carbon sink. There is also evidence that agricultural activities to produce food, such as rearing animals, can release greenhouse gases such as methane.

Test yourself

Investigate your chosen industry to identify how it might contribute to climate change. Then identify what **adaption strategies** and **mitigation strategies** the industry is adopting.

Policies and initiatives to manage these changes at national and local level

Given the global importance of climate change, the United Nations holds a meeting each year to discuss it called the Conference of the Parties (COP) to the United Nations Framework Convention on Climate Change (UNFCCC). There have also been several international initiatives intended to promote action to combat climate change and its impacts, for example:

▶ **2005 Kyoto Protocol**: the countries that signed the treaty pledged to reduce their greenhouse gas emissions.
▶ **2016 Paris Agreement**: all countries agreed to work to limit global warming to well below 2°C, ideally no more than 1.5°C above pre-industrial levels.

The United Nations 17 SDGs are intended to promote international prosperity, while protecting the Earth. While all the goals have some relationship with climate change, SDG Goal 13: Climate action specifically addresses climate change. It requires everyone to 'take action to combat climate change and its impacts'.

At national level, the UK government has embedded its international obligations and response to taking action against climate change through a number of policies and initiatives, for example 25 YEP and the Climate Change Act 2008. The government also passed legislation making it a legal obligation to achieve **net zero** carbon emissions by 2050.

Key terms

Adaption strategies: actions and activities undertaken to limit the negative impacts of climate change

Mitigation strategies: actions and activities undertaken to prevent or reduce any contribution to climate change

Net zero: achieving a balance between all greenhouse gases (including CO_2, CH_4 and N_2O) released to the atmosphere and the greenhouse gases removed from it; it differs from the term 'carbon neutral' which is narrow in scope and normally refers to achieving a balance between CO_2 released to the atmosphere and CO_2 removed from it

SUSTAINABLE DEVELOPMENT G⚫ALS

▲ Figure 2.11 United Nations' 17 sustainable development goals

▲ Figure 2.12 United Nations' SDG 13 Climate action

Ten Point Plan for a Green Industrial Revolution

In 2020, the UK government launched the 'Ten Point Plan for a Green Industrial Revolution'. The ambition was to leverage £12 billion of government investment, alongside investment from the private sector, to create and support up to 250,000 green jobs by 2030. The plan focused on the following areas:

1 Advancing offshore wind
2 Driving the growth of low-carbon hydrogen
3 Delivering new and advanced nuclear power
4 Accelerating the shift to zero-emission vehicles
5 Green public transport, cycling and walking
6 'Net zero' and green ships
7 Greener buildings
8 Investing in carbon capture, usage and storage
9 Protecting our natural environment
10 Green finance and innovation.

However, the UK government's climate action plan (Net Zero Strategy) was successfully legally challenged in the High Court in 2022 and most recently in 2024. The court concluded that the plan did not provide a credible framework to enable the government to meet its legally binding climate commitments. Consequently, the government is expected to develop a revised action plan.

Test yourself

Select one of the areas within the Ten Point Plan. Consider how this might impact you as an individual in terms of your career opportunities and the technology changes that might impact your chosen industry.

Assessment practice

1 Identify **three** potential consequences of climate change. (3 marks)
2 Identify **two** signs that suggest a business may be greenwashing its environmental credentials. (2 marks)
3 Identify **three** human activities which contribute to climate change. (3 marks)
4 Explain why biodiversity net gain must be considered during developments and what benefits it brings society. (3 marks)
5 Identify **three** of the key government intentions set out in the Environment Act 2021. (3 marks)
6 Describe **two** levels within the waste management hierarchy which have the potential to reduce the quantity of waste needing disposal. (4 marks)
7 Explain how a land-based business can comply with legal responsibilities when managing waste. (6 marks)

8 Maya owns a kennel and cattery business. She is considering what practical changes she could make to the business to become more sustainable.
For each of the three sustainability pillars, describe **one** change she could make. (6 marks)
9 Sami has been asked by their employer to review the impact of their business on the climate and produce an action plan. In addition to reducing the impact on climate, the aims include saving money, encouraging staff to participate and improving brand reputation.
Explain a range of potential initiatives Sami might consider in the action plan. (6 marks)
10 Explain why natural capital is important for human wellbeing. (6 marks)

Further reading

You may find some of the following helpful for keeping up to date with issues associated with sustainability:
► Joint Nature Conservation Committee
► Office for Environmental Protection
► Outcome Indicator Framework for the 25 Year Environment Plan by the Department for Environment, Food and Rural Affairs
► MAGIC website developed by the Department for Environment, Food and Rural Affairs
► Natural England
► Environment Agency
► Climate Change Committee
► State of Nature's 2023 report on the UK's current biodiversity
► Intergovernmental Panel on Climate Change
► United Nations' Sustainable Development Goals
► Baker, J., Hoskin, R. and Butterworth, T. (2019) *Biodiversity net gain. Good practice principles for development: A practical guide*, CIRIA.

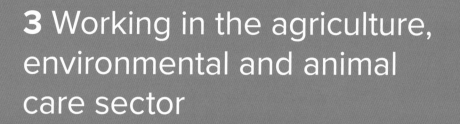

3 Working in the agriculture, environmental and animal care sector

Introduction

The land-based sector is a dynamic and diverse sector in which to work. As it comprises a high proportion of small- and medium-sized businesses, employers may not always have human resource facilities to support new entrants. It is, therefore, important that both employers and those who work for them are aware of employment rights and responsibilities.

Additionally, individuals should be aware of how they can positively contribute to effective team working, in order to achieve desired outcomes for their employer.

Given the increasing role of technology, which is transforming the workplace, those working in the sector must also ensure they have, and maintain, the necessary capabilities and competencies to play an active role in the development of their careers. This will demonstrate their work commitment and ambitions to current and future employers.

Learning outcomes

By the end of this chapter, you will understand:
- the different types of employment contracts and their contents
- the rights and responsibilities of different employment contracts
- the the expectations of professional conduct and behaviours in the workplace
- the importance of monitoring staff and colleagues for indications of modern slavery, people trafficking and signs of exploitation
- the impact of union membership on the employer and the employee

- the types of teams and how they are developed
- the importance of team dynamics and behaviour and their effect on team performance
- the techniques used to monitor and manage individual and team performance
- the benefits that continuing professional development (CPD) brings to the individual and their employer
- the methods and sources of personal and professional development support.

3.1 Employment rights and responsibilities of the employer and employee

The land-based sector presents a rich and diverse variety of employment opportunities across a range of industries (Table 3.1). Given the options available, it is possible to specialise and progress within a single industry (for example floristry), but it is also possible to work across or between multiple industries (for example transition between agriculture and horticulture). There are also other career opportunities which support the sector and may require technical and vocational sector knowledge (for example agricultural auctioneer or health and safety consultant). Irrespective of the individual career route someone takes, there is core knowledge and understanding which is common to everyone.

▼ Table 3.1 Example occupations within the agriculture, environmental and animal care sectors

	Industry	Technical occupations	Higher technical occupations	Professional occupations
Animal care and management	Equine care and management	• Equine groom (riding or non-riding) • Farrier • Senior equine groom (racing, riding or non-riding) • Veterinary nurse	• Equine dental technician • Stud manager	• Veterinary surgeon
	Animal care and management	• Animal care and welfare assistant • Working dog handler • Dog groomer • Keeper and aquarist • Detection and protection working dog specialist • Animal care and welfare manager • Veterinary nurse	• Animal trainer • Animal warden • Animal welfare officer • Livestock veterinary technician • Specialist veterinary nurse	• Animal nutritionist • Animal physiotherapist • Veterinary surgeon • Wildlife rehabilitator • Zoo curator
Agriculture, land management and production	Agriculture crops and livestock	• General farm worker • Livestock unit technician • Poultry technician • Poultry worker • Crop technician	• Assistant farm manager • Livestock buyer	• Agricultural inspector • Agronomist • Nutrition and fertiliser advisor • Farm manager
	Land-based engineering	• Land-based service engineer • Land-based service engineering technician	• Agricultural diagnostic technician	• Agricultural engineer
	Forestry	• Forest craftsperson (harvesting or establishment and maintenance)	• Forest works manager	• Professional forester
	Arboriculture	• Arborist • Utility arborist	• Arboriculturist	• Professional arboriculturist
	Production horticulture	• Crop technician • Packhouse line leader	• Production horticulture manager	• Horticultural scientist
	Landscaping and turf management	• Golf greenkeeper • Advanced sports turf technician • Horticulture or landscape construction operative (horticulture operative) • Horticulture or landscape construction operative (landscape operative) • Sports turf operative • Horticulture or landscape supervisor (horticulture supervisor) • Horticulture or landscape supervisor (landscape supervisor)	• Golf course manager • Horticulture and landscape technical manager • Garden designer	

	Industry	Technical occupations	Higher technical occupations	Professional occupations
	Countryside, wildlife management and gamekeeping	• Countryside worker • Field biologist • Underkeeper • Water environment worker	• Head keeper	• Ecologist • Environmental practitioner • National park or nature reserve warden
	Aquaculture and fisheries management	• Fisher • Fisheries technician		• Aquaculture manager
	Viticulture and oenology		• Viticulture and oenology manager	
	Floristry	• Florist • Senior florist		

Source: IfATE occupational map for the agriculture, environmental and animal care sector

Note: Some of these occupations cover a number of job titles, for example a countryside ranger may also be referred to as a community ranger, an estate ranger, an estate supervisor, a park ranger, a ranger, a recreation ranger or a reserve or countryside warden.

Different types of employment contracts and their contents

Everyone at work has specific rights in return for certain responsibilities. However, these rights vary between the employer and employee, and are dependent on the type of employment contract that exists between them.

In simple terms, the contract of employment is a legally binding agreement between an employee and an employer. The employee agrees to perform specific tasks and, in return, the employer will provide agreed remuneration (benefits such as a salary).

The contract may be agreed verbally or in writing (such as a job offer via email or letter). Both types of contract are legally binding and enforceable. A contract can also be agreed through demonstrated actions or behaviour. For example, if an individual undertakes work and is paid for it, this indicates an employment agreement exists, even when there has not been any oral or written contract.

A contract of employment usually consists of three types of terms:
▶ **express terms**: terms put in writing
▶ **implied terms**: terms assumed to be included because they are obvious (for example do not steal from the employer and mutual trust), legal requirements (for example entitlement to statutory redundancy pay) or custom and practice (for example if an annual bonus is normally paid to all staff)
▶ **incorporated terms**: terms included but referenced elsewhere, such as in a staff handbook.

The Employment Rights Act 1996 (see Chapter 6, page 97) states that employees or workers (including agency workers) have a legal right to a 'written statement of employment particulars' from their employer on or before their first day of work. Often this statement is referred to as the 'employment contract'. However, its purpose is to formalise the contract and provide evidence the contract exists. It also contains detailed additional information about the job that goes beyond the basic requirements of the contract.

Content of a written statement of employment particulars

The statement must contain a minimum number of express terms, which are usually laid out in a similar order to Figure 3.1

There is additional information that must be given to the employee, which can be included at the same time within the statement, or separately, but must be provided within two months of the employment start date. This includes:
▶ pension arrangements (if this information is not included in the document, the employer must state where the employee can find it)
▶ any terms and conditions that apply to other employees too (known as 'collective agreements')
▶ details of any training provided by the employer that is not compulsory (if this information is not included in the document, the employer must state where to find it)
▶ disciplinary rules and disciplinary and **grievance** procedures (see Chapter 6, page 102 for more about grievance procedures and how these complaints should be managed).

Key term

Grievance: a formal complaint made by an employee about their treatment at work by their employer or someone else they work with

Written statement of employment particulars	Notes
Express terms: 1. Employer's name 2. Employer's address 3. Employee's or worker's name 4. Date the employee or worker starts work 5. Date that 'continuous employment' started for an employee 6. Job title or a brief description of the job 7. Place or addresses where the employee or worker will work 8. How much, how often and when the employee will be paid 9. Working hours the employee or worker must work 10. Holiday and holiday pay 11. Sick leave and sick pay 12. Any other paid leave 13. Any other benefits, including non-contractual benefits 14. Notice period the employee or employer must give when employment ends 15. How long the job is expected to last 16. Any probation period 17. Any terms that apply if the employee will work abroad 18. Training that must be completed by the employee or worker Additional information which may be included: 1. Pension arrangements 2. Terms and conditions that apply to other employees too 3. Details of any training provided by the employer that is not compulsory 4. Disciplinary rules and disciplinary and grievance procedures	 5. *Working for the same employer without a significant break* 7. *One specific worksite or multiple worksites* 8. *For example £1,200 per month, paid on the last Friday of each month* 9. *Should include which days and if their hours or days can change* 10. *Should include how this is calculated if the employee or worker leaves* 11. *Or where the employee can find this information* 12. *Or where the employee can find this information* 13. *For example childcare vouchers or company car* 15. *If it is temporary or fixed term* 16. *Including its duration and conditions* 17. *May not be included if it is not relevant* 18. *May include timescales* 1. *Or where the employee can find this information* 2. *Known as 'collective agreements'* 3. *Or where the employee can find this information* 4. *Or where the employee can find this information*

▲ Figure 3.1 Example of a written statement of employment particulars

Industry tip

As the land-based sector predominantly comprises **small- and medium-sized enterprises (SMEs)**, employers usually rely on the use of template documents to help them ensure they include all the necessary information within the contracts they use. This also applies to employment contracts. Sometimes contract templates are provided by trade associations as a benefit of being a member. Alternatively, employers can access free templates for both employees and workers from the Advisory, Conciliation and Arbitration Service (Acas) (the difference between these two employment statuses is covered later in this chapter). It is important to always use the most up-to-date templates available on the Acas website, rather than saving a copy onto a computer and using it for all future contracts. This ensures that if employment law changes, the employer is using the most current and compliant version of a contract when they take on someone new.

Key term

Small- or medium-sized enterprises (SMEs): in the UK, a business is usually considered to be an SME if it has fewer than 250 employees and a turnover of less than £50 million

An employer may choose to provide additional information (such as incorporated terms) within the statement, or else provide it within a document such as a staff handbook or signpost staff to where they can find it, for example on the organisation's intranet. This could include organisational policies and procedures such as:

▶ travel expenses policy (for example what expenses are allowable and how they can be claimed)
▶ absence due to illness (for example telephoning the employer or manager by a specific time)
▶ use of internet and email (for example access to the internet for personal reasons is restricted to during breaks or outside working time and email can only be used for work purposes).

Industry tip

As workplaces and roles are dynamic and can change over time, it may be difficult for an employer to define exactly what an employee may be asked to do. Therefore, it is widespread practice for land-based employers to include a clause within the contract which requires an employee to perform additional reasonable duties as required. This does not mean the employer can ask the employee to perform *any* task, as it must be reasonable and within the ability of the employee.

Employers may also include a **restrictive covenant** or **exclusivity clause** within a contract, which should be contained within the statement for clarity. For example, a livestock feed merchant may be concerned that if a sales manager leaves and gains employment with a competitor, the manager might take customers' contact details with them to the new employer. Therefore, the merchant may include within the contract a restrictive covenant that the sales manager must not approach the merchant's customers after they leave their employment for a specified period of time. Similarly, the merchant may be concerned that a sales manager might take the opportunity to sell agricultural implements for a machinery dealer to the merchant's customers. Therefore, the merchant might include an exclusivity clause that prohibits the sales manager from working for another employer while they are employed by the merchant, unless this is agreed.

The extent to which an employer can limit what other work can be done depends on the individual. For example, it might be reasonable to limit what other work a full-time employee might do, but not necessarily what a part-time worker might do. Therefore, employers must make decisions according to each individual staff member's circumstances.

Industry tip

Often employers are concerned that staff may undertake additional work either for themselves or someone else, which means they may not get sufficient rest between periods of work. Particularly where the work is physically demanding or requires concentration and focus, insufficient rest can increase the risk of an accident happening. Therefore, employers may include a restrictive covenant or exclusivity clause within a contract to help them fulfil their legal obligation to ensure the individual concerned is not putting themselves or others at increased risk because of a lack of sufficient rest.

Rights and responsibilities of different employment contracts

An employment contract will reflect the employment status of the individual and their legal status at work:
- **Employee**: these individuals usually have regular hours or a working pattern and are required to be available and undertake work (unless on leave) for an agreed salary. They have the most obligations to their employer but also have the most employment rights. However, some of these rights are subject to a minimum length of **continuous employment**.
- **Worker**: these individuals may not have regular or guaranteed hours or working patterns and may not be obligated to be available for work. However, they still have employment rights.
- **Self-employed person**: these individuals have the flexibility to choose when and what work they undertake, determine what fees they charge and are not paid a formal wage. They have the fewest employment rights. However, they still have protection against unlawful discrimination and for their health and safety while working at a client's workplace.

Both employees and workers share some employment rights, including:
- being paid at least the national minimum wage
- receiving a wage slip/payslip showing the hours worked and the associated rate of pay
- being protected against unlawful deductions from wages
- receiving the statutory minimum rest breaks
- being protected against unlawful discrimination
- being protected for whistleblowing
- receiving statutory maternity, paternity, adoption and shared parental pay.

Key terms

Restrictive covenant or **exclusivity clause**: a contract clause that sets out what work an employee may or may not do (such as working for someone else) during their employment or when they leave their employment

Employee: someone who works under a fixed-term or permanent contract

Continuous employment: when an employee works for an employer without a break in employment; it is calculated from the first day they started working for that employer; some breaks in employment count towards continuous employment, for example annual leave or sickness, maternity, paternity, parental or adoption leave, but other breaks do not, such as when the employee is on strike

Worker: someone engaged under a casual contract

Self-employed person: someone who works independently for themselves, normally operating under either a service contract or consultancy agreement

However, an employee has the following additional employment rights compared with a worker (see the Employment Rights Act 1996 later in this chapter):

▶ protection against unfair dismissal
▶ a minimum period of notice if employment is terminated
▶ statutory redundancy pay
▶ the right to request flexible working
▶ time off for emergencies
▶ statutory maternity, paternity, adoption and shared parental leave and pay.

The employment status of an individual is important for many reasons in addition to their legal rights. For example, an employer is responsible for income tax deductions and National Insurance contributions (NICs) on behalf of an employee. However, an individual's employment status may not reflect their working hours or pattern and thus, the type of contract they are given.

Industry tip

Although there is an important legal difference between employees and workers, for convenience a single term such as 'staff' or 'workforce' is often used to describe both. This helps to reduce perceived differences in status and thus potential discrimination where both types of individuals are undertaking the same or similar work (see Chapter 6, page 100 for more about discrimination). For example, workers may be treated less favourably because they are not employed on a permanent contract.

Full-time and part-time (permanent) contracts

There is no specific number of hours worked which differentiates between whether an individual has a full- or part-time role. However, full-time is widely considered to be 35 (or more) hours per week and part-time is fewer than 35 hours per week.

Fixed-term contracts

These contracts last for a specified period of time or until a specified task is completed.

Casual contracts

In the land-based sector, it is common for employers to engage staff on temporary or casual contracts, for example seasonal workers involved with planting, harvesting or packing crops or with animal rearing, such as lambing at a specific time of the year. Zero-hours contracts can be used in situations where an individual may be available for work as and when the employer needs them. Other temporary staff may include consultants and contractors. Temporary and casual staff may be self-employed or agency workers contracted through an employment agency.

An employment agency or individual who supplies labour for the agriculture, horticulture, shellfish gathering and food processing and packaging sectors is termed a 'gangmaster'. They must be licenced by the Gangmasters and Labour Abuse Authority, which is the government body responsible for preventing workers from being exploited and ensuring they are treated fairly by employers. For example, after 12 weeks' continuous employment an employer must ensure agency workers get the same terms and conditions as a permanent employee.

Industry tip

There may be subtle differences in responsibilities of individuals under the Health and Safety at Work etc. Act 1974. For example, an employer may expect a specialist contractor to provide their own tools, equipment and personal protective equipment because they have specialist knowledge and understanding of the work being undertaken. However, irrespective of the employment relationship between an individual and their employer, the employer still has a duty of care to each individual. For example, they should provide information and instructions on hazards and risk control measures and if necessary challenge poor behaviour and practices.

Test yourself

Identify two reasons why an employer may not want to engage someone as an employee on a permanent contract.

Legislation that supports employment rights and responsibilities

There are several key pieces of legislation that offer individuals rights and place responsibilities on employers, including the Health and Safety at Work etc. Act 1974 to minimise risks to health, safety and welfare at work (see Chapter 1, page 4) and the Equality Act 2010 to offer protection against discrimination (see Chapter 6, page 96).

Employment Rights Act 1996

In addition to the requirement to provide an individual with a written statement of employment particulars, this Act establishes the rights of individuals at work in specific situations. For an employee:

▶ Reasonable notice must be given by both the employer and the employee before a contract is terminated. The period of notice to be given by the employer depends on the length of time the individual has been employed for. The period of notice to be given by the employee might depend on how long the employer needs to recruit a replacement.

▶ Employees have a right to compensation if they are made redundant, so long as they have worked for the same employer for at least two years. The amount of compensation is dependent on the age of the employee and their length of service.

▶ Employees have the right to request flexible working arrangements.

▶ Employees are entitled to statutory maternity, paternity, adoption and shared parental leave (in addition to pay), unlike workers who are only entitled to pay.

▶ Employees are entitled to statutory sick pay. This is calculated as a fixed weekly amount and paid for up to 28 weeks, so long as they meet the eligibility criteria which includes being unable to work through illness for more than three days (including non-working days) in a row.

▶ The employer must provide a valid and fair reason for dismissing an employee. Dismissals for any of the following reasons are considered automatically unfair:
  – health and safety concerns
  – assertion of statutory rights
  – request for flexible working
  – pregnancy or maternity.

▶ Any claim for unfair dismissal must normally be made initially to Acas and subsequently to an employment tribunal within three months of the dismissal (see Chapter 6, page 103).

National Minimum Wage Act 1998

This Act establishes the minimum pay per hour a worker is entitled to. This hourly rate is determined by the worker's age and whether they are an apprentice. The rates are set by the government and come into effect at the start of April each year.

The relevant hourly rate is a legal entitlement and His Majesty's Revenue and Customs (HMRC) has the authority to take legal action against employers who fail to pay this. In addition, workers may also make a claim to an employment tribunal if they are paid less than the appropriate national minimum wage.

Although the national minimum wage is set at an hourly rate, it applies irrespective of how an individual is paid:

▶ **Time work** is paid by the hour (for example a tractor driver is paid for the time it takes to plough a field).

▶ **Salaried hours** are paid as an annual salary (for example a gamekeeper is paid in equal regular instalments throughout the year for a specified number of hours' work) although may be pro rata for part-time staff.

▶ **Output work** is paid by quantity or task and is sometimes referred to as 'piecework' (for example a dog groomer is paid a fixed fee for every dog they groom).

▶ **Unmeasured work** is paid in other ways (for example a landscape gardener is paid £200 to cut a hedge irrespective of how long it takes to complete the work).

Improve your English

The term 'pro rata' comes from Latin. Research this term online and write a definition in the context of part-time employment (for example, someone working two days per week) and full-time employment (for example someone working five days per week). Remember that salary and benefits such as annual leave entitlement are normally calculated on a pro-rata basis to ensure all employees are being fairly compensated for the quantity of work they do.

Improve your maths

An employer who manages an animal collection service advertises a vacancy for an animal care assistant. The existing employees in the same role are on a full-time salary of £25,000 with 30 days' annual leave. However, the employer only wants the new employee to work two days each week, when the animal collection is busy with visitors. Therefore, the employer advertises the role as being on a 0.4 FTE (full-time equivalent) contract. Work out what the employee would be paid pro rata for the two days a week they work, as well as how many days of annual leave they are entitled to.

Working Time Regulations 1998

These regulations implement the EU Working Time Directive 1993 and provide certain rights and protection to workers which help support their safety, health and wellbeing as follows:

▶ Individuals cannot **work** more than 48 hours a week, averaged over a reference period (normally 17 weeks).
  – Some individuals over the age of 18 can voluntarily opt out of the 48-hour week (sometimes referred to as a Working Time Regulation waiver) and work more hours than this. However, they cannot be dismissed or treated unfavourably for refusing to do so and can change their mind.
▶ There is an entitlement to rest breaks:
  – during the working day – a 20-minute rest break if the individual is expected to work more than 6 hours during the day
  – between working days – 11 hours' rest between finishing work and returning to work
  – between working weeks – 24 hours' rest every 7 working days, or 48 hours' rest every 14 working days.
▶ There is an entitlement to 5.6 weeks' paid statutory annual leave (up to a maximum of 28 days per year), calculated pro rata on the hours the individual works. However, it is important to be aware that an employer can include bank holidays and public holidays within this period. They can also choose to offer more holidays than the statutory entitlement.

Young workers have different rest break entitlements, such as a 30-minute rest break if they work more than 4.5 hours during the day and 12 hours' rest between finishing work and returning to work. In addition, they must not work at night during the 'restricted period'. Depending on their contract, this is normally:

▶ between 10.00 p.m. and 6.00 a.m or
▶ between 11.00 p.m. and 7.00 a.m. if their contract allows for them to work after 10.00 p.m.

However, depending on the type of work (for example agriculture), young workers can work until midnight or from 4.00 a.m. onwards, but only if there are no adult workers available to do the work and if it will not have a negative effect on the young person's education or training.

Expectations of professional conduct and behaviours in the workplace

Irrespective of contract type or employment status, employers expect workers to demonstrate a certain level of professional conduct and behaviour in the workplace. Not only does this contribute to the promotion of diversity and inclusivity within the workplace, but it also has an impact on the organisation's reputation and how it is perceived by its customers, clients and other stakeholders. These expectations include:

▶ punctuality
▶ cleanliness
▶ good conduct
▶ adherence to regulations
▶ respect for own and others' work and work area
▶ respect for positions of employment
▶ respect for the land, air and water (environment)
▶ respect for property and belongings of others and animals, including for volunteers.

Key terms

Work: this includes time spent directly undertaking the contracted role or task but also covers role-specific training, paid or unpaid overtime at the request of the employer, time spent at the workplace 'on call', working lunches and time spent travelling between home and the workplace if the individual does not have a fixed workplace; it does not include voluntary unpaid overtime, breaks when no work is done, holidays or travelling outside normal working hours

Young workers: individuals who are above the statutory school leaving age but under 18 (i.e. any worker aged 15, 16 or 17); young workers must not work more than 8 hours a day and 40 hours a week and employers should be aware that if they use young workers, they must not discriminate against them because of their age (see Chapter 6, page 97)

In addition to what might be commonly accepted expectations, workplace-specific expectations are set out for employees through briefings and within the documentation associated with their employment. These are normally shared with a new employee as soon as they start their period of employment, for clarity and transparency. For example, conduct and behaviours usually form part of the **induction** programme. The employee can then demonstrate their awareness of, and compliance with, these expectations by:

▶ meeting the terms of their **job specification**
▶ meeting contract terms (set out within the written statement of employment particulars)
▶ adhering to company policies.

Meeting conduct and behaviour expectations, in addition to compliance with workplace policies and procedures, is an important aspect of working within any industry. Not meeting expectations will most likely result in disciplinary and grievance procedures being instigated (see Chapter 6, page 102). Examples of activities that can lead to this include:

▶ failure to adhere to systems or policies
▶ failure to adhere to health and safety protocols
▶ breach of employment contract conditions
▶ intimidating behaviour, aggression or use of foul language
▶ harassment and bullying.

Dealing with workplace incidents and supporting health and wellbeing of employees

The role of a supervisor/manager is important in dealing with workplace incidents and events as soon as they arise. The aim is to informally address conduct and behaviours that do not meet expectations when they occur and before they reach the point where an individual raises a grievance, or there is a need to instigate a formal disciplinary procedure. However, even with proactive, vigilant and responsive management, instigation of either the grievance or disciplinary procedure may be appropriate. In these events, the supervisor/manager plays a key role. They should:

▶ follow their employer's written procedure
▶ keep information confidential
▶ explain to those involved how the process will work and what their rights are
▶ keep written records
▶ hold hearing meetings to investigate and gather evidence, ideally within five working days of the procedure being instigated
▶ remain impartial and decide on the outcome based on the investigation evidence
▶ ensure those involved understand that they have the right to appeal the outcome.

▲ Figure 3.2 A forestry engineer at work

A healthy and motivated workforce positively contributes to employee loyalty and retention, a culture of inclusivity, reduced absenteeism and ultimately workplace productivity. Therefore, employers have an interest in supporting the health and wellbeing of their employees. This goes beyond consideration of an individual's health and safety at work. Factors to consider include:

▶ financial health (for example employee recognition programmes or phased retirement opportunities)
▶ emotional health (for example 24/7 confidential support helplines or occupational health support)
▶ physical health (for example providing healthy snacks or promoting physical activity)

▶ social wellbeing (for example buddy schemes or opportunities for employees to make their voice heard)

▶ psychological wellbeing (for example opportunities for career development or workplace autonomy)

▶ work–life balance (for example customised working hours or working from home on specific days).

However, most employers take a holistic approach to wellbeing which goes above and beyond the statutory requirements such as support for attending medical appointments and sick pay entitlement (including agricultural sick pay for those employed before 1 October 2013). Indeed, a thoughtful employee assistance programme can be helpful in retaining existing staff, but it can also be used as a selling feature when recruiting new staff. However, it is important that employers recognise the diversity within their workforce when considering employee health and wellbeing.

Case study

Employers who want to provide wellbeing initiatives should consider all their staff when planning what they offer. For example, consider a national nature consultancy service. As well as having employees based and working full time at the organisation's office(s), it may also have employees who regularly work from home or part-time workers who may not be able to benefit from wellbeing initiatives.

▶ Why should an employer consider the individual context of all their staff when planning support programmes?

▶ Identify two ways an employer might encourage employee participation in wellbeing initiatives.

Test yourself

Research job adverts for vacancies within your chosen industry. Make a list of what benefits or 'perks' employers are offering that might contribute to the wellbeing of their staff.

Importance of monitoring staff and colleagues for indications of modern slavery, people trafficking and signs of exploitation

Employers and other stakeholders in the land-based sector must be aware of, and vigilant to, the risk of coercion and exploitation among workers, referred to as **modern slavery**. The land-based sector is a high-risk sector for this as it is particularly vulnerable to shortages in labour supply, with a high turnover of seasonal staff.

Everyone within the sector plays a vital role in monitoring staff and work colleagues for signs of trafficking or forced labour. However, the signs might not be immediately obvious and are often hidden, as victims might not understand their legal rights, or else feel ashamed about letting themselves be treated in such a way. Evidence of an individual being a victim of modern slavery can include:

▶ restricted freedom (for example being unable to leave their work premises, being forced to buy provisions from their employer or dependent, or having limited contact with family)

▶ behaviour (for example resorting to crime to get food, showing anxiety or being distrustful of authorities)

▶ working conditions (for example working excessive hours with no rest breaks or lacking appropriate clothing for the work they undertake)

▶ accommodation (for example not being able to share information about where they live, or living in poor accommodation)

▶ finances (for example having no access to money or being punished by fines for underperformance)

▶ appearance (for example having visible injuries that suggest they are being physically controlled or abused).

Employers have a responsibility to help protect their workers from modern slavery, by ensuring they are aware of their legal rights associated with the role and contractual terms and conditions (such as the Working Time Regulations). They should continually monitor their workforce (including agency staff) to ensure they are not knowingly or unknowingly being exploited. If they suspect someone is a victim of human trafficking, forced labour or worker exploitation, they should report it immediately. Depending on the circumstances, the following options may be appropriate:

▶ the police – 101, or in the case of an emergency 999

▶ the Gangmaster and Labour Abuse Authority

▶ the modern slavery and exploitation helpline

▶ the Health and Safety Executive (HSE).

Key term

Modern slavery: the exploitation of individuals for personal or commercial gain; it is a serious crime that violates the human rights of victims; the term covers human trafficking, slavery, servitude and forced or compulsory labour, and its victims are defined by the Slavery and Human Trafficking (Definition of Victim) Regulations 2022

Under the Modern Slavery Act 2015, all police forces and local authorities, as well as the National Crime Agency and the Gangmaster and Labour Abuse Authority, have a duty to notify the Home Office of anyone they believe is a suspected victim of human trafficking or modern slavery. In addition, the Public Services (Social Value) Act 2012 requires all public-sector organisations to monitor their supply chains to ensure what they buy creates additional benefits for society. As part of this, they should identify and manage risk of modern slavery within new procurement contracts, monitor contracts on an ongoing basis and take action when victims of modern slavery are identified.

While the duty to notify is not a requirement for other organisations, they are encouraged to complete a National Referral Mechanism (NRM) form or an MS1 (Notification of a Potential Victim of Modern Slavery) form (for further details visit gov.uk and search 'duty to notify' to download the forms and associated guidance). As part of the Modern Slavery Act 2015, all companies supplying goods or services in the UK with an annual worldwide turnover of £36M or more are required to prominently publish a statement each year indicating how they have challenged the risk of modern slavery within their activities and within their supply chain.

> **Case study**
>
> The Gangmaster and Labour Abuse Authority has received reports of chicken catchers not being paid for their travel time between different work sites, health and safety concerns with the suitability of accommodation (overcrowded and unsanitary conditions), individuals being paid less than the national minimum wage for piecework, and workers being controlled by employers withholding their identity documents.
> ▶ What are the potential consequences for an employer found to have exploited workers?
> ▶ What is the potential penalty for an employer who is found guilty of using workers supplied by an unlicensed gangmaster?

Impact of union membership on the employer and the employee

Trade unions play an important role in the workplace by providing an employee 'voice' and supporting the development of effective working relationships between an employer and their workforce. Trade unions have special rights in law to negotiate pay and working conditions. They also have the right to be informed and consulted on matters such as health and safety and redundancies.

Trade union officials provide a range of support for members, but immediate support in the workplace is normally provided by union representatives. These are unpaid members who receive paid time off (in line with the relevant Acas Code of Practice) to receive training for and perform to their role. Some representatives may undertake a specialist role. For example, equality representatives promote and raise awareness of issues associated with diversity and inclusion, and union learning representatives encourage employees to engage in training to enhance their work skill sets.

The Trade Union and Labour Relations (Consolidation) Act 1992 offers employees and some workers legal protection against being refused employment, being offered unfavourable treatment, or being dismissed because they are or are not members of a trade union. Members of a trade union are also offered protection for lawful activities associated with union membership.

3.2 Effective teamwork

Types of teams and how they are developed

Successful land-based businesses and organisations rely on effective team working. This is because often tasks cannot be completed by one individual and instead it may be more efficient to assign a number of people to complete a task, as the team will benefit from the diverse skills and knowledge of its members.

The structure and working parameters of each team will vary depending on the needs of the organisation, which might be driven by client or customer demand. When determining what teams are required, an employer may consider the:
▶ purpose of the team (for example providing a service or improving a work process)
▶ autonomy of the team (for example, individuals being able to make decisions by themselves without supervision)
▶ size and scale of the team (allocating the number of workers to a task depending on its difficulty and complexity)

- duration of the team (for example a permanent team or a temporary team working together for a defined period of time)
- physical requirements (for example the workers needing to be physically present in the same place).

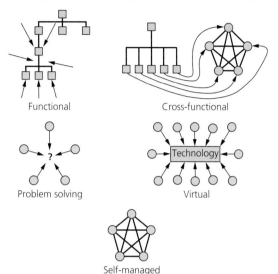

Functional

Cross-functional

Problem solving

Virtual

Self-managed

▲ Figure 3.3 Types of work teams

Having considered the goals of the team, an employer will usually select from one of the following types of team:

- Functional teams comprise individuals from the same department working together, with a leader whom members report to and who allocates responsibilities.
- Cross-functional teams (or matrix teams) comprise individuals from different departments, working with a leader whom members report to and who allocates responsibilities.
- Problem-solving teams (or task force teams) comprise individuals working on a specific problem, with a leader whom members report to and who allocates responsibilities.
- Project teams comprise individuals working on a specific project, with a leader whom members report to and who allocates responsibilities.
- Virtual (or remote) teams comprise individuals working in separate locations through the use of technology.
- Self-managed teams comprise individuals who work together towards a common goal but are responsible for managing themselves.

How teams are developed

Once an employer has determined the type, structure, scope and goal(s) of a team, they will develop the team. This may include allocating someone as team leader, whose role is to assign responsibilities to team members, co-ordinate activities, monitor progress and report to the employer. Teams are normally developed through the following five stages (Figure 3.4).

Forming or training

This is the initial stage when team members meet. As the team is new, members will be briefed on the purpose and working parameters and are likely to be highly motivated.

Storming

As the team members start to communicate and work with each other, they will likely share different perspectives and views. This may result in disagreement and conflict, so motivation may decrease. The team may start to split into smaller teams as a result of shared views or values. At this stage, members must learn to collaborate and overcome any disagreements.

Norming

The team members have overcome any internal challenges and are communicating effectively, providing others with mutual and constructive support. If a team leader has not already been appointed, it is at this stage that a leader will emerge.

Performing

The team is now starting to perform cohesively, is clear on working relationships and is focused on producing results. Members have a shared ownership and value team membership.

Adjourning or dissolution

This stage is reached when the work allocated to the team nears completion. This stage occurs naturally if the team was working on a specific project or task but may be reached if the team needs to be restructured for organisation or business reasons.

Importance of team dynamics and behaviour and their effect on team performance

Throughout the stages of team working, team dynamics and collective behaviour can have a critical effect on team performance and whether the assigned goals are met. Employers and team leaders can contribute to team effectiveness by:

- allocating the workload fairly (for example assigning work to individuals based on their skills, capacity and capability)

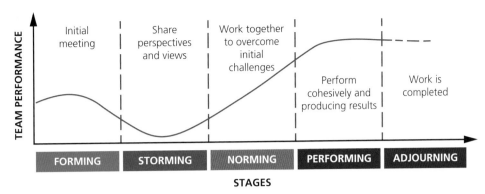

▲ Figure 3.4 Tuckman's five-stage team development model

- communicating effectively (for example providing clearly defined goals and frequent communication)
- defining roles and responsibilities clearly (ensuring individuals understand their contribution to the team)
- clarifying accountability and ownership (for example setting deadlines and response times for individuals)
- resolving conflict (identifying and addressing problems as they arise and encouraging collaboration).

While the team leader can have a significant impact on the effectiveness and efficiency of a team, the contribution and participation of individual team members is critical. Therefore, employers look for team members to possess and demonstrate a range of personal qualities. Most of these are commonly referred to as **soft skills** or **interpersonal skills**. These may include:

- open communication (asking questions if unsure and sharing progress)
- problem solving (recognising challenges when they arise and developing solutions, or preventing them escalating)
- listening (clarifying information shared by others so the meaning is understood)
- persuasion (sharing ideas and perspectives in such a way that they are accepted by others in the team)
- collaboration and support (working with others and helping where necessary)

- respect and tolerance (being tolerant of the views and opinions of others even if they do not agree with them)
- trust (being transparent and honest with others in the team)
- empathy (caring for others in the team)
- learning (reflecting on what could have been done differently when things go wrong)
- reliability (undertaking work allocated to the required standard and within the agreed timescale).

Employers normally put considerable thought and effort into selecting members of a team. This may mean bringing together individuals with diverse skills, knowledge and experience to solve complex problems. Therefore, putting the right individuals together can positively impact team working and project performance, for example it can:

- increase productivity
- save time and money
- reduce health and safety risks
- increase team collaboration and morale
- promote creativity and innovative thinking
- achieve desired results quicker.

▲ Figure 3.5 A group of crop technicians being briefed by their team leader

> ### Key terms
>
> **Soft skills**: attributes associated with an individual's awareness of, and ability to express and manage, their behaviours and emotions
>
> **Interpersonal skills**: abilities that relate to how an individual communicates, interacts and collaborates with others

Techniques used to monitor and manage individual and team performance

A manager/team leader can use a range of techniques to monitor and manage individual and team performance.

Establishing individual and team/organisational goals

Setting goals is helpful in determining general direction and outcomes. Goals are intended to be met over a long-term timescale. They are broad in their scope and may be intangible, so they can be difficult to measure.

Setting individual and team/organisational objectives

Objectives should be specific, narrow in focus and measurable. They are intended to be met in a short- to medium-term timescale.

Setting SMART targets

SMART is an acronym for Specific, Measurable, Attainable, Relevant and Time-bound. It relates to an approach commonly used for setting targets that can be met within a defined time period. This helps managers to monitor team progress and avoids work tasks exceeding deadlines.

> ### Key term
>
> **SMART:** acronym standing for **S**pecific, **M**easurable, **A**ttainable, **R**elevant and **T**ime-bound; a SMART objective incorporates all of these criteria to help focus efforts and increase the likelihood of achievement

Setting KPIs

KPI is an acronym for key performance indicator, also referred to as key success indicator (KSI). KPIs are metrics against which the performance of a team or an organisation is measured at any point in time, providing an insight into how well it is achieving its

Target	S	How is it Specific?	M	How is it Measurable?	A	How is it Attainable?	R	How is it Relevant?	T	How is it Time-bound?

▲ Figure 3.6 Example SMART target template

Financial growth KPI – To increase animal feed sales revenue from £200K to £250K											
January		March		May		July		September		November	
£200K	£201K	£210K	£205K	£220K		£230K		£240K		£250K	
Comments:											
Target owned by Director of Sales											
Revenue from confirmed sales											
Target sales						Actual sales					

▲ Figure 3.7 Example of tracking a key performance indicator (KPI)

objectives. They can be used to track, for example, use of resources or business assets, financial performance, customer satisfaction and progress against sales targets. A KPI usually requires a measure, an owner, a target, a data source and a reporting frequency.

Undertaking performance management reviews

These reviews can be formal or informal. They are normally held regularly (monthly or quarterly) and may be narrower in scope than a formal appraisal where they are used with an individual rather than a team. They provide an opportunity to review progress and can reward positive performance or identify underperformance.

Providing feedback within individual and team meetings

Regular meetings (weekly or biweekly) are an opportunity to provide constructive and developmental feedback which is intended to motivate and inspire individuals and teams. References can be made to performance against targets and managers may adopt a **coaching** approach.

Managing conflict

If the relationship between team members deteriorates and negatively impacts on performance, a manager may have to intervene. It may be possible to deal with any conflict informally (for example by talking to those involved to resolve any issues), or more formal mechanisms may need to be adopted. In the extreme, this may necessitate initiating the disciplinary procedure (see Chapter 6, page 102). Mediation may also be used within the workplace as an option to resolve conflict. This is a voluntary approach that relies on an impartial third party to create an environment within which those involved can hold open conversations. The mediator does not form any judgement or apportion blame but helps participants to find solutions that are mutually acceptable.

> ### Key terms
>
> **Coaching**: a process aimed at improving performance, where an individual learns by being helped to find the answer to their own problems; it focuses on the current position rather than what has happened in the past or what might happen in the future
>
> **Refresher training**: a CPD activity that allows an individual to reinforce their existing skills and knowledge and ensure they are up to date with current industry standards

3.3 Purpose of continuing professional development (CPD) opportunities

Importance of CPD

Continuing (or continuous) professional development (CPD) refers to learning experiences and activities that allow an individual to ensure their occupational proficiency is at a level appropriate to their role. It includes aspects of knowledge, skills or personal qualities that the individual has identified as areas of development or improvement; perhaps they have pinpointed a skill they would like to improve. It also includes learning undertaken by an individual relevant to their career interests to prepare for a new role in the future.

Once a CPD activity has been completed, it is important for the individual to reflect on whether the learning met the intended objective, how they will apply this learning to their work and how it will impact their proficiency. Through this reflection process, the individual might identify further learning or may conclude that they did not benefit from the activity undertaken. In the case of the latter, this should still be considered a positive outcome. The activity may have consolidated existing learning and may reassure the individual that this aspect of their knowledge or skills is current, sufficient and appropriate for their role. The pace of learning varies for each individual, so it is important to manage expectations around progress. It may be that the format of the activity was not right (for example online rather than in person) or something prevented the activity being as effective as it could have been (for example the content covered was not as detailed as expected), hence reflection is an important step when exploring and planning future CPD opportunities.

Most employers expect workers to take proactive ownership of their CPD, although this is also normally included within their appraisal or performance review. In addition, employers may require workers to undertake CPD for technical or legal reasons. For example, to demonstrate they have the requisite current skills and knowledge, workers may be required to hold or achieve a certificate of competence. In certain instances, individuals may be legally obliged to hold a licence to practice (see Chapter 1) and, if necessary, undertake additional or **refresher training**.

Training may be required when:

▶ changes to a work task affect health and safety risks (for example an animal keeper changes the species they are responsible for)
▶ an employer introduces new technology or equipment (for example a new self-propelled sprayer has been bought for the farm, but the controls are different to those on the existing trailed sprayer)
▶ working systems change (for example a forest harvesting contractor changes their working practices to minimise ground compaction on a sensitive site)
▶ skills and knowledge decline (for example a dog groomer has been absent from work for an extended period of time and has not used their skills recently)
▶ there is a contractual requirement (for example a tender for landscaping services may require a contractor to confirm their workers undertake regular refresher training to ensure competence)
▶ there has been an incident or accident (for example an estate manager may provide gamekeepers with training following a near-miss incident while riding an all-terrain vehicle).

Training can also contribute to an employer's defence to claims of negligence, for example if a tree climber is injured as a result of undertaking a work task.

▲ Figure 3.8 Refresher training on floral arrangements and techniques is part of CPD

Case study

The Provision and Use of Work Equipment Regulations (PUWER) 1998: Approved Code of Practice and Guidance (see Chapter 1, page 5) states that under Regulation 9 employers need to provide refresher training when necessary for those individuals who use work equipment. It suggests that those who use work equipment less frequently, or who may deputise for others, may need more frequent refresher training than those who use the work equipment regularly.

▶ Why might refresher training be required by individuals who use work equipment?
▶ What are the benefits to the individual of refresher training?

Record of continuing professional development

Date(s) of activity	Duration in hours	Location	Summary of activity undertaken	What were the aims of the activity?	What did I learn?	How will I apply my new learning?

▲ Figure 3.9 Example of a CPD template

Individuals may seek to obtain occupational credibility by joining a professional membership organisation. In order to maintain membership, these individuals must show commitment to the organisation's values and fulfil any CPD expectations set by the organisation. As this CPD may be subject to audit by the organisation, it should be formally recorded. This may be via an electronic or online system or retained as a paper-based record.

Case study

In order to maintain member status, both the Chartered Institute of Horticulture and the Institute of Agricultural Engineers require individuals to complete at least 30 hours of CPD each year.
▶ Why do membership organisations set CPD targets for their members?
▶ What might the consequences be of not undertaking sufficient CPD activities?

The benefits of membership of a professional organisation depend on the membership level but may include:
▶ opportunities for networking with other professionals within the same industry
▶ use of **post-nominals**
▶ access to regular specialist magazines, newsletters and/or emails about topical issues
▶ discounted or free access to relevant academic journals
▶ access to webinars, training events and study tours.

Test yourself

Research your chosen industry and select a relevant professional membership organisation.

Investigate what benefits it offers members, how an individual may progress through any membership grades and what its CPD expectations are.

There is not an exhaustive list of learning experiences and activities that count as CPD. Indeed, it can include things which are not directly work related. However, some of the main types of CPD include:
▶ work or industry experience (such as job shadowing)
▶ training (for example soft skills courses or internal company training courses)
▶ coaching or mentoring (informal guidance provided by someone experienced in the role)
▶ self-study and independent research (such as reading books, magazines or journals)

Key term

Post-nominals: combinations of letters placed after a person's name to indicate achievement of an academic qualification (such as a degree) or a professional qualification (for example Chartered status), membership of an organisation or award of a national honour (for example Member of the Order of the British Empire, MBE); they are often used by individuals in their email signature, on business cards and in social media profiles to summarise their achievements and provide an indication of their expertise or credibility

▶ seminars and events (for example webinars or technical visits)
▶ academic study and qualifications (for example an apprenticeship or a degree)
▶ volunteering and personal qualities (for example development of leadership or interviewing skills through charity work).

Benefits of CPD to the individual and their employer

Benefits of CPD to the individual include:
▶ increased career opportunities (such as internal or external promotion)
▶ the potential to specialise (for example achieve a higher salary and/or access niche markets)
▶ the ability to contribute to business performance/ keep up to date with industry developments and opportunities, such as new and emerging technology
▶ the chance to demonstrate occupational credibility
▶ increased job/career satisfaction
▶ the ability to maintain currency of qualifications, skills and knowledge
▶ improved work–life balance
▶ career progression/talent development
▶ improved confidence/motivation.

Benefits of CPD to the employer include:
▶ a skilled workforce benefiting employer performance
▶ staff retention
▶ workforce succession opportunities (developing individuals to fill business critical roles in the future)
▶ business continuity and contingency (for example workers being able to cover for colleagues in the event of sickness)
▶ reduced costs of external consultancy/contractors.

Methods and sources of personal and professional development support

CPD requirements are specific to an individual's previous training, education and experience, their current employer's needs and their future career ambitions. Therefore, CPD is personal and will be different for everyone. However, it is helpful to discuss and share potential learning needs with colleagues on a regular basis. This will help identify development needs and goals in order to select from the range of CPD opportunities available.

Sources of support

As CPD requirements are specific to an individual's learning needs and career, there is a wide range of sources of support. These may be internal and/or external to the individual's employer, and it is normal for an individual to access multiple sources, to varying extents, over time. These sources of support include:

▶ awarding organisations (via regulated qualifications or accredited courses)
▶ trade organisations (via trade shows and competitions)
▶ professional bodies and membership organisations (via webinars and conferences)
▶ training providers (via seminars and online workshops)
▶ employers (via internal training and secondment)
▶ colleagues (via coaching and work shadowing)
▶ peers (via observations and feedback).

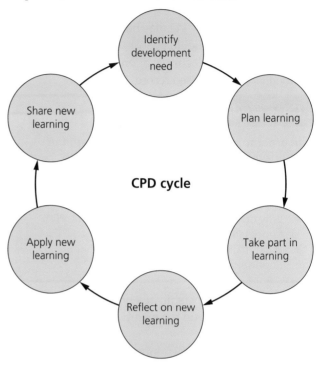

▲ Figure 3.10 The CPD cycle

▲ Figure 3.11 CPD enables employees to keep up to date with industry developments and emerging technologies

Assessment practice

1 Describe the key difference between fixed-term and permanent contracts. (2 marks)

2 Identify **two** advantages employees have over being self-employed. (2 marks)

3 Identify **two** reasons why an individual may want to undertake temporary or seasonal work. (2 marks)

4 Identify **two** reasons why an employer may want to vary the periods of notice that different employees must provide when terminating their contract of employment. (2 marks)

5 Identify **two** reasons why the risk of modern slavery may be high in the land-based sector. (2 marks)

6 Malc's Salon is a small, successful dog-grooming business consisting of two salons. The owners decide to open a third salon in a nearby town because of an increase in customers from that area. To do this, they must recruit two additional groomers and two grooming assistants.

Describe how the owners of Malc's Salon might promote a positive workplace culture that builds a team culture and encourages professional behaviour among the employees. (6 marks)

7 Explain **two** ways a land-based organisation can raise awareness about modern slavery and workforce exploitation. (4 marks)

8 Explain **two** potential advantages for an employee of being a member of a trade union. (4 marks)

9 Sam manages a family farm which has three employees. They decide to take on Jimmy, a 19-year-old, as an apprentice to help with livestock tasks.

Explain what Sam should include within the induction programme for Jimmy during his first week at work. (6 marks)

10 Explain **three** ways in which an employer might support and encourage their staff to engage in CPD activities. (6 marks)

Further reading

You may find the websites of some of the following organisations useful:

▶ Advisory, Conciliation and Arbitration Service (Acas)
▶ Equality Advisory and Support Service (EASS)
▶ Equality and Human Rights Commission (EHRC)
▶ Gangmasters and Labour Abuse Authority (GLAA)
▶ Health and Safety Executive (HSE)
▶ Unseen UK.

4 Ethics

Introduction

This chapter introduces ethical principles and values for working in land-based industries in the UK. The topic of ethics and its impact on business decisions and operations is wide, varied and complicated, as it not only affects individual businesses but also stakeholders, customers and suppliers.

The chapter outlines ethical principles and how these are applied in the workplace. This includes the Equality Act 2010 and protected characteristics. In addition, the action of whistleblowing is explained and how it is protected by legislation.

The chapter also looks at ethical principles and values and how they are used by businesses through their policies and behaviours, as well as how they can influence stakeholders and impact business operations.

The request for personal information about an individual links to data protection and GDPR and is covered more fully in Chapter 10 Information and data.

Learning outcomes

By the end of this chapter, you will understand:
▶ the definition of morals and ethics
▶ ethical principles and how they are applied in the workplace
▶ the definition and purpose of whistleblowing – to eradicate unethical behaviour in the workplace
▶ how ethical principles and values are used

▶ how ethical principles and values are represented by ethical behaviours and incorporated into business ethics using codes of conduct
▶ what ethical principles and values impact on business operations, including interaction with stakeholders and the supply chain.

4.1 Ethical principles and values

Definition of morals and ethics

Morals

Morals are the principles of right and wrong behaviour.

There are two types of moral principle:
▶ Absolute principles are unchanging and universal morals generally accepted by society.
▶ Relative principles are based on opinions and circumstances, and they can change depending on the situation/social culture of the time.

In the context of this chapter, morals relate to the standards of behaviour that businesses set and conduct. These principles govern how the business operates in its entirety, whether that is externally with its customers and regulators (whom it conducts business with) or internally (how it treats its employees).

Ethics

Ethics are principles that govern a person's behaviour or the conduct of an activity.

Business ethics influence what decisions are made. They can cause conflict or challenges, as the interpretation of what is considered 'ethical' may vary from person to person since the definition of ethical behaviour is influenced by an individual's background, experiences and values. For example, one individual's interpretation of ethical business practice could be linked to social impacts on the local community, whereas another person could be more focused on environmental factors. Sometimes these interpretations can mean decisions need to be made on topics where there is no clear right or wrong answer.

Ethical principles and how they are applied in the workplace

Honesty

Honesty is one of the key ethical principles. It requires individuals to be clear, open and truthful, regardless of the consequences. However, this does not mean disclosing all sorts of personal information to everyone, breaking data protection and compromising information security (this is covered in more detail in Chapter 10).

Honesty encourages trust within an organisation, both between colleagues and within the organisation

hierarchy and structure. It also encourages trust between the business and the public, their customers or clients.

Transparency

Transparency is when a business provides detailed and accurate information to all stakeholders both internally (such as employees, shareholders and boards) and externally (such as customers, regulators, insurance providers, industry bodies and membership bodies). Transparency within a business helps promote ethical operations.

Internally in a business, transparency can be about financial information such as profit margins, or externally with customers it can be about costs and pricing. For example, when providing a quote for a service such as felling a tree, garden maintenance or dog grooming, it could mean being transparent about how the quote or cost has been calculated, i.e. showing breakdowns of costs for materials, labour and VAT. See Chapter 9, page 132 for information on profit margins.

> **Industry tip**
>
> Land-based employers must be transparent with the information they communicate without sharing details that competitor businesses could use to their advantage. For instance, information shared publicly on a website or in marketing materials should not include labour or material costs, as this could enable competitors to change their pricing to ensure they get more business, as well as give insights into any deals a business has with suppliers on material costs. It is advisable instead to use publicly available information to invite potential customers to contact the business for a quote.

Transparency can also link to the company's policies, procedures and processes, from organisation structure to how recruitment, promotions and pay structures are arranged.

Having transparency within a business' ethos helps to develop trust with all **stakeholders**.

> **Key term**
>
> **Stakeholder**: any person, group or organisation that has an interest in the activities and performance of a business; they can be internal and external, from individuals to local communities to the government

Justice

The ethical principle of justice deals with the fair treatment of individuals and encourages and rewards diversity and inclusion. This means that in the workplace, businesses should have policies and procedures in place that cover equality and equity, and that deal with harassment and abuse, should they occur. See Chapter 6 for more about the Equality Act, protected characteristics and harassment.

Equality

Equality means each individual or group of people is given the same resources or opportunities. For example, every employee is given personal protective equipment (PPE).

Equity

Equity is about being fair and impartial while recognising that each person has different circumstances and allocating the exact resources and opportunities needed by that individual to reach an outcome that is equal with the rest of the group. For example, every employee is given PPE that fits them and meets their individual needs to carry out their role (see Chapter 1). This can mean having to conduct assessments on each employee to find out what they need, not only in terms of individual pieces of equipment but also sizing, and holding confidential or sensitive information. Therefore, whoever collects this information must ensure they conduct themselves in an empathic manner and are clear about how the information is used and stored. In this example, buying PPE on an individual basis can also create increased costs for the business, as it might not be able to purchase items in bulk.

Harassment

The Equality Act 2010 legally protects people from discrimination in the workplace and in wider society. It sets out the different ways in which it is unlawful to treat someone and includes harassing behaviour.

Harassment is when someone repeatedly behaves in a way to make an individual feel scared, distressed or threatened. It is not a one-off incident or situation. Harassment is unlawful under the Equality Act 2010 if it concerns these protected characteristics:

▶ age
▶ sex

▶ disability
▶ gender reassignment
▶ marriage and civil partnership
▶ pregnancy and maternity
▶ race
▶ religion or belief
▶ sexual orientation.

▲ Figure 4.1 Workplace harassment is unlawful

Harassing behaviour includes spreading malicious rumours, unfair treatment, regularly undermining someone and preventing promotion opportunities. In some cases it can also include physical abuse. Harassment and abuse can happen at all levels in a business, between colleagues, across departments or from supervisors and managers down the workplace structure.

Harassment can be in person, face-to-face, anti-social behaviour during work time or out of work, or it can be online 'cyber-stalking' using social media, telephone calls, emails, text messages or sending unwanted gifts.

Businesses should have policies in place for harassment to be reported, investigated and dealt with. These can be a mix of informal procedures, such as talking to all parties to resolve the unwanted behaviour, and formal grievance processes if the informal procedures do not resolve or stop the behaviour. Formal procedures can involve managers, the human resources (HR) department or trade unions. If these still do not resolve the harassment problems, employees can take legal action and go to an employment tribunal.

Consent

The term 'consent' is used widely in day-to-day life, but in all situations it means 'an individual's agreement to allow a certain action to take place'. In the workplace, consent could be requested for a company to carry out a background check or **DBS check** as a requirement for employment. These checks help employers make safer recruitment decisions by checking whether someone has a criminal record. Such checks are required when working in certain positions of trust, such as working with children, young people and vulnerable adults. They can also be part of a company's policy. For example, a DBS check could be required if a school is visiting a zoo or farm as part of a school trip and a member of staff is going to be spending the day with the school children showing them round and interacting with them on a one-to-one basis, such as during talks, animal encounters or activities.

Privacy

Privacy covers the various ways of accessing, controlling, monitoring and protecting an individual's data and information. This principle can be complicated: when a business takes an individual's data and information, it is taking on responsibilities such as trust, security and legal, which all overlap. Not undertaking these responsibilities can result in security threats and breaking laws such as GDPR (this is covered in more detail in Chapter 10). In basic terms, failure to maintain privacy of an individual's information can mean people lose trust in the company and how it performs business. There are also legal consequences and loss of information security.

When a business is collecting and storing an individual's information, it therefore needs to understand how the data is going to be used, ensure privacy and security safeguards are in place and only collect and store information that is needed. For example, when a customer's payment is taken for an order, it is important that their payment details are not stored. The business should also ensure that certain database details are restricted to particular staff or departments: for example, a plant supplier may have an order from a garden landscaping company but the

> ### Key term
>
> **DBS check**: a process carried out by the Disclosure and Barring Service (DBS) that provides a criminal record data check of an individual; the individual receives a certificate that has no official expiry date, but the disclosure is only accurate at the time it is processed; it is recommended that it is updated or renewed every three years, but this depends on the employer requirements and role being carried out by the individual

billing address of the garden landscaping company is only available to the plant supplier's finance team and not the delivery driver for the order; the delivery driver only needs the delivery address.

Confidentiality

Confidentiality is ensuring that information about an individual is not shared without their permission. This could be to a third party, to another part of the business (such as the marketing team) or for use in advertisements or social media activities. For example, when posting online about an activity or event that has taken place, the business must ensure that anyone cited in the text and/or appearing in the photographs has given permission for their details to be used.

An example of this within land-based businesses would be when a florist who has provided the floral display and bouquets for a wedding seeks permission from the customer (wedding party) and the venue to use any photographs or information in their social media posts. This can be obtained before the event, so that the customer has the ability to 'opt out' and keep information about their event confidential.

When purchasing online, companies now have to ask permission to share any information, and this is normally a mandatory field or tick box to complete a purchase.

British values

This section introduces the 'British values' that the Department for Education (DfE) requires schools to teach and discuss with the purpose 'to create and enforce a clear and rigorous expectation on all schools to promote the fundamental British values of democracy, the rule of law, individual liberty, mutual respect and tolerance of those of different faiths and beliefs'.

The aim of these values is to create social unity and prevent extremism.

Democracy

This value means everyone having the right to have their voice heard. In the workplace, this can be through meetings and performance reviews with supervisors or managers, team meetings or (if the company has them) employee boards or trade unions. Some companies conduct anonymous employee surveys to get feedback and opinions about specific topics or questions. This data and information can be used by the company to inform business decisions and to improve working conditions and morale, for example introducing new processes, changing team/company structure, pursuing investments and establishing employee benefit and reward schemes.

Rule of law

The British values reinforce how to differentiate between right and wrong and being accountable for your own actions. This is achieved by understanding the rationale for rules and laws and the consequences of them being broken. For example, the purpose of the Wildlife and Countryside Act 1981 is to protect wild animals in the UK by limiting or prohibiting activities such as trapping, killing and taking animals, or the introduction and release of animals. It also protects certain species, such as bats. The consequences of breaking this law can include fines, imprisonment or confiscation of work equipment and limiting work activities.

> ### Case study
>
> In October 2023, Natural England successfully prosecuted a Derby-based property developer for breaching the conditions of a European Protected Species Bat Mitigation Licence. He was ordered by the court to pay a total of £14,435.17 in fines and costs.
> ▶ What must be completed before applying for a European Protected Species Mitigation Licence?
> ▶ Under the terms of the licence, what activities break the law?
> ▶ What are the potential penalties for breaching the conditions of the licence and to whom do they apply?

▲ Figure 4.2 Bats are protected by law

Individual liberty

Individual liberty is the value of freedom of choice and pursuing personal ambition for things in our lives outside government control and legislation. This includes freedom of speech (the right to respectfully express opinions and beliefs in a safe environment) and freedom to make choices about our lifestyles, for example in relation to diet, gender, religion and sexual orientation. These choices need to be made while taking responsibility for our own behaviour, respecting others and following British values.

Respect

This means respecting people from different cultural. socio-economic, educational, religious or political backgrounds. Respect develops understanding that others may have beliefs that differ from our own, and that even if we do not agree with someone's opinions or beliefs, we should respect them nonetheless. This directly links to the British value of 'tolerance'.

Tolerance

This is the value of recognising and respecting the views and practices of people from different cultures, religions and belief sets, which includes being non-religious (agnostic or atheist). The value of tolerance is important for a diverse and harmonious society and helps prevent discrimination.

Definition and purpose of whistleblowing

Whistleblowing is when individuals, employees or contractors expose wrongdoing in a company/business, for example fraud, bribery, danger or other illegal behaviour, such as not holding correct qualifications to perform an activity, risking people's safety or not having the correct insurance. For example, if you know a company does not hold public liability insurance or someone uses a business/company vehicle without insurance or a driving licence, you could become a **whistleblower**. It usually relates to something that is witnessed firsthand, but it does not have to be.

A whistleblower might expose a practice or behaviour that is dangerous, for example if managers do not follow the health and safety requirements of a risk assessment, or do not use the correct PPE.

> ### Key term
>
> ***Whistleblower***: a person who discloses information about unlawful or immoral activity in the workplace; whistleblowing is also known as 'making a disclosure in the public interest'

The whistleblower will need evidence of this bad practice taking place, such as an email trail or other paperwork. This kind of malpractice can be reported internally within the company or to an external regulator. In the land-based sector, this could be one of the following:

▶ the Health and Safety Executive (HSE) is the UK's national regulator for workplace health and safety

▶ the Department for Environment, Food and Rural Affairs (Defra) is primarily involved in protecting the environment

▶ the Royal Society for the Prevention of Cruelty to Animals (RSPCA) works to improve the lives of animals

▶ the Chemical Regulatory Directorate (CRD) is the directorate of the HSE with the primary aim of ensuring the safe use of biocides, industrial chemicals, pesticides and detergents to protect the health of people and the environment

▶ the Animal and Plant Health Agency (APHA) safeguards animal and plant health for the benefit of people, the environment and the economy

▶ local authorities/local planning authorities are local councils and district councils and they can be involved in licensing inspections and issuing permits; they also have enforcement responsibility for workplace health and safety in certain contexts (see Chapter 1, page 13).

A whistleblower can raise a concern at any time, past, present or future. This means that if you know of an event that has already occurred or something that is planned or potentially going to happen, it can be reported. It does not have to be happening at that moment in time. See Chapter 10 for more about data protection and privacy considerations.

The purpose of companies having whistleblowing policies and procedures is to eradicate unethical behaviour in the workplace.

In the UK, whistleblowing is covered by the Public Interest Disclosure Act 1998. This means that whistleblowers are protected by law and must not be treated unfairly or lose their job if they 'blow the whistle'. If they do lose their job, they should get legal advice about unfair dismissal.

Unfair treatment or detrimental treatment includes:
▶ reduction in hours
▶ bullying
▶ harassment.

If still legally employed or working, unfair dismissal cannot be claimed; however, if someone believes that they are receiving unfair treatment, legal advice should be sought, as this is a complicated area of the law.

Case study

Over the years, there have been a number of high-profile whistleblowing cases. One of the largest international cases was in regard to Julian Assange and the Wikileaks website, which made the news in 2010 when they released sensitive military material passed to them.
▶ What was the content of the sensitive military material that was released by the Wikileaks website?
▶ How did the government respond to the leaked information?

How ethical principles and values are used

Codes of conduct

A code of conduct is usually part of a company's employee handbook and is managed by the HR department. Each company will have its own code of conduct and its own procedures for how it is enforced. It is an internal policy and outlines a company's expectations of its employees' behaviour while they are at work. It sets out rules and guidelines for employees to help avoid work conflict situations and ensures the company is compliant with appropriate workplace legislation, for example in regard to workplace bulling and harassment. It can include things like confidentiality, professional behaviour and competence, attendance and absence, breaks/mealtimes, use of company property, travel, conflicts of interest and dress code.

Codes of conduct can also outline a company's values, ethics and morals. These are sometimes published externally to help promote these aspects of the business to customers, regulators, future employees and other stakeholders.

Employment terms and conditions

Following on from Chapter 3, these are required to be included in an employment contract and outline the rights for the employee and the business. The content is dependent on the individual business but can include:
▶ rights
▶ responsibilities
▶ duties
▶ job specifications.

The terms and conditions of the contract must be followed until the contract ends or until the terms are changed (usually by agreement between the employee and employer).

An employment contract is not a 'contract to provide services'. For example, in the land-based sector if a person agrees to fell a tree in a garden or groom a dog, this is a contract for services, not an employment contract.

Workplace policies

These are the general guidelines that set out a company's expectations regarding employee behaviour and performance and how the company deals with certain situations or issues. The policies include codes of conduct (previously outlined in this chapter) and may further include the following areas:

- **Recruitment**: this sets out, and aims to promote consistency in, the hiring process.
- **Discipline and contract termination**: this can include handling employee misconduct and performance issues, the termination of contracts and resignations.
- **Grievances**: this covers filing complaints and how grievances are handled and resolved.
- **Internet and email use**: this sets out how employees are to use their email accounts and the internet. Some companies do not allow personal use, whereas others may allow it during breaks or at lunchtime.
- **Mobile phone use**: this covers the rules of mobile phone usage in the workplace for personal and company-issued devices. In some businesses, the use of mobile phones can be restricted for security or safety reasons, as the signal can interfere with equipment.
- **Health and safety**: this sets out the rules for maintaining a safe and healthy workplace, including reporting accidents and injuries, handling hazardous materials and dealing with emergencies.
- **Drug and alcohol use**: this sets out the rules for drug and alcohol use in the workplace or even during the time before starting work, for example when using machinery employees may be restricted from consuming alcohol for a certain number of hours prior to starting work.

Workplace procedures are different from workplace policies, as these explain the specific actions taken to carry out the policy.

Test yourself

List **three** workplace policies a business could have and give examples of what information they would contain.

Supply chains

A company's ethical principles and values can influence its decision-making on its supply chain. When making decisions on suppliers, a company will consider numerous factors that will be specific to its principles but also to its needs, for example:

- **working conditions**: child and slave labour, safety, hygiene, fair pay, working hours, humane and non-discriminatory treatment
- **environment**: sustainable and renewable resources, farming practices, animal welfare, deforestation, pollution, recycling and waste disposal, use of plastics, impact on natural resources and ecosystems, carbon footprint, distance
- **politics**: laws and practices of the supplier country in regard to gender equality, human rights, justice systems, behaviour and actions to other nations, for example conflicts, communication and transparency, historical events, political stability and government system
- **socio-economic issues**: supporting businesses and development in poorer areas, opportunities for work and financial stability.

▲ Figure 4.3 Deforestation for palm oil plantations has far-reaching effects for wildlife and climate change

In 2023, the World Association of Zoos and Aquariums (WAZA) developed a mobile phone app 'PalmOil Scan' that allows consumers to check whether products such as peanut butter or chocolate spread use palm oil. When the user scans the product's barcode, it will reveal whether it contains palm oil and whether it is sustainable.

This links to the issue of global deforestation for palm oil plantations and how this impacts wildlife species. This is a particular issue in Borneo, where deforestation has caused such a severe decline in orangutan numbers that they are at risk of extinction.

The app aims to create more consumer awareness of the supply chain of the products that consumers buy, the impact this has on the environment worldwide and how they can help make more ethical decisions when choosing products, such as buying products that only use palm oil that is sustainably produced.

▶ Along with WAZA, which other organisations helped create the app?
▶ What is palm oil?
▶ Why is palm oil used in food, products and manufacturing?

▲ Figure 4.4 Clearing forests endangers the lives and habitats of many species, including orangutans

How ethical principles and values are represented by ethical behaviours and incorporated into business ethics using codes of conduct

The ethical principles and values of a business are demonstrated in its behaviour, not only in how it treats its employees, but also how it expects its employees to behave. Employees represent the business. They are therefore an extension of the business and, as such, are the external face of the business. This is why a business' code of conduct is so important, as it demonstrates and formalises these ethical principles and values. It can also help establish a link between the business' purpose and its ethical values to create a culture that drives ethical behaviours and guides decision-making.

Ethical principles and values that impact on business operations, stakeholders and the supply chain

Sharing the same ethical values

The ethical principles and values of a business not only impact the behaviours of employees but also how the business operates, who the business' stakeholders are, the overall supply chain from where it purchases resources, and its customers.

For example, if an egg farm is organic and free-range this impacts:
▶ the physical farming production system (large outdoor space including a barn/hen house, no use of pesticides on the land, land maintenance, planting to feed hens organically)
▶ animal welfare and husbandry practices (organic diet, feeding methods, zero use of chemicals or antibiotics, veterinary treatment available, total number of hens and hens per m²)
▶ the employee job role (for example eggs collected manually rather than on a conveyor belt or robotically)
▶ the number of people employed (potentially more staff needed).

The stakeholders will also be different to stakeholders in intensive farming methods, as the farm will be subjected to audits and testing. The organic farm needs to obtain organic status and free-range certification, as well as standard farm inspections, to advertise and sell its product. It can also mean that it must install biosecurity precautions and protocols for Defra and the HSE, as the birds are free roaming and at higher risk of contracting diseases such as avian flu.

All of these factors will increase the farm's operation costs and, in turn, increase the price to the customer. This means that the target customer profile and expectations will be different from 'standard eggs', so the communication methods and messaging will need to take this into account, as well as the transparency and detail of the information available.

▲ Figure 4.5 Collecting eggs manually may mean more employees are needed

Non-exploitation of workers/employees

When working with suppliers and businesses outside the UK, it is important to know the working conditions and policies for their employees and that they are in line with the company's own policies as well as UK legislation. This is because the business' ethical principles will be judged by its association with the companies that it does business with, and this in turn can impact customers' decisions. In the UK, the Human Rights Act 1998 is the legislation that ensures ethical working practices, including ensuring suppliers do not engage in slavery or human trafficking (see also Chapter 3, page 60).

For example, in 2020 Channel 4's Dispatches produced a documentary that showed children working a 40-hour week in gruelling conditions to pick coffee beans that were exported to large companies in the UK and USA. Since this exposure, the coffee industry's businesses and consumers are becoming more ethically aware of where coffee beans are sourced, and the conditions under which the coffee pickers work. These conditions include age, hours, rate of pay and provision of health care.

UK businesses and consumers are becoming more aware of the impact that they can have on people's working conditions. Businesses that have been found to work with, and use, suppliers who exploit workers, including child labour, have been publicly criticised in the media.

Non-discriminatory against personal characteristics

This ethical consideration is not only about the supplier's own policies on discrimination but also the laws in the supplier's country and its policies on human rights and discrimination. In some countries, not all personal characteristics are protected, nor do people have the same laws and freedoms. This can include discrimination against religious beliefs, sexual orientation and gender equality. Certain characteristics or lifestyle choices may be illegal and punishable by imprisonment or even the death penalty.

This can make decisions about working with businesses who operate in particular countries challenging, as these businesses may have laws and practices which go against the values and ethics of the UK. This is especially problematic if it affects the financial viability of the resource or product, which in turn impacts the operational costs of the business.

Improve your English

Write a paragraph about a country outside of Europe outlining the differences in its laws and practices in comparison to the UK and the Equality Act's nine protected characteristics.

Complying with relevant legislation

A business must be compliant with all relevant legislation, and this is vital to its reputation and success. If a company is found to be non-compliant, there may be consequences such as fines, but there may also be a restriction or removal of work permits, an increase in insurance costs and audits, and negative reporting and media coverage. This could in turn impact customers' and other stakeholders' decisions to use the business.

Businesses that comply with all relevant legislation will have:
▶ ethical financial practices to meet tax requirements
▶ clear policies and procedures for their employees
▶ ethical working environments in relation to humane conditions, health and safety and working hours.

Some of the UK legislation that businesses need to adhere to includes the:
- Equality Act 2010
- Human Rights Act 1998
- Health and Safety at Work etc. Act 1974
- National Minimum Wage Act 1998

- Employment Act 2008
- Employment Rights Act 1996
- Working Time Regulations 1998.

For more on legislation, refer to Chapter 1 Health and safety and Chapter 3 Working in the agriculture, environmental and animal care sector.

Assessment practice

1 When must the terms and conditions of a contract be followed until? (1 mark)

2 Which piece of legislation covers whistleblowing? (1 mark)

3 Which process provides a criminal record data check of an individual? (1 mark)

4 List **three** actions that can be classified as harassing behaviour. (3 marks)

5 List **three** possible consequences if a company is found to be non-compliant with legislation. (3 marks)

6 If a country's laws and regulations do not match the Equality Act 2010's nine protected characteristics, how could this impact a UK business trading with it? (6 marks)

7 What is the purpose of the 'British values'? (6 marks)

8 Describe what is meant by a 'stakeholder'. (3 marks)

9 Using your own example, explain the difference between equality and equity. (3 marks)

10 What is the ethical principle of 'transparency' and how can this benefit a business? (2 marks)

Further reading

You may find some of the following references helpful for keeping up to date with UK ethics and legislation:
- UK legislation: **www.legislation.gov.uk**
- *DBS checks* on the Disclosure and Barring Service website
- *Public Interest Disclosure Act 1998 (PIDA)* on the Protect (Speak up, stop harm) website
- *Whistleblowing for employees* on the UK Government website
- Health and Safety Executive
- Department for Environment, Food and Rural Affairs (Defra), part of the UK government.

5 Business

Introduction

This chapter introduces different types of businesses in the UK, including sole traders, partnerships, limited companies and public corporations. It outlines their advantages and disadvantages, as well as the financial, legal and commercial implications for each type of business.

The chapter covers some of the objectives a business can utilise, such as key performance indicators (KPIs), and introduces project management principles and how these can be applied.

The content of this chapter is linked to Chapter 3 Working in the agriculture, environmental and animal care sector and Chapter 9 Finance.

Learning outcomes

By the end of this chapter, you will understand:
▶ advantages and disadvantages of types of business organisations, including sole trader, partnership, limited company and public corporation
▶ structures of businesses – not for profit/charity, freelance, franchise, social enterprise, public sector and private sector
▶ types of objectives and values associated with different types of businesses and structures, including key performance indicators, social responsibility objectives and environmental objectives
▶ financial, legal and commercial implications for each type of business
▶ typical organisational policies (health and safety, equality) and their relationship to legislation
▶ the principles of enterprise skills
▶ how the principles of enterprise skills are applied to develop business growth and change, including sales opportunities and diversification of the business

▶ types of business risk (financial, reputational, compliance, operational, economical, security and fraud)
▶ risk management methods and controls (insurance, diversification, risk register, strategic planning, external advice and guidance)
▶ definitions of business measures and how these are applied to determine success
▶ typical data sets used to interpret and determine if success measures are met to support business and future budget planning
▶ the importance of the ISO 9000 quality standard, its purpose and its application to organisations
▶ quality standards expected by internal and external stakeholders and associates
▶ the principles of project management
▶ how to apply the principles of project management through the implementation of a project plan
▶ factors to consider in the implementation of a project plan.

5.1 Types of business organisations

Advantages and disadvantages of different types of business organisations

Sole trader advantages

A sole trader business is owned by one person, so it is small in size. In the land-based sector, examples of sole traders include dog groomers, florists, gardeners, machinery service engineers and agronomists.

Sole traders rely on their own finances, such as savings or personal bank loans, to fund and support their business.

An advantage of being a sole trader is that they can keep any profits made from the business for themselves, after tax deductions. Sole traders can run the business how they want, making any decisions themselves. This can include which work to take on, work patterns and holidays.

Setting up as a sole trader is legally the easiest type of business ownership, as it has fewer rules and regulations compared to other types of business. It also has no set-up fees. Sole traders complete a self-assessment form with His Majesty's Revenue and Customs (HMRC) to pay income tax and National Insurance (NI); this is the only requirement.

Sole trader disadvantages

A disadvantage of being a sole trader is that they take on all the risks of the business and unlimited liability, meaning they are personally liable for any debt of the business. This means that personal assets, for example a car or house, are at risk of being sold to pay off the business' debts. As sole traders personally fund their business, this means they can only raise a limited amount of finance though savings. They can only get bank loans if the bank is confident that the business will work and the loan will be paid back.

Sole traders have full responsibility for their business, so they often try to keep running costs at a minimum by not outsourcing and take on as many tasks as possible, meaning they often work long hours.

There is no legal distinction between a sole trader's business and personal affairs. This means that should

they accidentally cause a loss to another in the course of their business activities, such as personal injury or property damage, because they were careless, they are personally responsible for 'negligence'. Negligence can relate to an act or omission that breaches a duty of care owed by one party (defendant) to another (claimant) and consequently causes loss and damage to that party (claimant).

Partnership advantages

Partnerships have between two and twenty partners in the business, and this is stated in the Partnership Act 1890, although there are some exceptions to this rule. A partnership is set up by a 'deed of partnership' document which covers the terms for the partnership, such as how much money each partner has invested in the business and the role that each partner plays in the business. If someone invests in a business but is not involved in its day-to-day running, they are known as a 'sleeping partner'. Examples in the land-based sector include veterinary practices, landscaping businesses, tree surgery businesses and machinery dealerships.

There are three types of partnership:
- An **ordinary partnership** is two or more individuals involved in a business to make profits.
- A **limited partnership** is unincorporated with two levels of partners (general or limited).
- A **limited liability partnership (LLP)** is an incorporated entity with separate legal identity to the partners, which must be registered with Companies House as a limited company.

As there are several people involved in a partnership business, they are able to raise more finance than a sole trader and have more people responsible for the success of the business. This means that banks are more likely to lend to the business.

Having different people involved means that a range of skills can be brought into the business. For example, a partnership running a landscape and garden design business may have some partners who are excellent at working with clients to create garden designs and other partners who are highly skilled at hard landscaping and planting.

In a partnership, the workload and responsibility of the business can be shared or delegated between the partners, thereby reducing the individual workload and working hours for each partner.

▲ Figure 5.1 In a partnership, one partner may be more suited to creating garden designs

Partnership disadvantages

As there are multiple people involved in a partnership, one disadvantage is that the partners can disagree with each other about business decisions and direction. This can cause barriers and slow down business operations and progression.

Another disadvantage is that partners are jointly and severally liable when the business incurs liabilities. This means that all partners are as liable as each other if one partner breaches a contract or is found to be negligent.

The profits of the business must be shared between the partners, as well as the debts. This means that all partners are personally liable for any debt for the business and, like sole traders, if there are any outstanding debts, personal assets are at risk of being sold to pay them off.

Limited company advantages

A limited company is legally separate from the people who own it and it has its own legal identity. This means that the finances for the business are separate from the investors' personal finances.

The ownership of a limited company is divided into equal parts, known as shares. Whoever owns shares is known as a shareholder. Shareholders do not own the business, they are investors. Shareholders receive their share of the profits as a dividend. A limited company is private when its shares are not available on the stock market to be bought or sold by the public.

Limited companies have limited liability, which means an investor only loses their initial stake (money used to set up the business) if the business folds and goes bust. The investors are protected by the rules of limited liability. This is an advantage in comparison to sole traders and partnerships who have personal responsibility for their business.

Limited companies can raise additional funds by borrowing and through the **share issue** of **ordinary shares**.

As limited companies must be registered at Companies House, this can make them appear more legitimate to customers and other stakeholders.

Limited companies pay corporation tax (see Chapter 9, page 132), and this can be more efficient than paying income tax if in the higher bracket. The tax brackets can change each tax year so for current information check the HMRC website, but for the 2024/25 tax year, there are three marginal income tax bands: the 20 per cent basic rate, the 40 per cent higher rate and the 45 per cent additional rate. Also, the personal allowance starts to shrink once earnings hit £100,000.

Limited company disadvantages

Limited companies have expensive legal set-up costs and they must be registered with the Registrar of Companies. They must complete Memorandum of Association and Articles of Association documentation. Due to the complexities and increased administration in operating, limited companies usually require the support of an accountant, which is an additional cost to the business (although this in itself may be **tax deductible**).

> ### Key terms
>
> **Share issue**: when a limited company offers equity in the form of shares to investors; this is an effective way for a public limited company to raise capital by selling either existing or new shares to the public, employees or a group of investors; a share issue can be either an issue in accordance with existing shareholders' pre-emptive right to subscribe or a directed share issue
>
> **Ordinary shares**: also called common shares, these are normal shares issued by a limited company and are stocks sold on a public exchange; each share of stock generally gives its owner the right to a single vote at a company shareholders' meeting; unlike in the case of preferred shares (share issue), the owner of ordinary shares is not guaranteed a dividend
>
> **Tax deductible**: expenses that are able to be deducted from taxable income or the amount of tax to be paid

As profits are shared between the shareholders through the issuing of dividends, it can be harder to motivate and control workers who are not shareholders.

Public sector advantages

The term 'public sector' is very broad and embraces political, economic and legal organisations responsible for the administration and welfare of the nation and its people.

There are two main administrative levels for businesses in the public sector: government and local authorities.

At government level, public sector organisations (also known as public corporations) are run by the government and founded by an Act of Parliament. They provide public services and are funded through a range of taxes, including:
▶ National Insurance
▶ income tax
▶ VAT
▶ air passenger duty
▶ fuel duty.

Local authorities are responsible for the services and infrastructure of a local area, such as health and social care, environmental services, education, economic development and planning decisions. Local authorities are funded through three main sources:
▶ government grants (money from central government for local services)
▶ council tax (a property tax levied on residential properties)
▶ business rates (a property tax levied on business premises).

An advantage of public corporations is that because they are underpinned by an Act of Parliament and funded via taxes, they enable policy to be implemented, and their performance is measured and monitored. Because they are owned by the government, planning and co-ordination is easier, since the government controls certain items. Also, decisions can often be made more quickly, as bureaucracy is reduced. Additionally, due to the way that they are set up they enable larger infrastructure projects and investment.

Public sector disadvantages

Due to the size and complexity of public corporations, there can be disadvantages. They can experience problems delivering policy targets, be difficult to manage and be expensive to maintain and operate.

Additionally, as they are overseen by the government, they can be subject to misuse of power and political interference, thus ignoring consumer interests.

Case study

The British Broadcasting Corporation (BBC) was established as a public corporation in 1927. It is not directly run by the UK government and is funded by the TV licence fee.

Over recent years, the running and funding of the BBC has received much public scrutiny and criticism, often making headline news.
▶ What is the BBC's mission?
▶ What are the BBC's five purposes?
▶ Who regulates the BBC?

Structures of businesses

Different business types each have their own structure.

Not for profit/charity

The term 'not for profit' does not describe an organisation's legal structure but instead its mission. It refers to various independent organisations whose purpose is not to make profits for directors, members or shareholders.

Not-for-profit organisations have one of three main structures:
▶ charitable incorporated organisation (CIO)
▶ community interest company (CIC)
▶ unincorporated association.

A CIO is a special type of limited company, designed to benefit the community rather than private shareholders. CIOs must provide the following information:
▶ a community interest statement explaining the company's plans
▶ an asset lock, which legally ensures that the company's assets will only be used for its social objectives and sets limits on payments to shareholders
▶ a constitution – a body of fundamental principles or established precedents, according to which the company is acknowledged to be governed.

A CIC is another type of limited company, that exists to benefit the community. It differs from a regular company because it prioritises social objectives over private profit. CICs must provide the same information as CIOs.

An unincorporated association is an alternative to a business. The structure is suitable for more informal groups with shared interests and objectives that do not plan to make profit, for example a voluntary group.

In the land-based sector, there are a number of not-for-profit organisations, including animal rescue centres and charities, trade bodies and advisory groups.

Franchise

A franchise is operated by a contracted franchisee, who is either a sole trader or a limited company, using a registered trademark. Being part of a franchise, the business gets access to things like the business model, brand, information and data, support and sometimes a supply chain.

Social enterprise

A social enterprise is an organisation that exists with a clear goal to help the community but is run like a business. Any profits are reinvested back into the organisation.

Public sector

Public sector organisations are run by the government to provide public services. This can include:

▶ healthcare (for example doctors, nurses, GPs, paramedics and administrative assistants)
▶ education (for example teachers, teaching assistants and school librarians)
▶ social care (for example carers, social workers and probation officers)
▶ law enforcement (for example police officers, lawyers and those in the armed forces)
▶ local council (for example councillors, administrators and refuse collectors)
▶ banking (for example bankers working for the Bank of England).

The public sector also includes central government departments and government bodies that are responsible for specific areas. For example, His Majesty's Revenue and Customs (HMRC), the Department of Health and Social Care (DHSC), the Home Office, the Department for Education (DfE), the Department for Environment, Food and Rural Affairs (Defra) and the Ministry of Justice (MoJ). Each department focuses on its own distinct functions within the government structure.

Local government is made up of 32 local authorities, which are also known as councils, and they manage services at the community level. These services include housing, libraries and refuse collection.

As already discussed, there are also public corporations which are organisations founded by an Act of Parliament and (usually) funded by the taxpayer, for example the BBC is funded by the TV licence.

Private sector

The private sector includes several different types of business ownership. The most common types are:

▶ freelance (for example consultant or advisor)
▶ sole trader (for example dog walker or florist)
▶ partnership (for example garden maintenance company, dog groomers or veterinary practice)
▶ private limited company (for example large tree maintenance and arboriculture company, farm/agricultural business or land-based machinery dealership).

▲ Figure 5.2 Dog walkers are an example of a sole trader business

Types of objectives and values associated with different types of businesses and structures

Key performance indicators (KPIs)

KPIs are individual criteria which can be measured and quantified and therefore used to evaluate the success of a business or an employee in terms of meeting objectives for performance. These can be targets such as sales, production or time to complete a task.

Social responsibility objectives

These are the objectives of a business that do not include profits or increasing shareholder values; instead they demonstrate how a business is going to operate to benefit society. If a business aims to be socially responsible, it should adopt policies that promote the wellbeing of society and the environment while reducing negative impacts on them.

Environmental objectives

Environmental objectives are the goals that a business or organisation sets to improve environmental performance through its environmental management system (EMS). These goals can apply to the whole business, or to certain sites or tasks that the business performs. They are split into two parts: objective and target. For example, an objective could be to reduce landfill waste and a target would be to reduce it by 20 per cent within 5 years.

Financial, legal and commercial implications for each type of business

Not-for-profit/charity

There are a number of legal and commercial considerations for not-for-profit organisations and charities. The first is to ensure that they meet the requirements to qualify for charitable status. Charities and not-for-profit organisations receive tax benefits, but these are subject to specific regulations. To be considered a charitable organisation, they must be in one of the categories defined by the Charities Act 2011. These include advancing education, relieving poverty, promoting health or advancing religion. All charities must demonstrate that they provide a public benefit.

The second consideration is to have a legal structure, which can be a charitable trust, CIO or CIC, as described earlier in this chapter.

Not-for-profit organisations and charities must have a governing document that outlines their purpose, structure, governance and operational guidelines, including how trustees are appointed and removed. This document is known as a trust deed or a constitution.

The third consideration is that not-for-profit and charitable organisations must by law register with the Charity Commission if their income is over a certain amount.

Franchise

The business model of franchising is when a franchisor licenses its **intellectual property (IP)** and business

> **Key term**
>
> **Intellectual property (IP)**: creations of the mind, such as inventions, literary and artistic works, designs, symbols, names and images used in commerce; IP is protected in law by, for example, patents, copyright and trademarks, which enable people to earn recognition or financial benefit from what they invent or create; the IP system aims to create an environment in which creativity and innovation can flourish by ensuring the right balance between the interests of innovators and the wider public.

model to a franchisee in exchange for a fee. The franchisee will then operate a business under the franchisor's brand and system. See Chapter 10 for more about intellectual property.

In the UK, there is no specific law that governs franchising, although there are several laws and regulations that apply to franchises, including the following:

- The Consumer Protection from Unfair Trading Regulations 2008 prohibit franchisors from making false or misleading representations to prospective franchisees.
- The Competition Act 1998 prohibits franchisors from engaging in anti-competitive practices, such as price fixing or market sharing.
- The Data Protection Act 2018 requires franchisors to collect and process personal data lawfully and transparently.

A number of industry codes of conduct apply to franchising, with the most important being the Quality Franchise Associations' Code of Conduct. This includes providing prospective franchisees with complete and accurate disclosure of material information about the franchise.

If a franchisor or franchisee breaches any of their legal and contractual obligations, they may have legal action taken against them. The most common types of legal action include breach of contract, misrepresentation and unfair trading.

Social enterprise

Social enterprises are not legally different from any other commercial businesses, but they reinvest any profits back into their social purpose. These businesses need to have balance between social impact and financial security. See also page 84 earlier in this chapter.

Typical organisational policies and their relationship to legislation

This section links to Chapter 1 Health and safety, Chapter 3 Working in the agriculture, environmental and animal care sector (both cover different legislation in detail), Chapter 4 Ethics (which covers the different types of health and safety and equality policies and their purpose) and Chapter 6 Equality (which covers equality considerations and protected characteristics).

Health and safety (Health and Safety at Work Act etc. 1974)

The Health and Safety at Work etc. Act 1974 sets out the general duties that businesses (employers) have towards their employees and members of the public, that employees have towards themselves and each other, and that self-employed workers have towards themselves and others.

Under the Act, businesses need to have a policy that outlines their approach to managing health and safety. This policy usually covers the following:
▶ statement of intent – the business' aims and objectives
▶ employer's and employees' roles and responsibilities
▶ risk assessments
▶ safety procedures
▶ training of workers
▶ emergency and evacuation arrangements.

Procurement (Environment Act 2021)

The Environment Act 2021 provides a framework that aims to enhance environmental protection and sustainability by setting targets for clean air, biodiversity, water quality and waste. It also covers the recall of non-compliant products and sets out provisions for recalling products that do not meet environmental standards.

This Act impacts UK business policies and practices as they must align with the targets set out in the legislation and contribute to environmental protection. Businesses need to have policies in place to meet the requirements of the legislation, which can include how they work with local authorities for waste management, recycling and green waste.

The introduction of the legislation has led to the creation of a new regulatory body, the Office for Environmental Protection (OEP). Businesses need to engage with the OEP, comply with its guidelines and address any environmental concerns it raises.

The Act also requires that new development planning applications provide a biodiversity net gain (BNG). This means businesses involved in construction, infrastructure and land development must consider biodiversity enhancement in their policies (see Chapter 2).

Businesses should also be aware of local nature recovery strategies (LNRSs), which aim to restore and enhance local natural habitats. These strategies may impact land use, development and conservation efforts.

Recruitment (Equality Act 2010)

The Equality Act 2010 aims to prevent discrimination in the workplace. It is illegal to discriminate against individuals based on nine protected characteristics.

> **Test yourself**
>
> What are the nine protected characteristics under the Equality Act 2010?

Businesses must have policies and procedures in place to ensure there are equal job opportunities for all and that they follow all nine protected characteristics of the Equality Act 2010. They must also prevent discrimination across all aspects of the organisation. If any accusations of discrimination or harassment are made by employees, businesses must investigate these and take appropriate action.

During recruitment, businesses must ensure there is no discriminatory wording in job adverts and no discrimination during the recruitment process. Additionally, staff must be trained on the requirements of equal opportunity legislation.

If a business fails to comply with the Act, it may be prosecuted.

5.2 The principles of enterprise skills

Enterprise skills

For a business to be successful, its employees need to employ a range of skills, as outlined below.

Risk taking

Embracing or taking risks enables entrepreneurs and businesses to learn to manage uncertainty, make informed decisions and adjust their strategies based on market feedback and changing circumstances. It can also be trying out something new when the results are largely unknown.

Innovation

Innovation is a specific skill utilised by entrepreneurs. It is the means by which they exploit change as an opportunity for a different business or a different service. It can be presented as a discipline and can be learned or practised. The new idea is often associated with risk taking.

Resilience

Resilience is an important skill in business. It can be defined as 'the role of mental processes and behaviour in promoting personal assets and protecting an individual from the potential negative effect of stressors'. This can be achieved by being able to adapt to gradual but significant change, as well as sudden disruptions. This can mean transforming culture, workplaces and workflows by investing in new collaboration tools and technology.

> ### Industry tip
>
> As well as looking after their physical health, it is good practice for a business to have policies in place that support its employees' mental health and wellbeing.

Problem solving

Problem solving is a skill or activity that has a number of stages:
- defining a problem
- determining the cause of the problem
- identifying, prioritising and selecting alternatives for a solution
- implementing a solution.

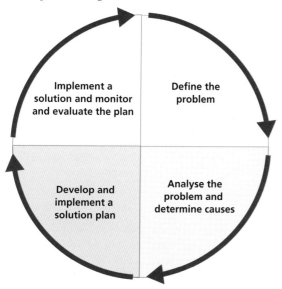

▲ Figure 5.3 Stages of problem solving

Strategic development

Strategic development (or strategic planning) is a process that businesses use to analyse their internal and external environments to determine the resources and actions they require to stay competitive and successful. It involves setting strategies to help reach objectives by adjusting direction in response to changing conditions. It is fundamental to creating and running a business.

Market analysis

Market analysis is the activity of gathering information about conditions that affect a marketplace and how a business is performing. This information can also be used to inform the forecasting of profits and losses.

Commercial awareness

This is knowledge of how businesses make money, meet customer needs and expectations, and identify problems in particular areas of the business.

Decision making

Decision-making skills allow businesses to make informed and rational decisions. This involves assessing all the facts, understanding the business' current state and goals and then deciding on the best course of action.

Prioritisation

Prioritisation is deciding which tasks to complete first, followed by the order of subsequent tasks. This can involve completing a number of tasks at the same time, but giving one of them more attention or effort than the others, as it has a higher priority.

How the principles are applied to develop business growth and change

Market analysis to support prioritisation

Analysing markets can help businesses prioritise activities within their business plan. There are a number of data sets that can be used to inform business decisions for growth and change. This section will focus on buying patterns, market trends and competitor offers.

Buying patterns

Buying patterns are the reasons (how and why) customers make purchasing decisions; they are the habits and routines that consumers have for the products and services they buy. Buying patterns include times, frequencies and quantities, and they are used to help businesses better understand and potentially expand their target audience. Each customer will have their own buying patterns, and there are many factors that can influence them.

Buying patterns can fit into four behaviour categories:
- routine purchases (such as weekly food shopping)
- limited decision-making purchases (such as buying from a new garden centre recommended by a friend)
- extensive decision-making purchases (big purchases such as a vehicle or piece of machinery)
- impulse purchases (such as a packet of sweets at a checkout or pay point).

Buying patterns are most predictable for routine purchases. The most straightforward way for a business to get information on its customers' buying patterns and purchase decision-making is to ask them, either face to face or through online feedback surveys. Some examples of the questions that could be asked to gain buying pattern data include:
- Why did you first purchase [product/service]?
- Where do you go when looking for [product/service]?
- What is your budget for [product/service]?
- How far would you travel to buy [product/service]?

Businesses can then use this data to inform activities such as marketing, promotions and product displays.

Test yourself

Think about your own buying patterns and the reasons behind them. Describe how this information could be used by a business to inform its plans.

Market trends

Market trends refer to the price directions of assets over a given period. They apply to all assets and markets where prices and trading volumes fluctuate. If in a set period the asset or market has an overall price increase, it is called an uptrend, and if it has an overall price decrease it is called a downtrend. Market trend data helps businesses identify trading opportunities.

There are four main factors that influence a market trend:
- **Government policy**: using fiscal and monetary policy, governments can influence the growth of market trends.

Key term

Commodities: economic goods or resources that can be bought or sold, for example coffee, copper and barley

- **Market sentiment**: market trends can be shaped by the sentiment among market participants' attitudes towards a business. If traders and investors have a positive opinion of and faith in the direction of a country's economy or a business' outlook, a positive sentiment can shape an uptrend. However, a negative market sentiment among traders and investors can push the asset's price lower, leading to a downtrend.
- **Supply and demand**: the asset price tends to fluctuate following shifts in dynamics between supply and demand. This is especially relevant for **commodities**. For example, when the economy is booming, demand for food items such as bread increases, so flour prices tend to rise. Adverse weather conditions may also affect the supply of wheat used to make flour, leading to a shortage and therefore boosting its price.
- **Corporate and economic news**: positive results in a business' quarterly reports or economic readings that exceed expectations can all contribute to an uptrend. However, negative news could push prices lower and cause a downtrend.

There are different types of market trends, classified according to their duration and the driving force behind them, as shown in Table 5.1

▼ Table 5.1 Market trends

Trend	Duration	Driver
Secular	Years to decades	Structural changes in economy and demographics
Primary	Months to years	Changes in the business cycle, political and economic events
Secondary	Weeks to months	Changes in investor sentiment as well as technical factors
Intermediate	Days to weeks	Changes in supply versus demand and market volatility
Minor	Up to a few days	Current news and changes in trading volumes

Market trend data can be used by a business to inform its trading strategy.

Competitive offers and pricing use the process of selecting strategic price points to take advantage of a product- or service-based market relative to the competition. This type of pricing strategy is generally used once a price has reached a level of equilibrium, which occurs when a product or service has been on the market for a long time and there are many alternatives available.

A business can set prices for its products or services below, the same as or above the competition.

Setting the price below the competition could mean that the business takes a loss initially, but if it believes that the customer will purchase additional products and services or provide repeat business after the initial offer, this could subsidise and make up for any losses incurred. This is known as a loss leader strategy.

A business can choose to charge the same price as competitors or use the given market price. If a business sets the same prices as competitors, it can differentiate itself through marketing.

To set a price above the competition requires the business to justify this premium price. This can be by offering generous payment terms or extra features, or it may compete on the quality of the service it offers in comparison to competitors.

Potential horizontal or vertical diversification opportunities, risks and rewards

Horizontal diversification is when a business adds new products or services that are not directly related to its current offer and that are aimed at existing customers or clients. This strategy is used by businesses when they are trying to compete within a single industry, for example the pet care industry.

It works by identifying a need for a product and seeking to fill that need with a new product that does not already exist in the company's product portfolio. To determine where it might need to engage in horizontal diversification, a company might conduct market research via customer surveys, look at consumer behaviour or analyse sales performance. The benefits of horizontal diversification include product line growth, increased promotion opportunities, ability to serve more customers and improved product quality.

An example of a company using horizontal diversification is Apple Inc. Apple was set up in 1976 by Stephen Wozniak and Steve Jobs to manufacture computers. As Apple became more established, it moved on to develop, manufacture and sell mobile phones, smartwatches and music players, as well as music and TV streaming services. It is now a global leader in technology and media.

Vertical diversification is when a business expands its existing product portfolio with related products and services within its supply chain. This can help to reduce costs and increase production efficiency, as well as increase the range of products and services that it offers.

There are many processes and businesses involved in a supply chain, including sourcing raw materials, processing raw materials, manufacturing materials into a product, transporting and distributing the product, and finally selling the product. Usually, there is one business per process in a supply chain, but if one of the businesses takes on more roles this is referred to as vertical diversification.

There are two types of vertical diversification:
- **Backward diversification** is when a business integrates backwards, meaning that it starts to produce the raw materials for the products that it currently makes. This allows the business to reduce its dependence on outside suppliers and reduce production costs.
- **Forward diversification** is when a business moves up in the supply chain into finishing, distributing or selling its products. A business could start selling its products online and create a direct relationship with its customers. This means that the business has greater control over distribution. For example, a farm starts to sell its produce in its own farm shop as well as to supermarkets.

There are two factors to consider before using a vertical diversification strategy:
- Costs: it is not advisable if the cost of making the product in-house is more than the cost of buying it from a third party.
- Scope: if it does not reduce or negatively impact the business' capabilities and performance, then it is an appropriate way for it to diversify.

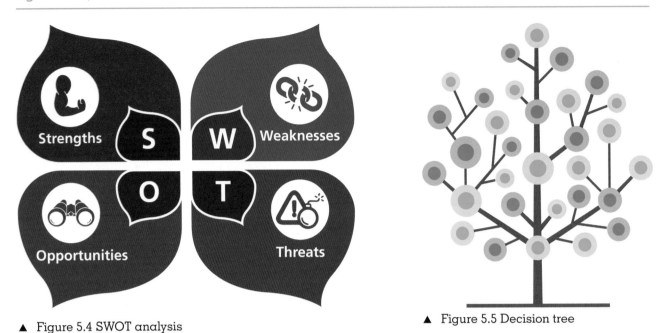

▲ Figure 5.4 SWOT analysis

▲ Figure 5.5 Decision tree

Decision-making tools

SWOT analysis

SWOT stands for strengths, weaknesses, opportunities and threats (Figure 5.4). It is a framework used to evaluate a business' competitive position and to develop strategic planning. It assesses the current and future potential of the business along with internal and external factors.

A SWOT analysis uses realistic, fact-based, data-driven information that looks at the strengths and weaknesses of the business (internal factors) and external factors that may impact business decisions, opportunities and threats.

A SWOT analysis is mainly used to inform a single objective or decision that a business is facing.

Decision trees

A decision tree (Figure 5.5) is a hierarchical model that visually represents decisions and their potential consequences. It uses conditional controlled statements to make decisions. A decision tree looks like a flowchart, where each node represents an attribute, the branches represent the test outcomes and the leaf nodes represent the decisions made after considering all attributes.

Types of business risk

Financial

A business can face a variety of financial risks:
- **Internal risk** is caused by poor management leading to flawed operational processes and an inability to grow.
- **External risk** stems from competition, the overall market and changing customer needs.
- **Market risk** is the risk of a change in position in the market as a result of movements in market prices.
- **Credit risk** is the risk of loss of credit rating and the ability to borrow as a result of failing to repay a loan or meet contractual obligations.
- **Liquidity risk** is the risk of not being able to meet short-term obligations.

Reputational

A business' reputation can be at risk either as a direct result of its actions or processes, or because of the actions of those who work for and therefore represent the business. Reputation can also be put at risk by the other businesses or individuals the business is associated with. This can be suppliers of raw materials or components, or businesses that provide it with services, for example transport and waste disposal, or who sell the business' products, for example retailers and online platforms. The reputation of a business can lose or gain customers and therefore impact profits.

Compliance

There are a number of areas where non-compliance can be a risk to a business. These include privacy breaches, environmental and sustainability concerns, corrupt and illegal practices and processes, health and safety breaches and poor employee behaviour. If a business is found to be non-compliant, this can lead to legal action.

Operational

This is risk associated with inadequate or failed internal processes, people and systems, or from external events.

Economical

Fluctuating interest rates, exchange rates and taxes in the UK economy may all impact on how well a business performs.

Security

This can be the security risk of information held by a company (linked to GDPR legislation), or the security of property, buildings and contents, including raw materials.

> ### Key term
>
> **Fraudulent action**: an intentionally deceptive act or omission that misleads, or attempts to mislead, another in order to obtain a financial or other benefit or to avoid an obligation or incurring an obligation. Types of fraud include tax fraud, credit card fraud and bankruptcy fraud. Fraudulent actions are characterised by, involving or proceeding from fraud or dishonest action. The legal consequences of fraudulent action can include criminal charges, civil lawsuits, fines, imprisonment, probation, restitution or paying victims back for their losses, or significant financial losses for the business.

Fraud

This is the risk of unexpected financial, material or reputational loss as the result of **fraudulent action** of people who are internal or external to the business.

Risk management methods and controls

Insurance

Insurance is a way for a business to manage or protect itself from unexpected risks. If something negative occurs to the business, the insurance company could pay the business or claimant (i.e. another business or client) to cover costs, damage, losses or compensation. If a business does not have insurance and an accident happens, it may be responsible for all related costs.

Diversification

As explained earlier, diversification is a risk management strategy that enables a business to increase its income streams. The rationale is that if a business has numerous products or services to sell, it will have increased long-term returns and, even if one market fails, it has other products and services which will help to reduce the impact of that failure.

Risk register

A risk register is a document that identifies potential setbacks within a business project. It aims to collectively identify, analyse and solve risks before they become problems.

Strategic planning

The purpose of strategic planning is to achieve a desired future for the business. It is a process for defining and sharing the direction and goals of a business. A strategic plan uses specific business strategies, allocates resources and evaluates the results. It is based on the business' mission, vision, values and competitive analysis.

External advice and guidance

Businesses can use external sources for information, advice and guidance to reduce or avoid risks. This can include industry bodies, professional advisors, insurance providers, peer networks, online resources and external audits. Each can provide businesses with different information to support their operation. This can include general operating guidance but also technical information, industry standards, best practice and training. They can also advise on weaknesses or gaps in a business. All of this information can be used to help a business make decisions and reduce risks.

5.3 Measures that businesses use to determine success

Definitions of measures and how these are applied to determine success

Key performance indicators (KPIs)

Key performance indicators (KPIs) can be used to measure the achievements of a business or an employee against a set of targets, objectives or industry peers.

KPIs can be based on:
- income
- revenue
- productivity
- customer satisfaction.

▲ Figure 5.6 Key performance indicators

The benefits of KPIs include helping businesses to focus on their priorities, establishing benchmarking (see opposite), monitoring productivity and motivating staff. As KPIs are data driven, they can make management aware of specific problems and provide information that can be used for strategic planning.

They also hold employees accountable for their role and work within the business. KPIs do not discriminate against specific employees and they create reassurance that the business is being closely monitored. See Chapter 2, page 38 and Chapter 3, page 64 for more about KPIs.

Contract terms

Contract terms outline specific deliverables, deadlines and performance expectations of a business or an employee. These need to be managed not only to ensure that they are delivered correctly, but also to mitigate any risks. This is done via a contract performance management process that will track, monitor and manage the delivery of goods or services. Its primary goal is to ensure that all parties involved meet all the obligations outlined in the contract.

If a contract is effectively managed, the business can track how that contract contributes to the overall success of the business.

Service level agreement

A service level agreement is a contract between a service provider and a customer. It specifies the degree of service a customer can expect from a supplier, including:
- the service to be provided
- the level of performance to be expected
- how performance will be measured and approved
- consequences or penalties if performance levels are not met.

Benchmarking

Benchmarking is the process of measuring products, services and processes against those of businesses known to be leaders in one or more aspects of their operations. It provides insights that help businesses understand how they compare with similar businesses. It can also help identify ways for a business to improve performance.

Supply chain requirements

Setting the requirements of a supply chain and measuring the performance of a supply chain against them can provide insights into the efficiency, effectiveness and overall health of the supply chain. This information can help supply chain leaders make decisions, optimise processes and improve overall performance.

Typical data sets used to interpret and determine if success measures are met to support business and future budget planning

The data sets that businesses can use to support and inform budget planning include:

- enquiries indicating the potential for creating sales
- marketing/promotional activities to determine potential new customers and increase sales (physical events, online activity)
- income and expenditure against predicted forecast, indicating the success of the product or service and future opportunities
- quantitative data using survey results or customer feedback indicating the success/introduction of new products or services and potential repeat custom
- repeat custom indicating the potential sustainability and viability of the business through predicted future sales.

Importance of the ISO 9000 quality standard

ISO 9000 is part of a globally recognised group or family of standards relating to quality management. It provides guidelines for businesses to improve the quality of their products and services, while meeting customer expectations.

ISO 9000 has seven principles which other quality management standards use as a basis, including a strong customer focus, the active involvement and buy-in of top management, a process-oriented approach and a commitment to continuous improvement. ISO 9000 is important because it promotes a culture of quality, efficiency and continuous improvement, which ultimately results in organisational success and customer satisfaction.

The implementation of ISO 9000 encourages businesses to adopt efficient processes, have streamlined workflows, reduce waste and improve resource utilisation. It also emphasises 'risk-based thinking', where a business identifies potential risks and assesses their impact so that it can implement preventative measures. This approach can minimise operational disruptions.

ISO 9000 promotes continuous improvement, as businesses can regularly review processes, collect data and make informed decisions to enhance performance.

If a business or organisation is seen to be using ISO 9000 it can lead to improved customer confidence, as the business will be recognised as one which follows robust quality practices.

Adhering to ISO 9000 also helps businesses meet legal and regulatory requirements, thereby reducing legal risks and potential penalties.

Quality standards expected by internal and external stakeholders and associates

As described above, service level agreements or contract terms and conditions outline the standards expected by all stakeholders in a business. The consequences of not meeting quality standards include potential loss of income and risk to reputation.

5.4 The principles of project management

Principles of project management

The main principles of project management are described below:
- **Timescales**: set clear, realistic and achievable timescales, including contingency time.
- **Supply chain**: co-ordinate resources and activities to meet project deadlines and goals.
- **People management**: define roles and responsibilities of the project team and assign tasks to appropriate people, managing their progress throughout the project and supporting them when needed.
- **Resources**: include people as well as systems, materials and facilities needed to complete the project.
- **Budgeting**: plan how and when budgets are going to be used across the project and track spending, making adjustments when needed.
- **Effective planning**: create a project plan that includes all dates and information and communicate this with the whole project team and stakeholders.

How to apply the principles of project management through the implementation of a project plan

Part of successful project management is being able to clearly identify and define the project objective, the benefit of the project to the business, any difficulties or barriers the team may encounter and the risks involved in the project.

Goals should be established at the beginning of the project but should also be adaptable as the project progresses. The project manager needs to be flexible and able to respond to and manage any problems that occur along the way to ensure completion of the project.

A key tool of project management and implementation of the principles is the creation of a project plan, which contains the goals, objectives and tasks required to complete the project. It should include information for all phases of the project, including:

▶ scope
▶ timescales
▶ key dates/deliverables
▶ personnel involved and allocation of tasks
▶ plans for communication with all stakeholders.

The project plan needs to be kept up to date throughout all phases of the project and adapted where necessary. It can assist with monitoring of resources and people management and inform budget use.

A project plan can be created using a spreadsheet or specific project management software, depending on the business' resources and IT availability.

Factors to consider in the implementation of a project plan

The factors to consider in the implementation of a project plan include:

▶ defining the purpose and scope of the project
▶ setting clear goals and objectives that are SMART (see Chapter 3, page 64)
▶ defining roles and responsibilities
▶ setting realistic milestones and constraints on costs and time.

Assessment practice

1 What are the **three** types of business partnership? (3 marks)

2 What can a business use key performance indicators (KPIs) for? (1 mark)

3 Give **three** examples of public sector services provided by the government. (3 marks)

4 What are the **four** main factors that influence market trends? (4 marks)

5 What can a business use market analysis for? (1 mark)

6 For a business in your land-based industry, how would the Environment Act 2021 impact its procurement policy? (6 marks)

7 Describe **three** advantages and **three** disadvantages of being a sole trader. (6 marks)

8 What are the legal considerations for a not-for-profit or charitable organisation? (6 marks)

9 a Explain the term 'vertical diversification' with an example of how a business could utilise this strategy.

   b Explain the term 'horizontal diversification' with an example of how a business could utilise this strategy. (2 marks)

10 What should a project plan include? (6 marks)

Further reading

You may find some of the following references helpful for keeping up to date with UK business principles and practices:

▶ *Mission, values and public purposes* on the BBC website
▶ *Business regulation: guidance and tools* on the UK Government website.

6 Equality

Introduction

The attitudes you have towards work colleagues and the behaviour you demonstrate in front of them may directly impact their relationship with you. A respectful, tolerant and thoughtful workplace has benefits for the individual, as well as for the reputation and relationship the organisation has with customers, clients and the wider sector.

There is a legal framework of rights and protections to support employers and organisations to provide fair treatment to all and embrace and promote diversity and inclusion in the workplace. However, it is important that employees are also aware of their rights and responsibilities so that they can support their employer and challenge discrimination where it occurs.

Learning outcomes

By the end of this chapter, you will understand:
▶ the characteristics protected by equality legislation
▶ the purpose of current equality and diversity legislation and the protected characteristics detailed under the Equality Act 2010, Employment Rights Act 1996, Human Rights Act 1998 and trade unions, including its application in the workplace
▶ factors to consider when working with people from diverse backgrounds
▶ how to define negative behaviours and how they apply in the workplace

▶ the potential consequences of negative discrimination (grievance, disciplinary, potential legal action)
▶ how to show empathy and respect to those from different backgrounds
▶ methods that embrace and promote diversity and inclusion, including inclusive culture, recruitment and products.

6.1 Characteristics protected by equality legislation

The purpose of current equality and diversity legislation and the protected characteristics

There are a number of pieces of legislation associated with direct protection of **equality** and indirect promotion of diversity. The scope of each piece of legislation is different, but collectively they provide a comprehensive framework. However, while some legislation specifically applies to the employee–employer relationship (for example the Employment Rights Act 1996 and Trade Union and Labour Relations (Consolidation) Act 1992), other legislation is more widely applicable to everyone, irrespective of whether they are an employee or not (for example the Human Rights Act 1998 and Equality Act 2010) (see Chapter 3, page 57).

Human Rights Act 1998

This Act identifies fundamental freedoms and rights to which everyone is entitled. These are referred to as the 'Convention rights and freedoms' and have been incorporated from the European Convention on Human Rights (ECHR) into UK law. All of the Convention rights and freedoms are important in respect of equality protection and are set out in the following Articles:

▶ Article 2: Right to life
▶ Article 3: Freedom from torture and inhuman or degrading treatment
▶ Article 4: Freedom from slavery and forced labour
▶ Article 5: Right to liberty and security
▶ Article 6: Right to a fair trial
▶ Article 7: No punishment without law
▶ Article 8: Respect for your private and family life, home and correspondence
▶ Article 9: Freedom of thought, belief and religion
▶ Article 10: Freedom of expression
▶ Article 11: Freedom of assembly and association
▶ Article 12: Right to marry and start a family
▶ Article 14: Protection from discrimination in respect of these rights and freedoms.

For example, the notion of a private life under Article 8 includes protection associated with sexual orientation, while Article 9 includes protection for religious and non-religious beliefs.

Equality Act 2010

The Equality Act is the primary piece of legislation associated with protecting the rights of everyone against **discrimination**. It applies to everyone while at work and when impacted by the work of others. The Act brought together and merged a number of earlier Acts and regulations, in order to simplify the protection offered to certain characteristics. These are referred to as **protected characteristics** (see Section 4.1, page 71).

The Equality Act offers protection from discrimination in the following locations and situations:

▶ in the workplace
▶ when using public services like healthcare (such as visiting a doctor or optician) or education (while at school or college)
▶ when using businesses and other organisations that provide services and goods (for example petrol stations, shops and restaurants)
▶ when using transport (for example a train or bus)
▶ when joining a club or association (for example a local football or music club)
▶ when having contact with public bodies (such as a local council or government department).

While the Act places a responsibility on everyone, including organisations and businesses, not to discriminate, the main responsibility in the workplace lies with the employer. This responsibility applies to both intended and unintended treatment. Importantly, it also applies to the treatment of groups of individuals and is not restricted to treatment of individuals. Individuals are responsible for their own actions, but employers may also hold **vicarious liability** for the actions of their employees.

Key terms

Equality: providing the same opportunities to everyone by removing barriers to success and not unfairly providing an individual with less favourable treatment in comparison to others

Discrimination: disadvantaging an individual by offering them less favourable treatment in comparison to others; the treatment does not have to be an intentional or deliberate action, or series of actions, to be considered unlawful

Protected characteristic: a trait associated with an individual which it is illegal to discriminate against

Vicarious liability: when someone such as an employer or organisation is held responsible for unlawful acts or conduct of its employees or someone acting on its behalf

The Act also places a responsibility on public bodies to consider how their actions affect groups of people with protected characteristics. This is referred to as the public sector equality duty (PSED) and it requires public bodies to actively promote equality of opportunity and foster good relationships between those with a protected characteristic and those without. Public bodies are organisations which deliver a service to the public or government and include such organisations as the Animal and Plant Health Agency, British Wool, the Joint Nature Conservation Committee and the Veterinary Medicines Directorate. Public bodies are required to publish their equality objectives every four years and to publish information at least once each year to show how they are complying with the duty.

Employment Rights Act 1996

This Act covers the employer–employee relationship. It brought together and merged a number of pieces of legislation to establish and protect certain employment rights, for example the right of an employee to receive a statement of employment particulars before or on the first day of their employment (see Chapter 3, page 53). The scope of the Act is extensive, and regarding equality within the workplace, it gives an employee a number of rights including:

▶ the right not to be unfairly dismissed
▶ the right to request flexible working
▶ the right to maternity, paternity and adoption leave
▶ the right to take time off to care for dependents, attend antenatal or adoption appointments and perform employee representative duties.

The Act sets out what constitutes unfair dismissal by defining fair reasons to dismiss an employee. However, it identifies some specific circumstances where dismissal is automatically considered unfair (for example being dismissed due to pregnancy). In general, an employee must have worked for an employer for at least two years before they have the right not to be unfairly dismissed.

Trade Union and Labour Relations (Consolidation) Act 1992

This Act protects anyone taking part in lawful industrial action from being unfairly dismissed. It also provides protection for employees taking part in trade union activities from discrimination or dismissal associated with trade union membership (see Chapter 3, page 61).

Protected characteristics

There are nine protected characteristics defined by the Equality Act 2010 for which protection is offered to individuals and groups of individuals against discrimination.

Age

Age is defined in terms of an 'age group' and is intended to be interpreted flexibly. It applies to individuals who belong, or do not belong, to a certain age (for instance individuals aged 25) or an age range (for example older workers, the under 30s, people over 40). The definition of this protected characteristic may therefore depend on the circumstances of the alleged discrimination. For example, it is unlikely that a farm manager can advertise to recruit a 'young person' for a stockperson vacancy, as this may unlawfully exclude others who have the experience and skills to undertake the role from applying.

Disability

The Act defines a disabled person as someone who has 'a physical or mental impairment that has a substantial and long-term adverse effect on his or her ability to carry out normal day-to-day activities'. An impairment is considered substantial if the cumulative effects are more than minor or trivial for the individual. An impairment is considered long-term if it:

▶ has lasted for 12 months
▶ is likely to last for 12 months
▶ is likely to last for the rest of the individual's life.

It is important to consider that a disability might not be visible, and an individual's circumstances need to be carefully considered when determining whether or not they have an impairment. In this respect, employers may need to take specialist advice (for example from an occupational health specialist or the individual's medical practitioner). This is likely to be the case where someone has a **progressive condition**. However, individuals with certain conditions are automatically considered to be disabled from the point of diagnosis and are therefore automatically protected (for instance someone with cancer, HIV infection or multiple sclerosis (MS)).

> **Key term**
>
> **Progressive condition**: a health condition which gradually gets worse over time

The Act places a duty on employers and organisations to make **reasonable adjustments** to support a disabled individual to access services as easily as a non-disabled individual. Therefore, they should think about the adjustments they may need to make immediately or ahead of time. For example, a zoo should anticipate that it will have disabled visitors, so it must consider how it can improve access to the services it offers. This may include physical changes to infrastructure and facilities, support for carers or assistance dogs, consideration of dietary needs and provision of support aids (such as hearing loops or hearing protection), as well as making information available on its website to support those planning their visit. It is important to be aware that individuals must not be asked to pay for the cost of any reasonable adjustment that is made.

Gender reassignment

Under the Gender Recognition Act 2004, individuals over the age of 18 have the legal right to change gender and hold subsequent rights associated with that gender. However, to exercise some of these rights, such as obtaining a new birth certificate to reflect their new gender, they may need to obtain a Gender Recognition Certificate.

The Equality Act subsequently offers a transgender person protection at all stages, from proposing reassignment through to having undergone reassignment. However, the language and terminology associated with gender reassignment is evolving. It is commonplace to use the term 'trans' and considered polite to refer to an individual as 'a trans person'. In addition, there is increasing recognition that there is a growing and diverse use of the word 'trans' by individuals, including those who have a gender fluid identity. Therefore, although the law currently sets limitations on this characteristic, employers should focus on positive **inclusion** based on the gender role an individual presents. For example, land-based employers should consider their dress codes or uniform requirements and the language they use and remove unnecessary gender divisions at work.

Marriage and civil partnership

The Equality Act protects the rights of anyone who is married or in a registered civil partnership under the Civil Partnership Act 2004. This includes those who are legally married or in a registered civil partnership outside the UK. For example, a garden centre may not offer different working conditions to its staff depending on whether or not they are married.

Those who are single, not yet married or in a proposed civil partnership (for example engaged) and those who are divorced or have had their partnership dissolved are *not* protected under the terms of the Act.

▲ Figure 6.1 The Equality Act 2010 protects those who are married or in a registered civil partnership

Pregnancy and maternity

The Equality Act protects individuals from discrimination because of pregnancy and maternity if it occurs during the **protected period**. There is additional protection offered against unfavourable treatment if an individual is breastfeeding. For example, an agricultural contractor must not take an employee's absence (that is due directly to pregnancy) into account when making decisions about their employment status. This does not mean that the individual concerned is not protected outside the protected period, as unfavourable treatment may be considered sex discrimination. However, in relation to fulfilling health and safety responsibilities, an employer may need to make reasonable adjustments to a pregnant employee's working conditions (see Chapter 1, page 18).

Key terms

Reasonable adjustments: changes that an employer or organisation must make to prevent an individual with a disability from being disadvantaged; what is objectively deemed reasonable will depend on factors such as the practicality of the adjustment, the cost and resources required to make the adjustment, and the size and type of organisation

Inclusion: the creation of an environment in which all individuals feel they are respected, accommodated and welcomed

Protected period: period of time that starts when a woman becomes pregnant and continues through to the end of ordinary maternity leave (26 weeks after giving birth), or until she returns to work, whichever is sooner

Race

The Equality Act protects individuals and **racial groups** defined by their skin colour, **nationality**, or ethnic or national origin. An individual's race is made up of a combination of these aspects, for example white British traveller, British Sikh or black British of Nigerian national origin. However, an individual can be subject to discrimination associated with any one or combination of these aspects. For example, a landscape contractor cannot refuse to employ someone who has the legal right to work in the UK because of their national origin.

Religion or belief

The Equality Act offers protection for individuals of a particular religion. A religion does not have to be organised or well known, but it must have a clear structure and belief system. The Act also offers protection associated with a religious or philosophical belief.

For a philosophical belief to be legally protected, it must be:
▶ genuinely held
▶ not just an opinion or viewpoint
▶ associated with a substantial aspect of human life and behaviour
▶ considered sufficiently **cogent**, serious, **cohesive** and important
▶ worthy of respect in a democratic society, and compatible with human dignity and the fundamental rights of others.

These are known as the Grainger criteria, which were established by an Employment Appeal Tribunal (EAT) in 2009.

The Act also offers protection to anyone who does not hold a particular belief or belong to a particular religion. For example, the manager of an animal collection would likely be discriminating against a collection assistant if they made them redundant because the individual was an atheist. The owner of a florist shop might be discriminatory if they refuse to let an employee wear an article of clothing associated with their religion or belief.

Key terms

Racial groups: groups of people who share the same protected characteristic associated with race or ethnicity

Nationality: the status of belonging to a particular nation; it is associated with citizenship and may not necessarily reflect where an individual was born

Improve your English

The word 'cogent' is used to refer to something which is clearly presented and convincing. What do you think it would mean in the context of expressing a belief?

The word 'cohesive' comes from the Latin word which means 'to stick'. What do you think it would mean in the context of expressing a belief?

Sex

The Equality Act offers protection from discrimination to individuals of either sex. It considers the sex of an individual to be that recorded on their birth certificate or Gender Recognition Certificate.

Sexual orientation

The Equality Act offers everyone protection from discrimination based on a person's sexual orientation towards others of the same sex, the opposite sex or either sex. It also covers how individuals choose to express their orientation. This can include places they visit, their appearance and dress, and the people they associate with.

There are other laws which have a connection with equality issues in the workplace. For example, under the Data Protection Act 2018 (see Chapter 10, page 147) information that an individual is a trans person or has a trans history is considered sensitive data.

Industry tip

Employers usually set out in a workplace policy how they intend to demonstrate compliance with their legal responsibilities and how they will provide equality of opportunities. This policy may also set out how the employer values and promotes diversity. Awareness of the responsibilities of individual roles within this policy usually forms part of the induction programme any new employee receives when they start working. It is important that this policy is regularly reviewed to ensure it reflects any changes in legislation or best practice.

Employees should be trained to identify issues relating to equality and diversity, **commensurate** with their role. For example, the manager responsible for hiring new staff to a pet shop chain may require specific training to ensure their recruitment and selection processes are inclusive.

Improve your English

The word 'commensurate' comes from the Latin word which means 'the act of measuring'. What do you think it means in this context, in terms of an employee's role?

Test yourself

Select one protected characteristic. Investigate actions an employer could take to ensure an individual with that protected characteristic would not be subject to discrimination at the recruitment stage of their employment.

6.2 Factors to consider when working with people from diverse backgrounds

The workplace is rich in potential diversity of colleagues and others (such as clients, customers and the public). For example, you may be working with people with different cultural backgrounds, religious beliefs, disabilities, lifestyles, interests, behaviours, personal characteristics, age, gender, educational level and socio-economic status. Therefore, it is important to be aware of your legal and moral obligations towards them and how you can leverage this diversity to make the workplace a positive and welcoming environment for all.

Defining negative behaviours and how they apply in the workplace

You need to be aware of a number of negative behaviours which are detrimental to others. Some are undesirable (prejudice and bias) while others are strictly prohibited by law under the Equality Act 2010 (discrimination, harassment and victimisation). It is also important to recognise the difference between discrimination and positive discrimination or **positive action**.

Prejudice

Prejudice is a preconceived opinion about an individual or a group that is not based on actual experience. It can make the relationship with others in the workplace uncomfortable and it can create a negative experience. Where this results in unwanted conduct or less favourable treatment, it is likely to be considered harassment or discrimination.

Bias

Bias refers to demonstrating different behaviour or actions towards others, for example:

- advantaging an individual or providing them with more favourable treatment (positive bias)
- disadvantaging an individual or providing them with less favourable treatment (negative bias).

In both cases, it is likely that someone will be disadvantaged, and if this is associated with a protected characteristic, this may be considered discrimination.

Bias is usually driven by inaccurate assumptions or false **stereotypes** (negative bias towards someone), or preference or favouritism (positive bias towards someone). This may be conscious bias which is deliberate (for example an employer more frequently disciplines one worker for being late, who is not more frequently late for work than their colleagues) or unconscious bias which is not deliberate (for example an employer more frequently rewards a worker who is a member of the same sports club). Unconscious bias is a result of an individual's life experience that has shaped their views but might not be reasonable or correct. Where bias results in unwanted conduct or less favourable treatment, it is likely to be considered harassment or discrimination.

Direct discrimination

This refers to disadvantaging an individual by offering them less favourable treatment or treating them unfairly in comparison to others because of a protected characteristic. For example, an employer advertises a job vacancy but makes it clear in the advert that only those without a physical disability should apply, even when this is not occupationally relevant. An individual who is subjected to alleged discrimination does not need to have the protected characteristic the discrimination relates to, as they may be subject to

Key terms

Positive action: action taken by an employer to help or support an individual with a protected characteristic, for example providing upskilling language courses to support employees whose first language is not English

Stereotype: general and oversimplified assumptions, ideas or characteristics which are used to represent a type or group of people; stereotyping a group of people does not reflect the diversity or complexity of the individuals within that group

discrimination by perception or discrimination by association.

Case study

A veterinary practice plans a team bonding activity at a local paintball site. They need one member of staff to stay behind on reception to answer emergency calls from clients. The management team decides to leave one of the veterinary nurses who has long-term reduced mobility, because they are unlikely to be able to fully engage in paintballing as the site is in a woodland.
▶ Why might it not be considered reasonable to select this individual to remain on reception while the others are paintballing?
▶ How might the management team ensure the veterinary nurse is not excluded from the team bonding?

Indirect discrimination

This is where a provision, criterion or practice (PCP) applies which has (or might have) the effect of disadvantaging an individual because they hold a protected characteristic. For indirect discrimination to be proven, there are four requirements that need to be demonstrated:
▶ The PCP applies neutrally to everyone (it is a contractual requirement in an employment contract, or a general rule such as all staff must wear specific clothing).
▶ The PCP puts all those who share a protected characteristic proportionately at a general disadvantage in comparison to those who do not hold that characteristic (for instance changes in shift work timings put women at a general disadvantage in comparison to men).
▶ The PCP puts an individual with a protected characteristic at a personal disadvantage in comparison to those who do not hold that characteristic (for example, an individual can show they are or could be disadvantaged due to changes in the timings of new work shifts).
▶ The PCP cannot be objectively justified as a proportionate means of achieving the desired objective (for example an employer cannot provide a good reason why only individuals with specific qualifications can be promoted).

Situations where an objective justification argument is used should be considered exceptional and there must be a legitimate objective (for example a health and safety or business need). These situations require all other alternative options to be considered and judged to be not proportionate.

Case study

A dog-grooming salon is recruiting for an apprentice. In the advert, the salon owner states that it is essential for any applicant to have undertaken some dog grooming at school or college. There is a significant under-representation of males on the dog-grooming courses offered at the local schools and colleges.
▶ Why might it not be considered reasonable to make previous dog-grooming experience an essential requirement?
▶ How might the salon owner recruit an apprentice without potentially excluding male applicants?

▲ Figure 6.2 It is important to avoid discrimination when recruiting new staff

Key terms

Discrimination by perception: discrimination where the individual concerned does not hold the protected characteristic but is wrongly believed to hold it; for example an individual is wrongly believed to hold specific religious beliefs because of their name or place of birth

Discrimination by association: discrimination where the individual concerned does not hold the protected characteristic but is wrongly believed to hold it because they associate with someone else who holds the protected characteristic; for example an individual is wrongly believed to be trans because they regularly go out with and associate with trans people

Objective justification: when a proportionate and legitimate reason is used to justify applying a provision, criterion or practice in a situation when it would normally be considered direct or indirect discrimination, i.e. there is a justification to offer less favourable treatment to individuals or groups who hold a protected characteristic; for example, an employer is unable to recruit someone with a specific protected characteristic because of the occupational requirements of the job

Harassment

Harassment refers to aggressive pressure, intimidation or unwanted conduct that relates to a protected characteristic. The conduct is intended to violate, or has the effect of violating, an individual's dignity by creating an intimidating, hostile, degrading, humiliating or offensive environment. The main intention of harassment is to get an individual to do something they do not want to do, or to not do something they are entitled to do.

There is a degree of subjectivity associated with what is deemed to be harassment. The perception of the individual alleging harassment is important when making any judgement. It should be considered alongside whether the conduct is reasonable, given other relevant circumstances. Similar to discrimination, an individual does not need to have the protected characteristic the conduct relates to, as they may be subject to harassment by perception or association.

Victimisation

Victimisation refers to singling someone out or subjecting an individual to a detrimental action or disadvantaging them because they have done, or might do, a protected act. Protected acts are defined as:

- bringing proceedings under the Equality Act 2010
- giving evidence or information in connection with proceedings under the Equality Act
- doing any undertaking in connection with the Equality Act
- making an allegation that someone has not complied with the Equality Act (for instance an individual has been subject to discrimination).

While it might be the individual alleging they have been discriminated against who is victimised because they instigated proceedings, protection is also offered to any third party who acts in good faith in relation to a protected act. For example, if an individual provides evidence at an employment tribunal that they witnessed their workplace colleague being subjected to discrimination because of their sexual orientation, any subsequent punishment by the employer because they gave evidence would be considered victimisation.

Potential consequences of negative discrimination

There is a range of potential consequences of discrimination in the workplace, which include the following:

Financial:
- risk of civil claims
- difficulty recruiting and retaining staff
- cost of retraining of staff
- legal fees.

Emotional:
- increased mental health issues and stress.

Reputation:
- loss of reputation
- difficulty retaining existing and attracting new clients and customers
- difficulty attracting new staff
- negative publicity.

Employees:
- reduced staff morale and productivity
- increased staff turnover, absence and sickness
- increased potential for physical conflict.

In addition, an employer or organisation may need to manage an increase in grievance and disciplinary procedures and may potentially be subjected to legal action. If an employee believes their legal rights have been breached, they may take their dispute to an employment tribunal. If an individual who is not an employee believes their legal rights have been breached, they may take their dispute to the County Court.

▲ Figure 6.3 Discrimination can result in mental health issues

Grievance and disciplinary procedures

Employees who want to make a complaint about a work-related issue or incident can raise this formally with their employer as a grievance. The issue or incident may be an isolated instance, or a series of instances, and can vary in severity. Irrespective of the nature or scale of the grievance, an employee must follow their employer's grievance procedure. If either the employee or the employer fail to do so, this may be taken into consideration if the matter progresses to an employment tribunal.

Employees should ordinarily first raise any concern informally with their line manager, or another manager, by talking to them. If that does not settle the matter, or the concern is serious, they can raise a formal grievance. The employer should impartially and thoroughly investigate the concern. Depending on the concern raised, they may need to take action to support anyone impacted while the concern is being investigated (such as arrange for those involved to temporarily work in different locations or, where appropriate and necessary, suspend an individual pending the investigation). An investigation will require the employer to meet with those involved, who may have a right to be accompanied by a colleague, an appropriate workplace trade union representative or an official employed by a trade union.

Once the employer has concluded the investigation, they should inform the employee as soon as possible of the outcome. The employer must offer the employee the right to appeal if they believe the procedure was not followed, or was unfair, or the outcome does not satisfactorily resolve the complaint. If, after an appeal, the employee believes their complaint has not been satisfactorily resolved, they may be able to make a claim to an employment tribunal.

Employers use disciplinary procedures to formally deal with **capability** and misconduct concerns. Instigation of disciplinary action may be an outcome of a grievance procedure or may be the direct result of workplace actions. For example, a worker raises a grievance that they are being subjected to workplace bullying. If the outcome of the investigation is that this has been proven, the individual responsible for the bullying may then be subject to the disciplinary procedure.

Similar to dealing with grievance issues, an employer should have a formal disciplinary procedure which they must follow when managing allegations of

misconduct (such as harassment and discrimination). If the employer does not, it could potentially lead to a claim of unfair dismissal and may be considered if the matter progresses to an employment tribunal. The procedure is similar to a grievance procedure. There should be a fair and thorough investigation, a clearly communicated outcome and a right to appeal. The potential outcome from a disciplinary procedure will depend on the circumstances but normally includes:

▶ no action
▶ informal warning (usually verbal)
▶ first written warning
▶ final written warning
▶ dismissal (for example for gross misconduct).

Industry tip

Dealing with disciplinary and grievance issues in the workplace can be complicated. For example, personal data used as part of the investigation may need to be carefully managed in line with data protection requirements (see Chapter 10). Therefore, it is important that employers have procedures in place that clearly set out how issues will be managed. For example, a small agricultural contractor who does not employ a human resources (HR) professional may need to seek legal advice to ensure the procedures are appropriate and align with best practice such as advice provided by the Advisory, Conciliation and Arbitration Service (Acas).

Employment tribunals

Employment tribunals are public bodies which have the statutory jurisdiction to hear disputes between employers and employees. Examples of issues which may be considered by an employment tribunal are shown in Table 6.1.

▼ Table 6.1 Issues which may be considered by an employment tribunal

Act	Examples of issues which may be considered by an employment tribunal
Employment Rights Act	• Unfair dismissal • Maternity, paternity and adoption issues: pay and leave
Equality Act	• Claims of breach of equality clauses • Failure to provide equality of terms
Trade Union and Labour Relations (Consolidation) Act	• Unfair dismissal and other actions for reasons related to trade union membership or participation in industrial action

Key term

Capability: a judgement made about an individual's ability to undertake the role for which they are employed; an employer may choose to have a discrete capability procedure, rather than deal with performance issues through a disciplinary procedure

Normally, an employee must make a claim within three months minus one day from the date the workplace issue happened. However, if they want to make a claim to an employment tribunal, they must first inform Acas and will be offered the option of early conciliation to try to resolve the claim.

Legal action

The Equality and Human Rights Commission (EHRC) is the formal regulator of the Equality Act 2010. It has investigative powers, as well as litigation and enforcement powers. If necessary, it can apply for a County Court order to require an organisation to comply with specific requirements. However, it does not provide advice to individuals. This is provided by the Equality Advisory and Support Service (EASS).

If an individual brings a discrimination claim under the Equality Act to a County Court, they are required to send information about the claim to the EHRC. This intelligence enables the EHRC to monitor discrimination law cases and, if necessary, offers the opportunity for it to intervene by providing expert testimony.

How to show empathy and respect to those from different backgrounds

Recognising the benefits of working with individuals from different backgrounds, empathy is associated with emotional understanding of the perspectives of others which have been shaped by their individual backgrounds and experiences. It is also about appreciating others' feelings and consciously responding in a compassionate and respectful manner.

Empathy and respect are critical to building effective relationships both within and outside work, and showing others that they are valued. This can be demonstrated through being a good active listener, learning about different cultures and understanding traditions, avoiding criticising or judging the feelings of others, or even performing small acts of kindness such as making someone a hot drink. It also requires self-reflection, recognising when your own feelings, behaviours, actions or thoughts may not acknowledge someone else's legitimate feelings and consciously adapting your response.

Methods that embrace and promote diversity and inclusion

As already stated, there is a range of reasons why an employer or organisation should wish to embrace and promote diversity and inclusion within the workplace.

However, an inclusive culture requires a commitment across all levels of the organisation or business to be curious and respectful of differences in identity, skills, experiences and perspectives. Employers should also be aware of individual circumstances and that the notion of equality may not result in fair outcomes for all. Treating everyone the same way (i.e. providing them with the same level of support or resources) may not achieve the desired outcome.

To achieve positive outcomes for all, employers should implement an **equitable approach** to individuals in the workplace (Figure 6.4). For example, an employer who operates a landscape gardening business may invest in a battery-powered hedge cutter and lawnmower to support an employee who is unable to easily start or operate the existing fleet of petrol-powered equipment. This will allow that employee to feel valued and supported and increase their productivity.

> ### Key term
>
> **Equitable approach**: identifying existing differences and addressing these by individually adjusting resources and opportunities to allow everyone to achieve a positive outcome; in short, achieving a level playing field

Promoting an inclusive workplace

The following are some of the ways that an inclusive workplace can be promoted:

- Ensure policies and procedures recognise the benefits to the organisation of having a diverse workforce and are regularly reviewed to ensure they model best practice.
- Ensure recruitment practices provide applicants with a fair opportunity to access job roles, taking positive action to remove unnecessary barriers for applicants.
- Ensure human resource and personal practices minimise discriminatory progression opportunities and take positive action to support employees.
- Review how products and services are offered to customers and clients to ensure they are accessible, representative and inclusive.
- Anticipate opportunities to make reasonable adjustments in the workplace before they are requested.
- Communicate thoughtfully, using respectful language.
- Provide training appropriate to their role for all staff so they are aware of their responsibilities at work.

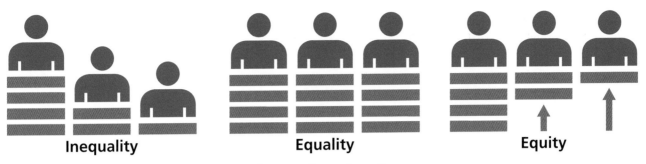

Inequality   **Equality**   **Equity**

▲ Figure 6.4 The difference between inequality, equality and equity

▶ Consider dress codes and appearance expectations to ensure individuals are able to express their identity appropriately.
▶ Remove unnecessary gender restrictions.
▶ Establish support groups and provide a supportive working environment that accommodates the diverse needs of workers.
▶ Be alert to the risks of stereotyping and unconscious bias.
▶ Take advantage of opportunities to celebrate diversity.

▶ Proactively challenge poor or negative behaviour as it arises.

Test yourself

Reflect on any work experience you have had. Identify two things the employer did which made you feel welcome and respected as an individual. For example, did they provide a well-planned induction programme or a workplace mentor you could go to for advice?

Assessment practice

1 Identify **three** characteristics protected by equality legislation. (3 marks)
2 Explain the public sector equality duty. (2 marks)
3 Explain the potential implications of vicarious liability for an employer. (3 marks)
4 Identify **three** behaviours that might be signs of workplace harassment. (3 marks)
5 Describe how unconscious bias can occur in the workplace. (2 marks)
6 Explain how the Equality Act 2010 protects individuals from discrimination in the workplace. (6 marks)

7 Describe the potential consequences of negative discrimination in the workplace. (4 marks)
8 Explain how an employer can promote diversity in the workplace. (6 marks)
9 Describe how employers might reduce the risk from stereotype bias during recruitment. (5 marks)
10 Describe how employees can help promote diversity and inclusion within their workplace. (5 marks)

Further reading

You may find some of the following resources helpful for keeping up to date with equality issues:
▶ Advisory, Conciliation and Arbitration Service (Acas)
▶ Equality Advisory and Support Service (EASS)
▶ Equality and Human Rights Commission (EHRC).

7 Communication

Introduction

Communication consists of two processes: giving information and receiving information. Types of communication include letters, emails, reports, websites and face-to-face social events. This chapter explains the different types of formal and informal communication and how they are used by businesses. It also starts to evaluate communication methods and outlines their benefits and limitations, and it introduces the use of imagery and videos.

This chapter also introduces the benefits and limitations of social media for a business, as well as the potential impacts if it is not used.

This chapter links to Chapter 4 Ethics and Chapter 5 Business for the coverage of topics such as use of social media, policies and social and environmental business ethics.

Learning outcomes

By the end of this chapter, you will understand:
▶ types of effective communication, including verbal, non-verbal, visual and written
▶ different types of communication and their suitability for different purposes
▶ formats used for the types of formal and informal communication and their associated business conventions
▶ the importance of communication, spoken

language, body language and tone, and how each is used to convey messages to different audiences for different purposes
▶ use of relevant images and visual aids and how these support written text and oral presentations
▶ the benefits and limitations of social media, including risk of misuse and positive and negative effects on the business.

7.1 Types of effective communication

This section covers verbal, non-verbal, visual and written methods of communication.

Verbal communication

Verbal communication is the way in which spoken words are used in the form of speeches, discussions, presentations and conversations.

It is typically two-way communication (between the sender and receiver), although sometimes it can be used to communicate information via webinars, social media videos and speeches where the audience (message receivers) are not face to face with the sender.

The effectiveness of verbal communication depends on:
▶ tone
▶ clarity of speech
▶ volume
▶ speed
▶ words used (language)
▶ body language
▶ inflection (how we know when somebody has finished speaking when there is a slight raise in pitch; this is important in non-visual telephone calls)
▶ listening skills (of the sender and receiver of the message).

It is important to adapt tone, volume, speed, language and body language to match the style of communication (formal or informal), in order to meet audience needs and ensure the information or message is understood.

Non-verbal communication

Non-verbal communication is the transfer of information without the use of words or spoken language. Non-verbal communication can occur in a range of ways, including:
▶ facial expressions
▶ gestures (sign language)
▶ body posture.

Visual communication

Visual communication uses graphics and images to deliver information rather than words/text and audio. It includes the use of:
▶ images
▶ typography
▶ charts
▶ diagrams.

▲ Figure 7.1 Different typefaces (fonts) help to communicate your message

Visual communication can be more accessible, compared to text, as it goes beyond language barriers and is not limited by the reading ability of the receiver. It can also include more context to the information being communicated. This is why it is said that 'a picture can paint a thousand words'. This method of communication is typically one-way (sender to receiver) and can be used alongside verbal communication in presentations. Images are also used to catch people's attention and communicate information quickly, which is why they are used in health and safety signage, and hazard classification pictograms are placed on the packaging of products.

> **Improve your English**
>
> Choose a picture and write a description of what it shows. Remember to include aspects such as colours, people's facial expressions (if appropriate) and the mood/emotions conveyed.

Written communication

Written communication is the process of conveying a message through written symbols. In everyday life and the workplace, this communication method is used widely in text messages, emails, social media posts, websites, letters, contracts and policies. This method of communication is typically one-way (sender to receiver).

Different types of communication and their suitability for different purposes

Informal

Informal communication is common outside the formal structures or processes of a business or education system (such as a school, college or university). It is unofficial, free-flowing and flexible. It does not follow rules, processes, formalities or the hierarchy within a business, so may mutate as the conversation develops. This means the information communicated can flow in any direction. Informal communication often uses verbal methods, is two-way and is therefore more personal.

Informal communication often occurs in social interactions between individuals with similar interests, although not always.

An example of informal communication in a workplace is the situation of the 'water cooler chat' or 'corridor conversation'. This is a term used to describe the conversations between work colleagues that often take place where people gather, such as around the water cooler or coffee machine. These conversations can help develop working relationships and encourage a positive work culture. However, as they do not include everyone in a team, they can result in people feeling excluded from business information or opportunities. Businesses need to ensure that any important information is not officially disseminated in this way, especially as the increase in remote working since the COVID-19 pandemic means that some people may be excluded simply by not being physically present in the workplace.

▲ Figure 7.2 A water cooler chat

Formal

Formal communication is structured and used for official messaging, for example a letter from a solicitor, doctor or college or a police statement. It is controlled and follows specific channels or methods, standards and rules set by the sender. This means that everyone receives the same messaging in the same way.

Formal communication usually follows an organisation's hierarchy or structure, meaning that higher-ranking employees, for example managers

and supervisors, use it to send various messages and instructions to people in their teams, such as operators or trainees. Examples of formal communication in a business include health and safety policies, holiday/annual leave allowances, pay rises, restructures and pension updates.

Benefits of formal communication include that it:
▶ provides an efficient flow of information within a business
▶ is not personal
▶ uses clear, polite and respectful language
▶ can create a professional image for a business
▶ features a set format
▶ reduces the likelihood of mistakes and errors
▶ gives the message or information more credibility.

Formal communication is used in many ways within a business, including:
▶ inductions – the process of making new employees familiar with the business and their role
▶ setting objectives – for a task, project or job role
▶ meetings
▶ training
▶ written policies, such as codes of conduct
▶ contracts
▶ emails.

Test yourself

Describe two benefits and two limitations of informal and formal communication.

Identify three situations where formal communication would take place.

Formats used for the types of formal and information communication and their associated business conventions

Reports

Within the workplace, a business report can be formal or informal depending on its purpose and audience.

Formal reports are detailed documents relating to a specific topic, project or set of data. They can contain tables, charts and graphics to explain or quantify the written information and help the reader to understand the contents. They usually follow a structure which is set out by the business, for example an abstract (summary), introduction, aim, methodology, results, evaluation and conclusion.

Informal reports do not have a specified structure and tend to be shorter than formal reports. They are used for quick communication with internal stakeholders.

Emails

Many businesses have policies covering email use. These can include the layout, language, use of attachments and format of signatures that should be used, as well as what can be communicated via email and by whom. It is important to remember that emails can be used as a legally binding contract if certain criteria are in place, including:

▶ clearly defined conditions
▶ all parties agreeing to the content and that they are bound to them
▶ details of payment or rewards.

Emails have a wide range of uses within a business. Internally, emails can be used for informal messaging between colleagues or for formal communication between managers, HR and business leads. Externally, emails serve as a means to formally contact customers, regulators and other stakeholders. The use of emails can be monitored by IT and HR departments to check that it is within policy guidelines.

Benefits of emails include:

▶ speed: delivery is instant and there are no delays with postal systems
▶ ease: there are no limitations as to when communication can be sent and delivered
▶ cost: they are a cost-efficient way of sending out written communications; there are no postal, printing and stationery costs
▶ documentation: copies are automatically saved for information and **audits**
▶ accessibility: they can be accessed away from the office via a laptop or mobile device
▶ digital storage and security: there is no need for filing cabinets with locks, as email uses password protection.

▲ Figure 7.3 Communication by email can be beneficial

Key term

Audits: official inspections of an organisation's records usually carried out by an independent body

Case study

In 2024, a former Post Office boss was accused of misleading the High Court by claiming she did not know that an IT system could be accessed remotely before 2018. The public inquiry used as evidence emails that revealed the Post Office boss was in fact told about the remote access as far back as 2010.

▶ What was the former Post Office boss accused of as a consequence of the email evidence?
▶ What were the consequences of these emails being withheld?

Industry tip

Employers may use emails to send out quotes, invoices and confirmations for work as they are low-cost. However, as they can form a legally binding contract, they should be checked and proofread before sending to avoid disputes with customers over any prices and work agreed that are mentioned within the email.

Test yourself

Explain the limitations and risks of emails.

Letters

A business letter is a formal communication used for official correspondence (Figure 7.4). It tends to have a set structure and format and uses formal language. It is usually printed on headed paper with the organisation's information preprinted on it and is sent out to recipients as a hard copy, but it can also be sent as an attachment to an email.

A business letter can be used for a range of purposes, including job offers, promotions and resignations.

The structure of a letter is usually as follows:

▶ Sender's name, job title and address
▶ Recipient's name, job title and address
▶ Date
▶ Salutation: addressing the recipient with 'Dear' along with their title and name, for example

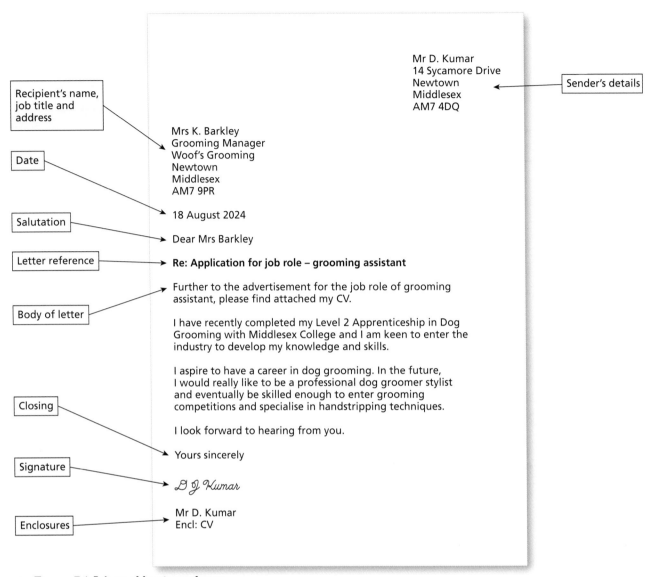

Recipient's name, job title and address

Date

Salutation

Letter reference

Body of letter

Closing

Signature

Enclosures

Mr D. Kumar
14 Sycamore Drive
Newtown
Middlesex
AM7 4DQ → **Sender's details**

Mrs K. Barkley
Grooming Manager
Woof's Grooming
Newtown
Middlesex
AM7 9PR

18 August 2024

Dear Mrs Barkley

Re: Application for job role – grooming assistant

Further to the advertisement for the job role of grooming assistant, please find attached my CV.

I have recently completed my Level 2 Apprenticeship in Dog Grooming with Middlesex College and I am keen to enter the industry to develop my knowledge and skills.

I aspire to have a career in dog grooming. In the future, I would really like to be a professional dog groomer stylist and eventually be skilled enough to enter grooming competitions and specialise in handstripping techniques.

I look forward to hearing from you.

Yours sincerely

D J Kumar

Mr D. Kumar
Encl: CV

▲ Figure 7.4 A formal business letter

'Dear Mr Smith', or if the recipient's name is not known 'Dear Sir or Madam' or 'Dear customer' etc.
▶ Letter reference, for example 'Re: Confirmation of interview'
▶ Main text of the letter
▶ Closing: formal phrases for this include '**Yours sincerely**', 'Yours faithfully' or 'Yours truly'
▶ Signature with name, job title and organisation name (if they have one) underneath
▶ List of any enclosures (if applicable).

Websites

A website is an effective way for a business or organisation to promote itself to a wide range of audiences and convey its desired image. Websites contain direct, clear, controlled and fixed

Improve your English

Write a formal letter applying for a job in the land-based sector in which you are interested in working. The letter should cover your background and skills applicable to the role. Remember to use the correct structure for the letter, together with a formal, polite tone.

Key term

Yours sincerely: a standard sign-off for a formal email or letter when you know the recipient ('sincerely' means genuinely and is used to emphasise your honest intentions towards the person); 'sincerely' can be replaced with faithfully or truly when writing to someone whose name you do not know (for example you have addressed them as 'Sir' or 'Madam')

information about a business' products, services, policies and contact details.

Websites also enable customers and stakeholders to find out information about an organisation at any time, when other lines of enquiry such as email, telephone or social media messaging may be less available.

There are fixed costs associated with the development and maintenance of a website, which need to be carried out by someone with relevant IT skills, and an external company may be hired to do this. Regular maintenance is important to ensure the information on the website remains current.

▲ Figure 7.5 Websites can help to promote your business

Social media

Social media is online communication that is increasingly being used by businesses to market and promote their image, products and services. It can cover a range of communication types, including short messages or statements, images, graphics and reports.

Social media can help businesses reach a wide audience and develop a social network at low cost, in comparison with more traditional methods such as leaflets or magazine advertising. It may also cost less and be easier to maintain than a website. Businesses can interact directly with customers, who can also increase the business' social media presence and reach by liking and sharing posts. It works in real time, providing direct, responsive and personalised contact with customers.

Social media platforms include Facebook, Instagram, LinkedIn, Threads, Snapchat and X (formerly known as Twitter).

▲ Figure 7.6 Social media helps businesses reach a wide audience quickly

Industry tip

When businesses use social media platforms, they should be mindful of the content that they post and the messaging that they convey, as it is immediately public, can be shared quickly, and if their posts are misinterpreted or say something incorrect this could impact the image of the business and influence customers. This includes the image you portray on your own social media accounts, which may reflect on the business.

Printed media

Although printed media is a more traditional way of advertising a business or organisation, it is still used by many. It can be in the format of posters, leaflets, brochures, adverts or articles in magazines and papers, as well as the use of business cards or letters.

Printed media is more expensive than digital forms, and it comes with other limitations, including:

▶ audience reach: it is usually limited to a local delivery range and is not always directed to targeted or engaged audiences
▶ lifespan: it is not always read by a wide enough audience; it can be missed or thrown away
▶ information: this is fixed at the time of printing or publication, so cannot be updated.

Printed media is used at trade shows to promote businesses, which attendees can refer back to after the event. It may also be used for a focus on a local area, for instance a local gardener or cleaner might advertise their services in the area where they already work.

Photographs and video clips

Photographs and video clips can be an effective way of conveying information in a clear and engaging format. They can be more effective than written communication as they can have a higher **retention rate** and can be easier to remember. They can supply context and are not limited by the reading ability of the individual receiving the message. They can also be used in digital communication via websites and social media.

When using imagery, you need to ensure that all content is checked for suitability and meets all legal requirements. The quality and content of the images used must meet legislative and industry requirements, as these will reflect on the public image and reputation of the business.

> **Industry tip**
>
> When using a photograph to advertise a business' services, ensure that all health and safety requirements are met, such as wearing PPE, handling equipment appropriately, animal welfare and safety. This includes checking the background, to ensure there is no litter or trip hazards. The photograph should also demonstrate that the business represents equality and diversity.

There are strict rules and legal requirements surrounding the use of images and video clips. For example, you must have the written permission of everyone shown in the image or clip to be able to publish it. Images should not include minors/children. Anyone shown in an image should be fully informed of its purpose and use.

Team meetings and individual meetings

Depending on the purpose of the meetings and the information being communicated, team and individual meetings can be either formal or informal.

Examples of formal meetings include business updates, project meetings and performance review meetings.

> **Industry tip**
>
> To ensure a formal meeting is effective and achieves its purpose, it is good practice to only invite the people required to attend, and to prepare and circulate an agenda in advance. A chair or facilitator should ensure that the meeting keeps to time and conversations stay on track. Notes or minutes should be taken of any discussions and agreed actions, and these can be kept as a record and circulated.

Examples of informal meetings include brainstorming and feedback sessions. These meetings help

> **Key term**
>
> **Retention rate**: the accuracy of the recall of information over a given period of time

develop relationships within organisations between management, employees and co-workers. They give the opportunity for open discussions to take place, in order to plan and implement improvements to the organisation as well as individual performance towards business targets and objectives.

> **Industry tip**
>
> It can be useful to record online meetings so that absent team members can review the recording and stay informed. The recording also provides an accurate account of what was discussed for future reference. Before recording, you must remember to get permission from all attendees and to inform them why the meeting is being recorded.

Face-to-face events

Face-to-face events give individuals and businesses the opportunity to network with a targeted audience at an industry-focused gathering. They can develop professional relationships using informal and personal communication styles with a range of stakeholders.

However, not only can these events be costly to attend or to have a stand at, but they can also be time consuming and resource heavy, as time is spent away from the business and day-to-day work roles.

In the land-based sector, there are a number of external face-to-face events that take place both at a local and national scale depending on the industry. These include conferences, trade shows, competitions and award evenings, such as Cereals, Crufts, the Game Fair, the ARB Show, the Chelsea Flower Show and Groomer of the Year.

Importance of communication, spoken language, body language and tone

Communication, spoken language, body language and tone are each used to convey messages to different audiences for different purposes, as outlined below.

Promotion of the sector/product through social media

Before creating the content for social media, it must be clear what the purpose of the promotion is, who the target audience is, and which platform it is going to be published on. This will influence how the messaging is put together and the language used. It will also set parameters on the format of the content, such as word count, time length for videos and sound bites, and image size. All of these should be checked before putting together the content.

For social media, it is important that the language used is personable and not too formal, in order to engage directly with the target audience. It should be technically correct and should not use colloquial terminology that will alienate the audience, as that will risk the meaning of the messaging being lost or misunderstood.

If using verbal communication rather than written text, the delivery should be clear, at an appropriate speed and use a positive, upbeat tone. Body language is also important; it needs to be open, positive and confident to create feelings of honesty and trust for the receiver of the message being communicated.

> **Test yourself**
>
> Search social media platforms for posts from businesses in your industry promoting their products or services and evaluate the written, verbal and non-verbal language used.

Legal records

Legal records use formal, non-emotive language and often contain specific terminology and phrasing only used in legal documents.

Legal records need to be accurate and contain appropriate factual information in the required format for legislative requirements. These records can be audited by regulators, such as the HSE, or used as evidence in investigations and court cases.

Contracts and policies are examples of legal records, but documents and records used in day-to-day work can also be legal records, for example risk assessments, accident books, veterinary medicine records, animal transport logs, plant passports and pesticide application records.

> **Test yourself**
>
> For a job role in your chosen land-based industry, identify five legal records that could be used.

Technical reports for quality standards

Technical reports communicate technical information to a specific audience such as managers and regulators and have a clear objective. They use formal language, technical terminology and precise information. They have a logical format and structure and usually contain data with an evaluation.

Technical reports can be used to identify gaps and areas for improvement, record compliance and measure performance after changes have been made to a process. They can drive changes to a business and improve efficiencies and outputs.

Use of relevant images and visual aids and how these support written text and oral presentations

Images and visual aids can provide context to written text or assist with understanding technical information.

Images and visual aids include:
- diagrams: theories and concepts
- graphs: representations of data sets
- photographs: real-life examples.

Any images used will usually need to be clearly labelled and referenced to ensure the reader understands their purpose within the text. Before using the image, you must check that you have permission from the copyright holder (if it is not you). See Chapter 10, page 139 for more about intellectual property.

Benefits and limitations of social media including risk of misuse and positive and negative effects on the business

Positive effects

As discussed earlier in this chapter, social media can have many positive effects on a business. It can maintain and develop new relationships with stakeholders and customers, it offers direct contact with a wide audience and it is personable. Social media is also convenient to use, as it can be accessed via many devices, for example a laptop, tablet or smart phone. Most platforms are relatively straightforward to use, so do not require special training, skilled staff and specific IT programmes (for example websites require web designers and design software). They also have the bonus of being relatively cost effective, as they are usually free to set up and do not incur charges to add or change content, unlike a website where domain names need to be bought and website sizes and maintenance have associated costs.

Social media creates opportunities for individuals and businesses to exchange and enhance knowledge, share best practice and create an open forum for discussions on specific topics and issues within a sector.

When used correctly, social media can be a tool to promote a business' services and products to existing and new customers.

Negative effects

Social media also has its downsides. Due to its wide, varied and unpoliced use, it can have the potential to lead to negative publicity for a business. It is easy for a dissatisfied customer or competitor to publish a review online, and by the time it is seen by the business and responded to, resolved or removed, it may already have been read by existing or potential customers, thereby damaging the reputation of the business.

There is no definitive cost–benefit analysis for the time spent on social media by a business. This is because it is difficult to substantiate the direct links between social media posts/advertising and financial gains/sales. Even if someone reads or likes/responds positively to a social media post, it does not mean that they will instantly buy from that company.

Social media accounts are also susceptible to hacking. Malicious attacks may involve posting damaging content on a business' social media site, resulting in loss of business or damage to reputation. This means that businesses need to ensure that they have policies and procedures in place to monitor use of business social media accounts, as well as restrictions on who uses them and how they can be used.

Test yourself

For a business in your industry, review some of its social media posts and list five potential positive effects and five potential negative effects.

Assessment practice

1 Which **two** processes does communication involve? (2 marks)
2 What does effective verbal communication depend on? (6 marks)
3 Name **three** types of visual communication. (3 marks)
4 Explain the difference between formal and informal communication. (6 marks)
5 What are the benefits of a business using emails to communicate with its customers? (6 marks)
6 State **four** items that would need to be included in the structure of a business letter to a customer. (4 marks)
7 State **three** disadvantages of a business having a website. (3 marks)
8 Explain the benefits and risks of using social media for a business. (6 marks)
9 State **three** limitations of using printed media to communicate with customers. (3 marks)
10 To ensure a formal meeting is effective, what **three** things can be implemented? (3 marks)

Further reading

You may find the following references helpful for further information on communication:

▶ *Technological influence on business activity – Eduqas: Digital communication with customers* on the BBC Bitesize website

▶ *Copyright notice: Digital images, photographs and the internet* on the Intellectual Property Office's website
▶ *Communication: Communications Act 2003* on the UK Government website
▶ *Data Protection: The Data Protection Act 2018* on the UK Government website.

8 Relationship management

Introduction

This chapter introduces the relationships between businesses and different sectors and the impact these relationships can have on a business, and it describes the role of stakeholders.

The chapter also explains the role and purpose of customer care and customer service and why these are important to a business, how to manage customer expectations, and how businesses can utilise customer feedback and satisfaction surveys.

The chapter outlines the importance of making a good first impression and how it can be achieved.

The chapter explains the legal requirements of the Consumer Protection Act 1987 and Consumer Rights Act 2015.

Learning outcomes

By the end of this chapter, you will understand:
- the role and purpose of customer care
- the importance of first impressions and accurate knowledge when representing the business and self and supporting customers
- the difference between customer care and customer service, and customer wants and needs
- methods and impact of customer care and how they can be applied and maintained when interacting with different stakeholders, including internal customers (volunteers, employees)
- how to manage customer expectations and expected timescales
- the benefits of customer care to the individual and business
- current legal requirements (Consumer Protection Act 1987, Consumer Rights Act 2015) when interacting with different types of customers and customer relationships, including business to business (B2B)

- the principles of customer service and how it can be maintained
- typical procedures used to deal with customer queries, disputes and complaints
- the consequences of not following procedures
- the processes used to promote customer relations and to establish and monitor customer satisfaction
- the roles of different stakeholders
- the definitions/roles, expectations and interrelationships of stakeholders (internal and external)
- the impact of different stakeholders on the business.

8.1 Role and purpose of customer care

Importance of first impressions and accurate knowledge when representing the business and self and supporting customers

▲ Figure 8.1 First impressions count

First impressions are important in all aspects of life, but they are especially important in work and professional circumstances. These impressions can influence your personal reputation and career. They can also influence the reputation of the business you work for, its success and the relationships it has with its customers.

First impressions are the opinions that are made within the first few minutes of meeting someone; they are formed from assumptions and physical observations about the other person. Therefore, the first impression someone gives can be different for different people, as each individual forms their opinions based on unique assumptions or biases.

One of the reasons why making a positive first impression is so important is that people may recall this and use it as the basis for any further opinions and assumptions as the relationship develops. It will also influence how they treat you. This means that it may be difficult to disprove or change these first impressions and opinions. For example, if the first impression someone has of you is that you are unconfident in your work, then they may assume that you are not very knowledgeable and it may take some time and effort to demonstrate that you are, in fact, well-informed and skilled in your role. If the first impression you give is a positive one, this can lead to

further positive assumptions about you. For example, when you meet someone for the first time you should make eye contact and indicate an optimistic outlook, as this body language conveys respect to the other person and indicates that you are pleased to meet them. From this they might also assume that you are confident, friendly and honest. It is also worth noting that having an overly positive attitude may have a negative effect, as it could suggest that you are promising a lot but that there is no substance to those promises. Adopting a position in the middle ground and portraying yourself as friendly, approachable, realistic, honest and helpful will ensure the impression you give is positive.

Another reason for making a positive first impression, rather than a neutral or indifferent impression, is that you are more likely to be remembered. This is particularly useful when working in job roles that involve sales and providing services to customers, for example dog grooming, pet sitting, garden landscaping or machinery sales. This is because the customer may make a link between the product they are buying and you. This could lead to repeat business and improve your company's sales figures. It is also beneficial for job interviews, as the interviewer may remember you above the other candidates when deciding whom to employ.

The following should be taken into account when trying to make a good first impression:
- **Appearance**: make sure your appearance is appropriate for the job role, business and situation.
- **Eye contact**: make sufficient eye contact with people, as this can show respect as well as confidence.
- **Smile**: smiling shows that you are happy to meet someone and that you are engaging with them.
- **Listen and speak in moderation**: this helps to show that you are confident and interested in what the other person is saying.

Having accurate knowledge is also important, as this will be part of the information someone will use to form their impression or opinion of you. If you provide inaccurate or false information, this can give the impression that you are untrustworthy and incompetent, which could cost the business sales and ultimately lose the business customers. If there is an occasion when you are unable to provide an answer, it is better to admit that you do not know and that you will find out, rather than pretending to know. People prefer honesty and helpfulness and will often recognise when someone is simply pretending that they know the answer.

Difference between customer care and customer service, and customer wants and needs

The terms customer care and customer service are often used interchangeably, but they have different meanings and applications.

Customer care goes beyond customer service because it focuses on emotional connections between brands, products and customers. It is a group of principles and strategies that businesses use to interact with their customers. It emphasises the importance of making each customer feel valued, whether the interaction is face to face or remote (via the telephone, email or social media). This can be achieved by responding to customers personally, helping them beyond their expectations, and listening to, and acting on, their feedback.

Customer service focuses on providing advice to customers about a product or service or dealing with complaints. It is a set of practices that a business provides to its customers including any assistive actions, for instance offering to help them find products or answering their questions. These practices can help customers evaluate the business' products or services, make purchasing decisions and resolve any issues that may occur. Customer service is centred around practical measures that employees can implement to improve their customers' experiences. For example, in a machinery dealership, this may include offering demonstrations of pieces of machinery to encourage customers to make a purchase. If customers can see how something works and therefore how it will make their lives easier, this will then become a factor in whether they purchase the product.

▲ Figure 8.2 Customer care is important to a business

Methods and impacts of customer care and how they can be applied and maintained when interacting with different stakeholders

For a business to have good, or even excellent, customer care, there are number of methods they can adopt.

For each stage of the sales process, a business needs to ensure that it focuses on keeping customers happy. These stages may include:
▶ finding potential customers – this can be face to face, over the telephone, or via email or social media
▶ finding out or discussing the customers' needs
▶ presenting products or services on offer
▶ facilitating customers purchasing products or services
▶ contacting customers post sales.

Engage with customers during and after the sales process

If staff are available to customers throughout the sales process, and help when they can, this will make customers feel more engaged with the business and may result in increased in customer loyalty.

After a customer has purchased a product or service, the business may need to provide aftercare. This could include:
▶ showing the customer how to use the product at home, for example giving a demonstration of how to use a new lawnmower or how to trim a dog's claws using a pair of nail clippers
▶ providing customer support via the telephone or online
▶ product servicing – some products require a regular service to keep them running properly, and businesses can contact customers when it is time for this to occur.

Test yourself

For two businesses in your industry, look up and compare their customer care and customer service policies, summarising how they might influence customer purchasing decisions.

Research an aspect of each business' products that you would like to find out more about. Use either the website information section or a chatbot function (if applicable) to compare the level of service provided by the two businesses. Examples of topics that could be looked up are returns and refund policies, delivery charges and timescales.

▲ Figure 8.3 Knowledgeable customer support will help your business

Product knowledge

Another method of customer care is to ensure that all employees have excellent product knowledge. Understanding the features and benefits of the business' products and services will enable staff to answer questions promptly and accurately and match the best product or service to the needs of each individual customer. For example, if staff are knowledgeable about the different features and prices of the equipment and machinery for sale, they can suggest the most suitable item that meets the customer's needs and is within their price range, meaning that the customer is more likely to make a purchase. If the piece of equipment suggested is outside their price range or does not fully meet their needs, they are less likely to make a purchase or return in the future.

Build customer relationships

Employees should try to build relationships with customers. This involves being polite and friendly and listening to customers. Having an approachable and inclusive attitude can help customers feel more comfortable.

Businesses can also enhance their customers' experience by ensuring that any facilities the customers use, such as waiting rooms, make their experience more enjoyable. This makes customers feel that they are valued by the business. An example would be comfortable seating at a dog groomer's establishment. Ensuring customers have somewhere comfortable to sit while they wait for their dog can encourage them to return.

Another method businesses can adopt is to make customers feel special. This could be by offering next-day delivery or click and collect for orders over the telephone or online, or by offering incentives such as free gifts and loyalty cards. Personalising the service to the individual customer can make them feel more valued. For example, a gardener who carries out routine services such as lawn mowing could take into consideration the routine and circumstances of each of their customers to ensure they carry out the work at a time that is convenient to them.

Providing good customer care

Customer care plays a vital role in a business' success. If a business offers good (or even exceptional) customer care, it can lead to:

▶ increased customer satisfaction and a substantial increase in customer loyalty and retention, with customers more likely to make future purchases from the business
▶ a positive image for the business, as customers are likely to share their experiences with their friends and family, which can bring new customers to the business and expand the customer portfolio/database
▶ trust and credibility with its customers, which can lead to long-term customer relationships that encourage repeat business.

A business can use key performance indicators (KPIs) to measure the impact of customer care on the customer experience and identify areas for improvement. See Chapter 2, page 38, Chapter 3, page 64 and Chapter 5, page 92 for more about KPIs.

Once a business has applied its chosen methods of customer care, it needs to ensure that these are maintained across the business by all stakeholders and employees, including any voluntary staff, apprentices or work-experience placements.

One way to maintain customer care is to provide training and support to employees to ensure that their knowledge and skills are kept up to date. This can include training on the products they are selling, as well as training related to their behaviours and communication skills. By regularly engaging with customers and asking for feedback on their experience and suggestions for improvement, a business can identify any staff training and support that is needed. Seeking feedback also helps customers to feel valued.

How to manage customer expectations and expected timescales

▲ Figure 8.4 How do you manage your customers' expectations?

Managing customer expectations and their expected timescales is all part of providing good customer care and service and crucial for building strong customer relationships and ensuring customer satisfaction. There are a number of strategies that contribute to this.

Communication with customers

A business and its employees should always communicate clearly and honestly with customers. This helps customers trust the business and the information they are being given, as well as setting boundaries and realistic expectations from the outset. This is especially important when dealing with a complaint or mistake. Effective communication and proactive management are essential for achieving customer satisfaction, both in the short and long term.

Monitor competitors

It is also beneficial for businesses to monitor what other businesses are doing, as customer expectations will be influenced by what they have experienced elsewhere and what they see other companies doing.

Service level agreements

A **service level agreement (SLA)** should be clearly advertised via the company website, **FAQ** pages, emails or messages on the business' telephone number. SLAs may detail response times to queries, delivery timescales and refund processes. Before setting SLAs, businesses must research how long on average they take to complete each task and how this compares to other businesses in their sector/area. It is important

to add in some contingency time when deciding on delivery timescales, as it is better to overestimate how long a task will take and to complete it more quickly, thereby exceeding customers' expectations. SLAs must be realistic and achievable because customers will measure the performance of the business against them, so if they are missed it can create a negative perception of the business.

Ask for feedback and continuously find ways to improve. This again helps make the customer feel valued, build up trust and create a positive image for the business.

▲ Figure 8.5 Frequently asked questions (FAQs) can be helpful for customers

Key terms

Service level agreement (SLA): a contract between a business and a customer that states the service to be provided, the level of performance to be expected, how performance will be measured and approved, and what happens if performance levels are not met

FAQs: frequently asked questions may be found on a company website or at the bottom of a page of instructions relating to a product or service; their location may depend on the business and not all businesses have them

Benefits of customer care to the individual and business

Good customer care not only benefits the customer. It can also help those employees who work and interact directly with the customers. Staff who receive positive feedback can develop increased motivation to provide higher standards of customer care, which in turn benefits the customers that they interact with and the business.

There are many benefits of customer care to the business itself. Having high standards of customer care increases customer loyalty and confidence. When a business has customer satisfaction as a goal and it engages with its customers emotionally, it increases the likelihood of the customer committing to buying its products or services. This means that it is more likely for the customer to return to the business and for the business to retain customers.

Customer care strategies create the opportunity to re-engage with customers and promote new or different products or services. These strategies may also inform market research into new products or services that will help the business diversify (see Chapter 5, page 89 for more about diversification).

Having high standards of customer care will also build a strong culture and reputation for the business. Reputation can grow through word-of-mouth recommendations, online customer reviews and recommendations, and through posts on social media.

All these factors will help the business increase its sales and revenue.

Case study

The UK Customer Experience Awards (UKCXA™) are held annually to celebrate the efforts of UK customer experience professionals. They provide industry recognition for hard work and noteworthy results. Visit their website to find out more and then answer the questions.
- How many award categories are there?
- What are the advertised benefits for businesses supporting the awards?
- Who judges the awards?

Current legal requirements when interacting with different types of customers and customer relationships

Legislation is a set of laws issued by the government to protect businesses, employees and consumers. The government uses legislation to regulate the behaviour of businesses. Businesses must operate within these laws to ensure the fair and safe treatment of any party they have dealings with. In the workplace, there are also policies which protect businesses, employees and consumers but are not a legal requirement. Both legislation and policies have clear guidelines for the rights and expectations of anyone involved with a company.

Consumer Protection Act 1987

This Act gives a customer the right to claim compensation if a defective product causes death, damage or injury. It also contains a strict liability test for defective products. This means that where a product is defective, then in most cases, the producer of that product is automatically liable for any harm caused by the defect. However, certain types of damage are explicitly excluded under the terms of the Act:
- loss or damage to the product itself
- damage to business products not ordinarily intended for private use
- damage to property with a value below £275.

Claims cannot be made more than three years from the date the customer became aware of the damage, or if it has been more than ten years after the date the product was last put into circulation.

Consumer Rights Act 2015

This Act protects consumers' rights and remedies in relation to contracts for goods, digital content and services. The rights of consumers are outlined below.

Goods contracts
- Goods must be of satisfactory quality, fit for a particular purpose and as described.
- Consumers have the right to reject faulty goods within a reasonable time.
- If the rejection period has passed, consumers can request repair or replacement.
- If repair or replacement is not possible, consumers can ask for a price reduction or a refund.
- There are specific rules for delivery, passing of risk and guarantees.

Digital content contracts
- Digital content (such as software, apps and games) must be of satisfactory quality, fit for a particular purpose and as described.
- Consumers have the right to repair or replacement if digital content does not meet these standards.
- Compensation is available for damage to devices caused by faulty digital content.

Services contracts

▶ Services must be carried out with reasonable care and skill.

▶ If services are not performed correctly, consumers can request repeat performance, a price reduction or a refund.

Case study

In 2021, a cat food manufacturer voluntarily recalled several of its products due to a possible link to an outbreak of a potentially fatal condition in domestic cats.

This precautionary measure was taken after the Royal Veterinary College (RVC) reported a sudden increase in cases of severe feline pancytopenia. An investigation into what caused this increase of cat illness was carried out.
▶ Who carried out the investigation?
▶ What products were included in the voluntarily recall?
▶ What were the consumers' rights if they were affected by the recall?

Principles of customer service and how it can be maintained

The principles of customer service are to:
▶ establish customer needs/expectations
▶ promote yourself, your company and your company's goods and services
▶ fulfil customer needs and expectations
▶ handle complaints from customers in a positive manner.

Typical procedures used to deal with customer queries, disputes and complaints

As an employee, you may need to respond to customer queries, disputes and complaints. However, you should only do so within the limitations and responsibilities of your role and in accordance with your organisation's policies. Businesses will have their own procedures for how to respond in these circumstances, and these are likely to include:
▶ responding to customers – SLAs methods and language used
▶ requirements and processes for issuing replacements or reservicing
▶ escalation to relevant individuals and departments within organisations to review the effectiveness of processes and procedures; this could also include escalating to a supervisor, manager or other department if the query or complaint is beyond the scope or responsibility of an employee's job role.

Consequences of not following procedures

If a business does not follow procedures when dealing with customer queries and complaints, the potential consequences include:
▶ reduced customer confidence in both the product and the retailer/manufacturer
▶ negative customer reviews on social media
▶ reputational damage, especially if errors are repeated.

If staff fail to follow procedures, it may mean that the process for dealing with queries and complaints is ineffective or not working, and the business should look at this again.

Processes used to promote customer relations and to establish and monitor customer satisfaction

Customer feedback

Customer feedback can be a very useful mechanism for promoting good customer relations, as well as obtaining information or data on how a business can improve. If a business responds positively to feedback and acts on it, customers will feel valued and more inclined to trust the business.

To improve as a result of customer feedback, a business must:

▶ collect customer feedback regularly and listen to customers' wants and needs
▶ turn customer feedback into action and make better, customer-centric decisions
▶ improve its products or services based on customer feedback and measure the impact of changes
▶ communicate with customers to let them know their feedback is valued and how it has been used
▶ create a customer feedback loop, where customer opinion is sought and used to implement continuous changes and improvements.

Customer satisfaction surveys

▲ Figure 8.6 Customer satisfaction survey

Customer satisfaction surveys are a form of customer feedback and are usually given out at the end of a sales process or after the service has been provided. They offer an opportunity to ask a set of questions that are not asked during the sales process. They also offer a comparable data set across all customers that complete it, because all customers will be asked to respond to the same questions, so responses can be compared or combined to give a better understanding of how the business is performing.

For a business to make the best use of customer satisfaction surveys, it must ensure that the questions being asked are precise, are **open-ended**, are not leading and avoid assumptions. Questions should be constructed so that the customer can respond with enough useful qualitative data for the business to analyse and base any improvements on.

The structure of the survey is also important. To increase the customer response rate, surveys should be short in terms of the total number of questions and ask one question at a time.

If a **qualitative data** scale is used for responses, such as that shown in Figure 8.7, it needs to be used consistently, with each end of the scale being the same for each question. For example, it is confusing and can skew results if in one question a strongly agree is on the right and in another it is on the left.

The scale can also be used to obtain **quantitative data** by using numbers for rating such as 1–5 or 1–10, as shown in Figure 8.8. In this scale, 1 indicates a strongly negative response and 5 indicates a strongly positive response.

I found the product registration process easy to complete.				
Strongly disagree	Disagree	Neither agree nor disagree	Agree	Strongly agree

▲ Figure 8.7 Example of a qualitative scale

Please rate your overall satisfaction:				
Highly dissatisfied				Highly satisfied
1	2	3	4	5

▲ Figure 8.8 Example of a quantitative scale

Key terms

Open-ended questions: questions requiring a detailed answer based on the respondent's knowledge, feelings and experience (qualitative data); they cannot be answered with a simple 'yes' or 'no' or with a specific piece of information (compare closed questions which are popular in questionnaires because they give a limited amount of options to choose from and collect quantitative data, which is easier to analyse)

Qualitative data: non-numerical data, such as words, images or observations; it is generally used to gain an understanding of human behaviour, attitudes and beliefs

Quantitative data: information with a numerical value that can be quantified by being counted or measured, for example length in centimetres or weight in kilograms; quantitative data tends to be structured and is suitable for statistical analysis

Customer follow-up procedures

A customer follow-up procedure is the communication provided to potential customers with the aim of persuading them to buy a product or service, as well as current customers with the aim of retaining them on a long-term basis. For example, if a dog-grooming business has a website and someone provides their email address in order to be kept up to date regarding services, having a customer follow-up system in place allows the dog groomer to contact them to see if they would be interested in making an appointment.

Businesses can also follow up with customers via telephone calls, text messages, printed newsletters, social media messages or responding to comments posted on social media. The type of business and its targeted customer demographic will influence the methods used for follow-up communications.

Customer visits

While this is perhaps less likely to be relevant to the land-based sector, it is worth considering whether visiting customers might be a good way to gather data and feedback from them. For instance, a company providing landscape gardening services could find it helpful to visit customers at their home or business to check the outcome of their work and their satisfaction with it.

8.2 Roles of different stakeholders

Definitions/roles, expectations and interrelationships of stakeholders (internal and external)

Within the context of a business or company, the definition of a stakeholder is a person, group or organisation with an interest or concern in the business' success.

The most common types of stakeholder are described below.

Owner

A business owner is the legal proprietor of the business and can be an individual or a group. They own the assets and profits, as well as being responsible for any debts. They have ultimate control over the business and decide on organisational roles and responsibilities.

Employee

An employee is a person employed for wages or a salary, especially at a non-executive level. They undertake roles and responsibilities specified by the owner(s) of the business.

Customer

A customer is a person or another business who buys goods or services from the business.

Supplier

A supplier is a person or another business that provides goods or equipment to the business.

Contractor

A contractor is a person or business that signs a contract to provide materials or labour in order to perform a service or a job.

Investors

Investors are people or organisations that put money into a business with the expectation of achieving a profit.

Creditors

Creditors are individuals or institutions that extend credit to another party to borrow money, usually by a loan agreement or contract. They are usually classified as personal or real. Personal creditors include friends or family, or a business that provides immediate supplies or services to a company or individual but allows for a delay in payment. Real creditors are banks or finance companies that have legal contracts and loan agreements with the borrower that permit the lender to claim any of the debtor's real assets or collateral if the loan is unpaid.

Media

This includes print media (national and local newspapers and magazines), broadcast media (TV and radio) and internet media (online publications, blogs and social media). The media may, for example, be interested in the public management of locally and nationally significant areas of forest. Journalists may investigate organisational practices and report on deals and decisions that affect the public. The media is also a way that the public or customers make their views known, for instance on planning applications for change of land use.

Communities

Businesses have a social impact and their activities may affect those living in the area where they are based. Communities have an interest in a business doing well because they want employment opportunities in their local area and good transport links etc. However, they

---

Key term

Creditors: individuals or institutions such as banks and finance companies that extend credit to a business or organisation to borrow money, usually in the form of a loan or contract, which must be paid back

also want a safe environment to live in, so businesses must ensure they take steps to minimise any negative impact on their local communities.

Trade unions

Trade unions are organisations that represent the collective interests of employees. They often focus on specific industries or professions, bringing together individuals who share common interests. Their key functions include negotiating pay scales and employment conditions with employers, offering legal support for issues such as discrimination and unfair dismissal, providing training and education opportunities, and working towards creating safe and healthy work environments.

Improve your English

Research the trade unions that operate in your occupational specialism and find examples of what they have achieved for the industry. This could include working conditions, pay or contract conditions.

Government departments and agencies

In the UK, there are over 400 government agencies and other public bodies, which are clearly designated units of central government departments; while administratively distinct, they legally remain part of those departments. They are specialised and technical, delivering the executive functions of policy and resources frameworks set by government departments. Their role might include:

- delivery of a service fundamental to the policy of their department
- carrying out statutory and/or regulatory functions on behalf of ministers
- delivery of a service to other parts of central government using specialist skills
- delivery of specialised functions separate to the core role of the sponsor department.

Table 8.1 shows some examples of government departments and agencies within the land-based sector.

▼ Table 8.1 Examples of government departments, non-ministerial departments and agencies involved with the land-based sector

Name	Industry	Role
Health and Safety Executive (HSE)	All	The HSE is the UK's national regulator for workplace health and safety. It provides guidance and support to employers and employees in how to comply with relevant legislation.
Department of Environment, Food and Rural Affairs (Defra)	All	Defra is a government department responsible for protecting the environment, with a focus on the green economy and supporting rural communities and many land-based industries such as fishing and agriculture.
Agriculture and Horticulture Development Board (AHDB)	Agriculture Horticulture	The AHDB is a public body that supports farmers, growers and other parts of the agricultural and horticultural supply chain with marketing and productivity. It is funded by a statutory levy from these stakeholders. The AHDB also conducts research and provides useful data about the market, which individuals and small businesses often could not afford to do themselves.
Forestry Commission	Forestry	The Forestry Commission is a non-ministerial government department responsible for protecting, expanding and promoting the sustainable management of woodlands. Forestry England is an executive non-ministerial department, partly sponsored by the Forestry Commission, which invests in managing forests for the benefit of wildlife and for the public's use and enjoyment. Forest Research is an organisation that supports tree-related research, providing scientific services and evidence to support sustainable forestry.

Name	Industry	Role
Environment Agency (EA)	All	In England, the EA is responsible for: regulating major industry and waste; treatment of contaminated land; water quality and resources; fisheries; inland river, estuary and harbour navigations; and conservation and ecology. In addition, the EA manages the risk of flooding from main rivers, reservoirs, estuaries and the sea. *Source: Environment Agency*
Animal and Plant Health Agency (APHA)	Agriculture Horticulture Animal care and management Forestry Arboriculture Floristry	The APHA is an executive agency of Defra, and also works on behalf of the Scottish Government and Welsh Government. The agency is responsible for animal, plant and bee health. *Source: Animal and Plant Health Agency*
Veterinary Medicines Directorate (VMD)	Agriculture Animal care and management	The VMD is an executive agency of Defra that protects public health and helps the industry meet high standards of animal welfare, by assuring the safety, quality and efficacy of veterinary medicines. The VMD also helps the Food Standards Agency to protect and improve the safety of food people eat. *Source: Veterinary Medicines Directorate*

Trade associations

Trade associations are groups of businesses within an industry or sector working together towards common goals. They are not-for-profit organisations which usually raise money through membership fees or subscriptions.

They can offer a range of services to their members, including advice, training and industry updates.

▼ Table 8.2 Examples of trade associations in the land-based sector

Name	Industry
British Florist Association	Floristry
Agricultural Engineers Association (AEA)	Land-based engineering
British Association for Shooting and Conservation (BASC)	Countryside management Agriculture
Agriculture and Horticulture Development Board (ADHB)	Agriculture Horticulture
CropLife UK	Agriculture
British and Irish Association of Zoos and Aquariums (BIAZA)	Animal care and management
Pet Industry Federation (PIF)	Animal care and management
Forestry Contracting Association (FCA)	Forestry
Arboricultural Association	Arboriculture
British Agriculture and Garden Machinery Association (BAGMA)	Land-based engineering
British Association of Landscape Industries (BALI)	Horticulture
Countryside Management Association (CMA)	Countryside management
Chartered Institute of Ecology and Environmental Management (CIEMM)	Countryside management

Impact of different stakeholders on the business

All stakeholders will have an impact on a business, but some will have more influence than others, giving them more power and control over the business' activities. Table 8.3 outlines the potential impact each stakeholder could have on a business.

▼ Table 8.3 Role and impact of stakeholders

Stakeholder	Role and impact
Owners	Owners have the most impact and control over a business. This is because they make decisions about the activities of the business and are financially responsible for it, so must provide or source funding.
Employees	Employees may have a limited amount of influence on business decisions, depending on their role. Some roles will have more authority and decision-making ability than others. However, all employees can affect the business directly, for example by refusing to work or not working as well as they should.
Customers	Customers buy products and services and give feedback to businesses on how to improve them. They can influence how successful a business is by recommending it to others or by warning them against it. They can also drive change through their purchasing decisions and patterns.
Suppliers	Suppliers can have a significant impact on a business if there are changes in the quality of the materials they provide or the reliability of their deliveries. Any problems with suppliers and the supply chain is a risk to the business.
Contractors	Contractors supply services on a contract basis, completing work that cannot be resourced by internal staff. This can represent a risk to the business if there are issues with the delivery of the contract, in terms of completion times or quality of work.
Investors	Investors can be key influencers in a business, as they are financially supporting the business with the expectation of receiving profits. They can drive forward change in the business' activities, depending on their investment contract.
Creditors	Creditors can also be key influencers, as they are financially supporting the business. They may also drive change in the business' activities, depending on their investment contract.
Media	The media are key influencers, as they can advertise the business but also report on the activities the business is carrying out. This can be either positive or negative coverage and can drive change in customer behaviour and the business' reputation.
Communities	Communities are affected by the social impact of the business. If the impact on the local community is negative, then people may protest or object through their local council. If it is positive, they can support the business by buying products and services.
Trade unions	Trade unions are key influencers and support the business/sector. They can improve the working conditions for employees and help them obtain fair pay. They can also try to influence customers' opinions.
Government agencies	Governments are key influencers and drivers of change. They can pass new laws, change tax rates and adjust levels of government spending in ways that affect the business and its operations.
Associations	Associations represent and support the business and sector. They can offer training, information and support services to their members to help with their businesses.

Assessment practice

1   State **three** reasons why a customer's first impression of you is important.   (3 marks)

2   What is the difference between customer care and customer service?   (6 marks)

3   What methods could a business adopt to have excellent customer care?   (4 marks)

4   What are the benefits of excellent customer service?   (6 marks)

5   Why is it important to manage a customer's expectations?   (3 marks)

6   What is the purpose of the Consumer Protection Act 1987?   (2 marks)

7   The Consumer Rights Act 2015 is a UK law that protects consumers' rights and remedies in relation to contracts for goods, digital content and services.
    What are the rights of consumers in the legislation?   (6 marks)

8   What are the typical procedures for dealing with customer complaints and what are the possible consequences of not following them?   (6 marks)

9   What is the purpose of customer follow-up procedures?   (1 mark)

10 For a named example of a business, identify the different stakeholders and describe their role.   (6 marks)

Further reading

You may find some of the following references helpful for keeping up to date with business relationship management, industry updates and UK legislation:

▶ Articles in the *Shopping, food & drink* news section on the Which? website

▶ Consumer Protection Act 1987

▶ Health and Safety Services on the Peninsula UK website

▶ Department for Environment, Food and Rural Affairs (Defra), part of the UK government

▶ The Forestry Commission's page on the UK Government website

▶ The Environment Agency's page on the UK Government website

▶ The Animal and Plant Health Agency's page on the UK Government website

▶ The Veterinary Medicines Directorate's page on the UK Government website

▶ British Florist Association

▶ Agricultural Engineers Association (AEA)

▶ British Association for Shooting and Conservation (BASC)

▶ CropLife UK (formerly Crop Protection Association)

▶ British and Irish Association of Zoos and Aquariums (BIAZA)

▶ Pet Industry Federation (PIF)

▶ Forestry Contracting Association (FCA)

▶ Arboricultural Association

▶ British Agricultural and Garden Machinery Association (BAGMA)

▶ British Association of Landscape Industries (BALI)

▶ Morris, S. (2021) 'Cat food recalled over potential link to serious illness', *Which?*, 22 June.

9 Finance

Introduction

This chapter introduces financial principles, definitions and terminology for businesses.

The chapter explains what businesses need to consider in order to function efficiently, as well as how profit and loss are calculated. It also discusses the types of cost involved in running a business and ways to maximise revenue.

The chapter explores the different types of taxation that a business must be aware of and explains the concept of Making Tax Digital (MTD).

The chapter also introduces financial forecasting and the different methods available and outlines the types of income and finance a business can have.

Learning outcomes

By the end of this chapter, you will understand:
- definitions of profit and loss, non-profit and cashflow and the significance of each to business
- key components of a profit and loss statement, including revenue, sales, inputs/costs of goods sold, expenses, returns, discounts and refunds, and taxation
- how to use the components of a profit and loss statement to calculate profit (including net, gross and gross profit margin) and loss
- types of cost incurred by a business (product, ancillary product, overheads, labour) and their classifications (direct, indirect, fixed, variable)

- measures to maximise revenue, including adjustments to cost, and implications to profitability, reputation and quality
- types of taxation (payroll, business, self-assessment, PAYE, VAT), sector rates of VAT (standard, reduced and zero) and tax related to food and drink, animals, animal feed, plants and seeds
- Making Tax Digital (MTD)
- how costs and revenue are forecast
- types of finance (loans, grants/bursaries, income) and the differences between them
- income, including direct sales, contracts and services.

9.1 The principles of finance

Definition of profit and loss, non-profit and cashflow and the significance of each to business

Profit

Gross profit is the money a business makes after deductions for the costs of producing and selling a product or costs associated with its services. Gross profit is also known as sales profit or gross income.

Net profit is the actual profit of a business. It is the balance after the amount spent in operating the business has been taken from the amount earned. These operational costs can include equipment and machinery, buying or hiring tools, mileage/fuel, insurance, rent, rates, utilities, marketing and taxes.

Loss

Loss refers to a decrease in a business' money due to unsuccessful investment, operational inefficiencies, legal obligations or unfavourable market conditions. It can also result from theft, damage to equipment, lawsuits or unexpected expenses. Losses affect a business' overall financial health and could impact its ability to maintain operations or achieve financial objectives.

Industry tip

Land-based businesses can experience losses from factors outside their control, for example changes in weather or climate, natural disasters (flood, fire, drought), pest infestation or diseases. It is important therefore for businesses to be able to adapt, diversify, seek alternative products/markets and make efficiencies, or to have reserves in the bank to cover any loss.

Non-profit

A non-profit business or organisation (often referred to as 'not-for-profit') does not aim to make profits for its owners, and its income is not more than its expenses and operational costs, i.e. its net profit is £0.00. If a non-profit has money after paying all costs, this money must not be taken by any individual but instead must be reinvested in the business or organisation.

Non-profit businesses and organisations include charities, political organisations, schools and social clubs.

Cashflow

Cashflow refers to the movement of money into and out of a business. It tracks the money coming in (sales revenue) and money going out (expenses).

Positive cashflow is when a business is bringing in more money than it is spending, is paying all its expenses and has enough money left over to invest into the business or save for the future.

Negative cashflow is when a business spends more money than it makes, is unable to pay bills, or risks running out of money.

It is important for a business to monitor and manage its cashflow. This can be achieved by:
- creating a budget which plans and allocates resources and outlines expected income and expenses
- tracking money coming in and money going out
- knowing when money needs to be spent and when it needs to be coming in
- preparing for unexpected costs
- setting clear terms and conditions with customers and suppliers for payment.

Key components of a profit and loss statement

The key components of a profit and loss statement (Figure 9.1) are as follows:
- revenue – all the income from the day-to-day operations of the business; also known as 'top-line income'
- sales – the money received by the business from selling goods or services
- inputs/cost of goods sold (COGS) – the direct costs involved in selling the goods of a business
- expenses – includes costs such as rental of equipment, cost of goods sold (COGS), freight/shipping, payroll, advertising and marketing expenses, utilities (water, electricity, gas), insurance, business rates and property rental or mortgage
- returns, discounts, refunds and losses
- taxation – income tax and National Insurance (NI) deductions, VAT (value added tax) (only applies if the business is VAT registered with HMRC (His Majesty's Revenue and Customs)).

Parker Landscaping Services

Statement of profit or loss for year ended 31 December 2024

	£	£
Revenue		55 000
		55 000
Less expenses		
Insurance	1 500	
Salaries	26 750	
Advertising	850	
Rent	8 550	
Heating and lighting	1 767	
Sundry expenses	430	39 847
Profit for the year		15 153

▲ Figure 9.1 A profit and loss statement

How profit (including net and gross) and loss are calculated

Profits are calculated by subtracting all outgoing costs of the business from the income for a given time.

An example of how profits would be calculated for a dog-grooming business is shown below (based on income and costs for one dog).

Income from customer for grooming a dog	Item	Cost £
£45.00	Shampoo and conditioner	3.50
	Tools (comb and scissors)	5.00
Gross profit		**36.50**
	Utilities	2.75
	Rent for business premises	7.00
	Staff wages	15.00
	Insurance	1.50
Net profit		**£10.25**

If the groomer had to refund the dog's owner for the price of the grooming as they were unhappy with the work carried out, this would be a loss to the business, as shown as below:

Income from customer for grooming a dog	Item	Cost £
£45.00	Shampoo and conditioner	3.50
	Tools (comb and scissors)	5.00
Gross profit		**36.50**
	Utilities	2.75
	Rent for business premises	7.00
	Staff wages	15.00
	Insurance	1.50
Net profit		**£10.25**
Refund to customer		**−£45.00**
Balance		**−£34.75**

▲ Figure 9.2 Dog-grooming establishments need to consider income and costs

Types of cost incurred by a business and their classifications

Product costs

Product costs are the costs that are incurred to create a product that is intended for sale to customers. They include direct materials (DM), direct labour (DL) and manufacturing overhead (MOH).

For example, on an arable farm the product costs for growing a crop of barley would include the costs of seeds, fertiliser, pesticides, irrigation and labour. For a florist making a bouquet, the product costs would be the floral stems, floral scissors or shears, wrapping, floral tape and labour.

Ancillary product costs

Ancillary products are goods or services that differ from or enhance the main product lines or services of a business. They are a further source of revenue for a business, alongside its main revenue-generating products or services.

Examples of ancillary products include a veterinary practice that starts to sell pet food, or an arboriculture company that starts to make and sell wood carvings.

Overheads

Overheads are costs related to the day-to-day running of the business. Unlike operating expenses or product costs, they cannot be linked to a specific cost unit or activity. Instead, overheads support the overall activities of the business. Overheads must be paid on an ongoing basis, even if the business is not selling its products or services. Overhead expenses can include:

- manufacturing
- administration
- marketing
- distribution
- research and development
- equipment
- rent of premises.

For example, an agricultural machinery servicing business pays rent for a workshop with additional space for a customer waiting room and office. Rent is one of the overhead costs of the business.

Labour costs

Labour costs are one of the biggest costs for a business and include employee wages and salaries, taxes, pensions, employee benefits and annual leave allowances.

Classifications of costs

- **Direct costs** are those related to producing a product or delivering a service and include materials, labour and distribution. They can be linked directly to a product or service.
- **Indirect costs** cannot be linked directly to a specific product or service. For example, at a garden centre this would include the utility bills (gas, water and electricity), as they are used by all parts of the business including the retail shop and customer toilets, and not just for growing plants for sale.
- **Fixed costs** do not change, even though the production of the business changes over the short term. For example, a farmer leases a tractor from a local distributor for 10 weeks at £770 per week, totalling £7700. The farm will have to pay this cost, no matter how often it uses the tractor or how much the farm produces.
- **Variable costs** fluctuate with production levels, i.e. they depend on the number of products the business produces. These costs increase as the production volume increases. Businesses can decide not to carry out an activity or production to avoid these costs, for example increases to fuel prices. An example of a variable cost is packaging. If a business packages its items before shipping, the more products it produces, the more the packaging costs increase. If the number of products decreases, packaging costs also decrease.

Measures to maximise revenue

Adjustments to cost

To maximise **profit margins** and revenue, a business can reduce or remove its production or service costs. For example, a dog groomer could try to find alternative products or suppliers to reduce the costs of shampoos and conditioners used in the grooming process. A tomato producer could look at the amount of fertiliser it is applying, and either reduce the amounts used or remove their use completely from production.

Implications to profitability, reputation and quality

When a business takes measures to maximise revenue, it must consider the implications these changes will have on profitability, reputation and quality. For instance, if a business decides to use a cheaper product or raw material but must use more of it to achieve the same quality/service level as before, then it needs to consider whether this decision has increased the profitability of the service or product.

If the dog groomer in the example above found an alternative shampoo that was £2.50 per 500 ml bottle instead of £3.50, but they had to use 50 ml per dog instead of 25 ml, then the cheaper shampoo would make their service *less* profitable, even though the initial cost of the product unit was cheaper.

> ### Improve your maths
>
> For the example above, work out the shampoo cost per dog for Shampoo A priced at £3.50 and Shampoo B priced at £2.50.

If a business tries to increase revenue by reducing costs, this can have a negative impact on the quality of its service or product, and there may be fewer clients willing to purchase the service or customers to purchase products. This would then lead to a decrease in business revenue.

The reputation of the business must also be considered when looking at reducing costs by sourcing cheaper raw materials or changing production processes. If the quality of the product or service is impacted, this may result in negative customer feedback and complaints.

Types of taxation

Payroll

Payroll taxation is deducted by the business from employees' wages and is based on what they earn each year. Employees whose tax is deducted from their pay by their employer pay tax via PAYE (pay as you earn); this is explained below.

Business

Corporation tax is levied on profits from conducting business and applies to:

▶ a limited company
▶ any foreign company with a UK branch or office
▶ a club, co-operative or other unincorporated association, for example a community group or sports club.

Taxable profits for corporation tax include the money a business or association makes from:

▶ doing business (i.e. trading profits)
▶ investments
▶ selling assets for more than they cost (known as 'chargeable gains').

If a business is based in the UK, it pays corporation tax on all its profits from the UK and abroad.

If it is not based in the UK but has an office or branch in the UK, it only pays corporation tax on profits generated from its UK activities.

Self-assessment

If someone is self-employed or earns money from **capital gains** or **dividends**, they need to register with HMRC to complete a self-assessment tax return. This is an online or paper form that has to be submitted to HMRC every year by those who owe tax and National Insurance on profits they have received.

> ### Key terms
>
> *Profit margin*: financial ratio that measures the percentage of profit earned by a company in relation to its sale revenue
>
> *Capital gains*: the increase in the value of a capital asset, for example a rental property or second home, when it is sold; put simply, a capital gain occurs when an asset is sold for more than what was originally paid for it
>
> *Dividends*: how companies distribute their earnings to shareholders; when a company pays a dividend, each share of stock of the company an individual owns entitles them to a set dividend payment (which can be in the form of cash, additional shares of stock or warrants to buy stock)

PAYE

PAYE (pay as you earn) is HMRC's system of collecting income tax and National Insurance from employees. It is deducted from the employee's monthly salary before they receive it into their bank account. It can also include student loan repayments.

Employers normally have to operate PAYE as part of their payroll.

PAYE is calculated based on an employee's salary and whether they are eligible for the personal allowance. The personal allowance is set by the government and refers to the amount an individual is able to earn tax-free each year; the rate of taxation and personal allowance can change from year to year.

For earnings above the personal allowance, employees will be taxed at either 20 per cent, 40 per cent or 45 per cent, depending on whether they are a basic rate, higher rate or additional rate tax payer. The rate of tax paid is determined by their income.

PAYE is also used to collect tax from those who receive pension income.

VAT

VAT is a tax that is added to most products and services sold by VAT-registered businesses. Businesses have to register for VAT with HMRC if their VAT taxable turnover is more than £85,000. Businesses can also choose whether to register if their turnover is less than £85,000.

Sector rates of VAT

There are three rates of VAT that can be added to products; the rate that is applied depends on the product or service and how it is used.

At the time of writing, the standard rate of VAT is 20 per cent* and most products and services have the standard rate applied to them.

The reduced rate of VAT is 5 per cent*. An example of a product that is charged at reduced VAT is home energy.

There are products and services that have a zero rate of VAT*. Examples of these products include:

▶ books and newspapers
▶ children's clothes and shoes
▶ most foods
▶ most goods exported from England, Wales and Scotland (Great Britain) to a country outside the UK
▶ most goods exported from Northern Ireland to a country outside the EU and the UK.

* These are the rates of VAT at the time of publication in 2024 and could change in the future.

Tax for food and drink, animals, animal feed, plants and seeds

Food and drink for human consumption is usually zero-rated, but there are some items that always have the standard rate of VAT applied. These include catering, alcoholic drinks, confectionery, crisps and savoury snacks, hot food, sports drinks, hot takeaways, ice cream, soft drinks and mineral water.

Restaurants must always charge VAT, whether the food is consumed on their premises or in a designated area such as a seating area in a shopping centre or airport. Restaurants and takeaway vendors must charge VAT on all hot takeaways and home deliveries. Cold takeaway food does not incur VAT, unless it is eaten in a designated area.

If animals, animal feeding products, plants and seeds meet certain HMRC requirements and VAT notices, they can qualify for the zero rate. If the items or products are packaged, such as pet food, they have the standard rate of VAT applied to them.

▲ Figure 9.3 Animal feed products may qualify for a zero rate of VAT

Making Tax Digital (MTD)

Making Tax Digital (MTD) is the UK government's plan to have a digitised tax system for VAT, income tax, self-assessment and corporation tax. The aim of MTD is to make tax returns simpler and more efficient, using software and digital accounting records. At the time of writing, the system is still due to be implemented. For up-to-date information on MTD, look it up on the UK Government website.

How costs and revenue are forecast

Forecasting is the process of predicting the costs and revenue of a business. It helps a business set goals

▲ Figure 9.4 Forecasting helps a business set goals and make plans and decisions about growth

and make plans and decisions about growth. It also helps to assess expenses and predict any profits or potential losses.

To forecast costs and revenue, a business' predicted financial performance over a specific time period is projected by analysing historical data, market trends and economic indicators. A number of methods are used:

▶ **Bottom-up**: this is a way of predicting future business performance by beginning with the lowest level of data from the business, which is broken down and a forecast for each item of data is made. This is then worked 'upwards' by adding all the different forecasted results to create an overall revenue forecast for the business.

▶ **Straight line**: this is used when a company's growth rate is constant. It gives a straightforward view of continued growth at the same rate and involves only basic maths and historical data.

▶ **Moving average**: this reflects the previous price movement of an asset. The data is used by analysts or investors to forecast the future direction of that asset price. It indicates the direction of a given trend after the price action of the underlying asset.

▶ **Simple linear regression**: this shows how one variable (the dependent variable) changes in response to changes in another variable (the independent variable).

▶ **Multiple linear regression**: this uses numerous predictors and gauges the influence of each on the dependent variable. It extends the simple linear regression model by incorporating multiple coefficients, one for each variable. This allows for a multi-dimensional analysis of data.

Types of finance and the differences between them

Loans

Loans are a type of finance (i.e. income) lent to individuals or businesses by banks and financiers. A loan will have an interest rate applied to it, which is dependent on a range of factors including the amount being lent, the term of the loan and the credit rating of the individual or business. A loan requires an application process to be completed to ensure the individual or business can afford it. There is a contractual agreement for a repayment schedule, which includes penalties and charges if the repayments are not made, or if the loan is paid back early.

Grants/bursaries

Grant schemes and bursaries are financial support systems offered by an individual, organisation or the government for a specific benefit. They usually do not require repayment. They have specific application requirements, criteria and processes, depending on who is giving the grant and its purpose.

Income

Direct sales

Direct sales are when the seller interacts directly with the customer without any intermediary. They are different from indirect sales, in which a producer relies on distributors, retailers or other third parties to sell their products or services, for example selling produce to a shop or supermarket chain that then sells on to the customer.

▲ Figure 9.5 Farm shops sell produce directly to customers

In the land-based sector, there are many examples of direct sales, including farm shops and markets where farms sell their produce directly to customers; dairies that offer milk deliveries direct to households rather than via a supermarket; and people who provide services directly to their customers, such as dog walkers, pet sitters and landscape gardeners.

Contracts

Contracts used in the land-based sector that provide income include:

▶ **full-time contracts**: permanent contracts that are usually based on a 35-hour week and include annual leave, pension and benefits schemes
▶ **part-time contracts**: contracts for employees who work less than 35-hour weeks

▶ **fixed-term contracts**: contracts offered for a specific period of time and often used for seasonal work or to complete a specific project
▶ **zero-hours contracts**: contracts that do not guarantee a minimum number of hours of work per week and are often used in industries where demand for labour fluctuates
▶ **freelance contracts**: contracts offered to self-employed individuals who provide services to a company on a project-by-project basis.

Services

This refers to income obtained from providing a service to, or carrying out a job for, a company or individual; for example an arborist felling a tree for a homeowner. Services are carried out under a contract or working agreement.

Assessment practice

1 Define the following financial terms:
   a gross profit
   b net profit
   c loss. (3 marks)
2 Explain what is meant by cashflow and how it can be managed. (6 marks)
3 Name **three** key components of a profit and loss statement. (3 marks)
4 Name **three** types of overhead expenses. (3 marks)
5 Explain the types of costs a business can incur. (6 marks)

6 When is corporation tax applicable to a business? (3 marks)
7 Describe the PAYE system. (6 marks)
8 State **three** products and services that have a zero rate of VAT. (3 marks)
9 Name **three** methods that could be used to forecast costs and revenue of a business. (3 marks)
10 Describe the types of contracts that a business can use. (6 marks)

Further reading

You may find some of the following pages on the UK Government website helpful for further information on business finance in the UK:
▶ Income Tax: introduction
▶ Self Assessment tax returns
▶ Corporation Tax
▶ VAT
▶ Making Tax Digital – Monitoring Businesses' Awareness of MTD
▶ PAYE Online for employers
▶ National Insurance: introduction.

10 Information and data

Introduction

Information and data are important assets that are potentially irreplaceable if lost or stolen. Therefore, it is important to know who has access to data and what they are using it for.

There are many good reasons for holding data, and the ability to analyse data can bring benefits to individuals, organisations, businesses and society. However, in our increasingly data-driven world, it can also be used for purposes for which the owner of the data has not given their permission. This may be accidental or deliberate. It is important therefore to understand the key requirements of current legislation and how individuals, organisations and businesses can minimise risks to the security of information and data.

Learning outcomes

By the end of this chapter, you will understand:
▶ types of information and data protected by legislation, including personal data, client data and intellectual property
▶ how businesses manage information and data and why these methods are used, including staff training, version control, access controls, indexing and cyber security
▶ the rights of individuals regarding their own information and data
▶ data storage requirements in relation to security

and protection and how they help to prevent common threats including cyberattacks, phishing, malware and trojans
▶ how to respond to security breaches
▶ the purpose of current legislation – Data Protection Act 2018 and the General Data Protection Regulation (GDPR) – and organisational procedures that are used to manage data and increase confidentiality
▶ data protection principles.

10.1 Key requirements of legislation relating to the security of information and data

Types of information and data protected by legislation

Information usually refers to data that is categorised or sorted into a format or has context that gives it meaning and makes it useful. Data conventionally was used to refer to raw numbers, facts, sounds, images, words etc., which on their own have no context or value. Despite the subtle difference, often the terms 'information' and 'data' are used interchangeably, with little distinction between them.

There are many types of information and data that people working in the land-based sector will encounter, either as part of their work or in their life outside work. Examples include sales records, pesticide application records, field survey information, breeding programme records, accident records, crop production records, wildlife survey information, machinery maintenance records, employee contracts and salary information.

> **Test yourself**
>
> Make a list of the types of data specific to your chosen industry that you are likely to use.

Some types of data are protected by legislation, and it is important that anyone working in the land-based sector is aware of when they may need to seek specialist advice or guidance. This protection exists to reduce the risk of individuals, organisations or businesses being harmed by impersonation, identity or financial theft, or discrimination as a result of unauthorised access to or use of data.

Personal data

Personal data is information that relates to an individual or their activities, for example their medical history or banking details. For something to be considered personal data, also referred to as an **identifier**, the law requires that the individual must either be:

▶ identified or identifiable directly from the information (for example it contains their full name and address), or

> **Key term**
>
> **Identifier**: a single piece of personal data that can be used to identify an individual

▶ indirectly identified or distinguished from other individuals or members of a group, from the information in combination with other information (for example a description of someone's physical appearance and their place of work).

Examples of identifiers include:
▶ full name
▶ address
▶ passport number
▶ driving licence number
▶ National Insurance number
▶ job title.

> **Test yourself**
>
> What other possible identifiers can you add to the list above?

Unfortunately, there is not a definitive list of identifiers, as they can include factors specific to the physical (external), physiological (internal), genetic, mental, economic, cultural or social identity of an individual. In addition, new identifiers are continually emerging as technology develops. There are also online identifiers which can be personal data if they relate to an individual person or their activities. Examples of these include:
▶ internet protocol (IP) address
▶ email address
▶ social media username.

Special categories of personal data

The General Data Protection Regulation (GDPR) includes additional special categories of personal data (more detailed information on GDPR rights and responsibilities is provided later in this chapter). These include information about an individual's:
▶ race
▶ ethnic background
▶ political opinions
▶ religious or philosophical beliefs
▶ trade union membership
▶ genetics
▶ biometrics (when used for identification)
▶ health

▶ sex life
▶ sexual orientation.

These special categories of personal data, as well as information about criminal convictions and offences, are considered especially sensitive and can only be processed in limited circumstances. This is partly to prevent them being used to discriminate against an individual. Individuals, both at work and outside work, are legally protected from discrimination by the Equality Act 2010 (see Chapter 6, page 96).

Industry tip

Employers in the land-based sector must be aware that they should not ask certain questions or request certain information during the recruitment process for new staff, for example questions such as 'Are you married?' or 'What religion are you?'. This is because this information is not normally required to decide if someone is appropriately qualified and suitable for the job. It can also suggest that the employer may use this information to discriminate against certain job applicants, depending on the answer they give.

Test yourself

When recruiting for new visitor experience staff, why might a zoo or an aquarium ask applicants to complete an application form rather than provide a curriculum vitae (CV)?

Information about organisations and businesses is not normally considered to be personal data. The exception is where someone is individually identifiable, such as when someone is self-employed as a sole trader and their name forms part of the business name, for example Sam Aldridge's Pet Supplies. However, even if information is not considered to be personal data, it may still be considered commercially sensitive and so may be stored and processed securely.

Client data

This refers to all the information collected, stored and used by organisations and businesses about their clients and customers. For example, a new customer enters contact and delivery details, as well as payment information, when they make an online purchase through a business' website. Client data can also include details about their appearance or information about the business' ongoing interactions with the client.

Client data may also include:
▶ behavioural data, such as how clients interact with the business (for example a customer emails every November to order a turkey for Christmas)
▶ communication data, such as clients' preferred communication methods and a record of previous interactions with each client (for example a note stating that one client always complains if their animal feed deliveries are made in the afternoon)
▶ demographic data relating to clients' income level or educational level and whether they are professional members of a specific trade association
▶ geographic data, such as postcode mapping showing where clients are located (for example customers who purchase new combine harvesters tend to be based in the East of England)
▶ transactional data, such as clients' requests for information, subscriptions, payments and purchases (for example an individual who always pays their membership subscription one month late).

Collecting client data is helpful, as it allows the business to track client trends over time and understand their preferences. These, in turn, allow the business to improve client support, provide tailored offers and support targeted marketing campaigns to promote other products or services.

Industry tip

While protection of client data is important for the clients themselves, businesses usually want to keep this data secure because of its commercial value to competitors. For example, a farm equipment machinery supplier may not want competitors to know when their clients' lease agreements run out. Therefore, the business may restrict who has access to this information.

It is possible for small organisations and businesses to store and manage client data using a basic spreadsheet or database. However, as an organisation or business grows, these basic software tools become too limiting, so client data is usually managed using customer relationship management (CRM) software. Many CRM systems are designed to be GDPR compliant and capable of storing, organising and analysing large quantities of client data. For example, a pet food supplier may want to know which customers have spent the most amount of money on their products and where these customers are based. In addition, the more sophisticated CRM systems either have built-in (or can integrate with) specialist finance and accounting platforms or inventory and stock management systems.

Intellectual property

Intellectual property refers to all created information, for example a new online seed catalogue, the logo of a farm shop, the design of an irrigation scheme, a new livestock vaccine or the design for a client's new garden. It has a broad scope but includes trade names or symbols, images and logos, commercial designs and inventions, as well as literary and artistic work. Intellectual property is often referred to as an intangible asset, because it is normally a non-physical asset. It can be owned by an individual, organisation or business, who has specific rights and protection associated with ownership.

> **Industry tip**
>
> The intellectual property of anything produced during employment is normally owned by the employer, not the employee who produced it. Therefore, it is important to check the terms of your employment contract, as you may not be able to take documents and photographs you have produced with you if you leave to work for yourself or another employer.

The Intellectual Property Office (IPO) is the UK government body responsible for intellectual property rights. Its role is to achieve a balance between protecting the creativity of innovators and the wider public interest. The specific legal protection offered to whoever created the information depends on the type of intellectual property.

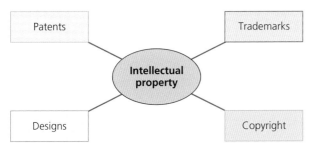

▲ Figure 10.1 Intellectual property refers to all created information

Patents

Patents are exclusive rights associated with inventions such as products or processes, for example agricultural seed-planting/drilling machinery, robotic mowers or precision grass-cutting equipment, dog-walking assistance tools and automatic watering devices ensuring animals or crops have constant access to clean water. Patents provide the owner with the legal right to prevent others from using the invention without the owner's permission for a specific period of time. A patent granted under the Patents Act 1977 (as amended) initially lasts for five years from the date the application was filed with the IPO, after which period it can be renewed annually up to a maximum of 20 years.

Trademarks

A registered trademark can cover words, logos, colours, sounds or a combination of these and usually has the symbol ® shown next to it. This indicates that the trademark is registered and makes others aware they cannot use it without the owner's permission. A trademark registration initially lasts 10 years, after which it must be renewed every 10 years with the IPO for the owner to keep the trademark protected.

Designs

A registered design can help protect the appearance of a product and covers physical shape, configuration, decoration, colour, pattern or a combination of these. Registering a design helps the owner to prove they created it, in case someone tries to use or copy it without their permission. A design registration initially lasts five years, after which it needs to be renewed every five years with the IPO up to a maximum of 25 years to keep the design protected.

Copyright

Copyright protection is different to other forms of intellectual property protection because the protection is applied automatically as soon as the intellectual property is created. Sometimes the owner may mark their property with their name, the year it was created and the copyright symbol ©. However, whether they choose to mark their property or not does not affect the copyright protection they automatically have.

Copyright protection applies to a wide range of property, including original literature (such as a tree survey report for a client), musical and artistic work, photography and illustrations (for example photographs showing stages of the building of an animal enclosure), sound and music recordings, film and television recordings (for example a video showing how to service a small engine) and the layout of published work (such as a catalogue of plants available from a nursery). However, the duration of the protection depends on the type of property, who created it and when it was created or published. For example, copyright of original written work usually lasts from the date the work was created until 70 years after the author's death. Once the copyright has expired, anyone can copy or use it.

In addition to visually marking work to clearly show ownership, copyright owners often hide features within their work which are not easy to spot, such as deliberate mistakes or fake information. For example, map makers often deliberately add fictional roads or details into their maps in an attempt to make it easier to spot copies of their work. There are also commercial organisations that offer copyright registration services. This provides verifiable evidence of the date the work was registered in the event of a suspicion of copyright theft.

Although it is possible for individuals and organisations to protect their intellectual property by registering it with the IPO, it is important to be aware that this may only offer protection in the UK and Isle of Man. There are different processes for registering and protecting intellectual property abroad. In the specific case of copyright, property might be protected under the Berne Convention for the Protection of Literary and Artistic Works (as amended) or other international agreements.

Test yourself

Imagine you have designed a new website to advertise your landscaping business. The website contains a gallery of photographs you have taken of previous work you have done for customers. What steps could you take to make it easier to prove the images are from your website if someone uses them without your permission?

Like most other types of property, intellectual property owners can sell or transfer their rights, or license others to use it. Where rights are permitted under a licence, this usually comes with conditions that the user must agree to comply with, such as what the user can use the property for, or how long they can use the property.

Case study

Land-based organisations frequently need to use intellectual property which might belong to someone else. For example, habitat or woodland managers might need to photocopy maps to show property boundaries, or to annotate when doing field survey work. Maps, including digital maps and data, produced by the Ordnance Survey are protected by Crown Copyright. Individuals, organisations and businesses need a licence to use its maps, and this may require a fee to be paid. The licence may be perpetual (i.e. there is no expiration date) or annual (i.e. it must be renewed every year from the date the licence starts). Often this fee is included within the cost of products bought through third parties, such as geographic information systems (GIS) or global positioning systems (GPS).
▶ What is the Ordnance Survey?
▶ Why might the Ordnance Survey prefer to license rather than sell its map data?

How businesses manage information and data and why these methods are used

The behaviours of organisations and businesses, including how they manage information and data, can be influenced by several factors. These can be categorised as either imperatives or incentives:
▶ Imperatives result from legislation or regulation and force organisations and businesses to act, for example a data processor's responsibilities under GDPR data principles (see page 147) or an employer's responsibilities under health and safety legislation.
▶ Incentives come from the benefits organisations gain from taking action. For example, changes to tax rules or availability of grants may allow a small business to expand the range of services it can offer.

There are usually undesirable consequences for an organisation or business for not managing information and data appropriately. For example, the consequences associated with a data breach which results in unauthorised access to confidential information could include financial penalties, reputational damage and loss of clients and customers. There are several tools and techniques that can be applied to minimise the risk of things going wrong.

Staff training

At some point, all employees will handle data and information as part of their role, so organisations usually provide staff with regular training. This helps support employees to understand the organisation's current policies and procedures and their individual responsibilities to ensure they protect personal data and business information. It is particularly important that staff training raises awareness of the ongoing risk to data security from **hacking** and other cybercriminal activity. The individuals who do this are referred to as hackers. Their intentions are not always malicious. For example, ethical hacking is undertaken by security experts to identify vulnerabilities and consequently strengthen the security of a computer system or network. However, malicious hacking disrupts the business activities of its victims and may result in significant harm.

Version control

Version control is used to ensure accuracy of information and to establish that employees are working with the most up-to-date information. For example, when updating a database or document, the new version is saved with a new file name and/or reference, which identifies when the information was updated. This helps to ensure that personal data is kept up to date and managers make informed decisions based on the latest information.

> ### Case study
>
> Jo is responsible for updating their employer's policies, including the data protection policy. It is good practice to review policies regularly to ensure they are current and fit for purpose, and Jo's employer expects every policy to be reviewed annually or sooner if something significant changes. Every time Jo needs to update or amend a policy, they save it as a new file and put the month and year at the end of the new filename. Jo also updates a table at the start of each policy which summarises the changes and when they were made. This helps anyone who needs to follow the policy to see what changes have been made without having to read the whole document.
> - How else could Jo maintain version control over their employer's policies?
> - What might be the consequences if Jo does not maintain effective version control?

> ### Key term
>
> **Hacking**: a collective term used to describe the use of computer networks to gain unauthorised access to or control over data

Access controls

Some information and data may be particularly confidential or sensitive in nature, for example the employee records held by an employer. Therefore, managers may restrict the number of people that need access to this type of data, to reduce the potential for data breaches. There are various ways this can be done, for example electronic documents can be password protected or stored in a secure drive or folder that only certain individuals can open.

Paper documents can be kept in a locked filing cabinet or storage room, to which only certain individuals have access. Records can also be anonymised by removing personal information, so that staff can access data they require to undertake their roles without compromising access to data they do not need to be able to view.

> ### Test yourself
>
> Think about the types of data that might be kept by a land-based employer. Make a list of those which they might not want to share with all employees.

Indexing

Managers need to be able to easily find information and data in a timely manner. Therefore, data is usually stored or catalogued in a way that allows it to be searched efficiently and effectively. This will help support managers to make the most informed decisions, work out the extent of any data breach quickly and respond to requests for information from a regulator or an individual making a subject access request for the information that an organisation or business holds about them. In addition, under the Freedom of Information Act 2000, public bodies in England and Wales must respond to freedom of information (FOI) requests from individuals or organisations to access information. Therefore, it is critical that organisations and businesses have quick access to information and data whenever they need it and that it is held securely.

Cyber security

There are numerous options available to protect data from illegal access such as hacking. Most electronic data users install and use reputable anti-virus software, which is regularly updated to detect and then delete suspicious code or software. Some also set up and use a **firewall**. This is a security device that monitors the data going to and from the device and, depending on the security rules set up by the device owner, either allows or blocks the data flow. Some users also undertake regular checks or audits to proactively identify any potential security vulnerabilities, so they can then take action to reduce cyber-security risks.

Key term

Firewall: a specialist security feature that selectively manages the communication of data into, within or out of a network; it is intended to block data that is considered potentially dangerous or is not trusted

Rights of individuals regarding their own information and data

In addition to the responsibilities set out in the data protection principles, the GDPR also provides individuals with rights regarding how organisations and businesses process their personal data (Table 10.1).

The GDPR sets out timescales and conditions associated with the exercise of these rights by an individual. Sometimes an organisation or business is permitted to request a reasonable administrative fee to cover the costs of dealing with a request, or may refuse a request if it has a legal obligation to process personal data about the individual. For example, an employer has a legal obligation to provide employee salary and tax details to HMRC, even if the employee requests they do not disclose this information.

Test yourself

Visit the 'Getting copies of your information (SAR)' section on the Information Commissioner's Office website and research how you can make a subject access request.

Imagine you have been a customer of a fencing supply business for several years and want to find out what information it holds about you. You intend to write an email to the business telling it you are making a subject access request. What details should you include in your email?

▼ Table 10.1 Rights relating to an individual's information and data under the GDPR

Right of access	Sometimes referred to as the 'right to ask', individuals can ask an organisation or business if it is storing or using their personal data, and request copies of their personal data being held. This is known as a subject access request (SAR).
Right to rectification	Individuals can request inaccurate data is corrected by an organisation or business or, if incomplete, ask for additional detail to be added.
Right to erasure	Sometimes referred to as the 'right to be forgotten', an individual can ask an organisation or business that holds their personal data to delete it.
Right to object	In certain circumstances, an individual can ask an organisation or business not to process, or to stop processing, their personal data.
Right to be informed	An individual must be informed if an organisation or business is using their personal data.
Right to restriction	An individual can ask an organisation or business to restrict the use of their personal data or not to delete it.
Right to data portability	An individual can ask an organisation or business to transfer their personal data to another organisation or business, or to provide a copy of the personal data in a format that is accessible.

Source: Information Commissioner's Office (2023)
A guide to individual rights

If an individual believes their personal data is not being processed lawfully, or their rights are not being respected, they can complain to the Information Commissioner's Office (ICO). The ICO is the independent body set up by the UK government to uphold information rights while balancing use of personal data in the public interest. It has an important role in improving information management practices. An organisation or business may have an obligation to report breaches in its data protection procedures to the ICO. The ICO can also take direct action, such as issuing fines, if an organisation or business fails to comply with its legal obligations.

Data storage requirements in relation to security and protection and how they help to prevent common threats

Cyberattacks

While a lack of internal controls can increase the risk of a data breach, organisations and businesses also need to be aware of the risk of a **cyberattack**. Although similar to hacking, cyberattacks are always malicious with the intent to cause harm. Where these attacks target government or national infrastructure, they can also be referred to as cyberwarfare or cyberterrorism.

Devices that access digital data are such a fundamental part of our working and private lives, for example online banking and accountancy tools as well as an increased reliance on smart technologies such as the use of GPS and automated machinery. Therefore, security steps must be taken to protect data and reduce the risk of illegal access by cybercriminals. These cybercriminals are becoming increasingly sophisticated in exploiting vulnerabilities, so individual device users, organisations and businesses should be aware of the common cybersecurity threats. Two of the biggest threats to users are phishing and malware.

Indicators of a cyberattack

Some cyberattacks are sophisticated and difficult to spot, but there are some potential indications to look out for:

▶ Spelling mistakes or inappropriate use of language: sometimes English is not the primary language of the cybercriminal, or else the language used is not appropriate to the context. For example, slang or informal language is unlikely to be used in a letter sent by a bank or HMRC.

▶ Poor quality images or images of text: text which appears as an image rather than type or blurry images are likely to have been copied from webpages and are unlikely to be original.

▶ Fake links: the text of a weblink may not be the true destination of where the link would take the user if they click on it. By hovering the pointer of the mouse over the link without clicking on it, the true destination will show.

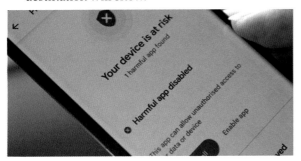

▲ Figure 10.2 Clicking on links may be harmful to your device

Phishing

This is a type of **spam** email used by cybercriminals to steal information from device users by pretending to be someone the user trusts. For example, the cybercriminal might pretend to be from the user's bank or building society, claiming there is a problem with the user's account in order to obtain security and account details so they can steal money, or they might send a plausible and official-looking email from a government agency to persuade the user to give them personal or sensitive information.

Most phishing attacks are undertaken via email. However, a similar approach is used with other communication methods, such as text messaging or telephone. In some sophisticated instances, cybercriminals also send information by post, asking the recipient to contact them urgently. In any phishing activity, the cybercriminals might use logos or addresses which look authentic. However, the contact details the recipient is asked to use, such as a website address, email address or telephone number, will connect them to the cybercriminal.

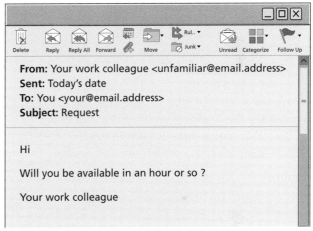

▲ Figure 10.3 Check emails carefully to ensure they are from a reputable source

Phishing attacks can be random and will be sent to many individuals in the hope that some will be fooled into thinking the message is real. Alternatively, attacks might be targeted at individuals working for a specific organisation or part of an organisation. These targeted phishing attacks

> **Key terms**
>
> *Cyberattack*: deliberate unauthorised attempt (successful or unsuccessful) to access a computer system or network, normally for an illegal purpose
>
> *Spam*: unsolicited and unwanted digital communications

are sometimes referred to as **spear phishing attacks**. They usually rely on having some existing information to create a message that appears to be from a colleague, for example asking the user to do something. Sometimes phishing messages contain links to malware which users unknowingly click before realising what they have done.

Malware

Malware is the name given to malicious software designed by a cybercriminal to damage or disrupt computer software or hardware. Cybercriminals develop malware for a variety of reasons. At the very least, malware can impact the performance of a computer device by using up resources such as disk space or processing capacity to make the computer device run slowly. At its worst, malware can lock users out of their devices or allow illegal activities to be undertaken on a computer without the user knowing, for example corporate espionage to steal intellectual property or stealing passwords of bank details for financial gain. There are many types of malware, but some of the most common are:

▶ **adware** which forces unwanted or irritating advertising, such as pop-ups, to be displayed on a device when the user is online
▶ **spyware** which enables a cybercriminal to monitor the actions of the device user without their knowledge (usually used to steal sensitive information like passwords or bank details).

Trojans

This malware is deliberately designed by cybercriminals to imitate harmless software. Because it looks harmless, it can trick users into installing it onto their computer. Users normally do this by either downloading what they believe to be normal software but which is actually from a malicious webpage or by following a link in spam email.

A **trojan** is not a virus or a worm, as it cannot self-replicate (i.e. execute itself). Instead, it requires the user to install it on their device. Once installed, a trojan attaches itself to the device startup routine and monitors what the user does. Once connected to the internet, the trojan allows the individual who designed it to take control of the user's device and steal, damage or perform harmful actions without the user realising. This can include accessing files, sending out spam emails to the user's contacts and running other programs.

Viruses

A **virus** is self-replicating software usually transmitted through internet connections that attaches to an

application. When the application is next used, the **virus** makes a copy of itself on the user's device and will either continue to run or may run every time the application is used. Once executed, a virus can corrupt data or provide cybercriminals with access to the device.

Worms

Like viruses, worms are self-replicating, but unlike viruses which attach themselves to an application, a **worm** is a standalone application and does not require a device user to execute it. A worm usually spreads through network connections, looking for and exploiting security vulnerabilities to install itself on other devices.

Malware usually relies on a combination of human and technical factors to enable installation on a user's device. Although malware commonly spreads through email, it can be attached to pirated software or installed by clicking on links in websites or pop-ups.

> ## Key terms
>
> **Spear phishing attacks**: targeted phishing attacks aimed at a particular person or department within an organisation
>
> **Adware**: a type of malware that causes unwanted advertising, such as pop-ups, to be displayed on a device when the user is online
>
> **Spyware**: a type of malware that enables a cybercriminal to monitor the actions of the device user without their knowledge and to steal sensitive information
>
> **Trojan**: a type of malware that, once installed in a user's device, attaches itself to the device startup routine and monitors what the user does once the user connects to the internet; it allows the individual who designed it to take control of the user's device and steal, damage or perform harmful actions without the user realising
>
> **Virus**: self-replicating software usually transmitted via the internet that attaches to an application inside a user's device and makes a copy of itself; it may continue to run or run every time the application is used, corrupting data and/or providing cybercriminals with access to the device
>
> **Application**: (also referred to as 'app') a program designed for a specific purpose
>
> **Worm**: a malicious program that is self-replicating but does not attach to an application and does not require a device user to execute it; it usually spreads through network connections, looking for and exploiting security vulnerabilities to install itself on other devices

Reducing the risk of a cyberattack

There are many actions individuals, organisations and businesses can take to secure their online presence and protect their devices, information and data. These include:

▶ only storing data that is needed for as long as it is necessary

▶ anonymising data to reduce access to non-essential information

▶ providing regular refresher training for staff regarding data protection

▶ using different email addresses to separate life and work

▶ reviewing access privileges for applications carefully during installation

▶ reviewing social media privacy settings to keep online activity private

▶ reviewing the settings on mobile devices to potentially restrict access to location information

▶ not buying or using pirated software

▶ keeping software such as operating systems and applications up to date by installing **patches** as they are issued

▶ using **strong passwords** and considering using a password manager application

▶ being aware of the security risks associated with using public Wi-Fi networks

▶ reviewing web browser security settings to block unwanted **cookies** and pop-ups, and restricting websites' ability to track browsing

▶ using **multi-factor authentication**.

Test yourself

Think about the passwords you use. How could you make them stronger and yet still memorable?

Two-factor or multi-factor authentication

This is a security mechanism to confirm the identity of an individual and give them access to a secure resource or information using two or more verification factors. For example, as well as entering a password, a user might be asked to:

▶ answer a secret question (for example something they know such as the name of their first pet or their place of birth)

▶ enter a unique PIN or access code emailed or texted to them, or gain access through an authentication app

▶ provide biometric information (for example scan their fingerprint or use a facial recognition system).

▲ Figure 10.4 Two-factor identification

Back-up of data

Organisations and businesses should also consider backing-up important information regularly. This will enable them to recover quickly in the event of data loss and will also help if the data being used becomes corrupted in any way. For a small-scale business, backing-up can be done using portable hard drives, but for organisations handling large quantities of data or highly confidential data, this may be via a remote storage facility or **cloud** storage.

Key terms

Patches: regular updates made by a software company to fix known problems with their software; some software products automatically check for patches when a device is attached to the internet and prompt the user to install them

Strong passwords: passwords that are designed to be hard for someone to guess or a programmer to work out; they usually contain at least 12 characters consisting of a mix of special characters/symbols, numbers and uppercase and lowercase letters

Cookie: a text file that contains data used to identify your computer/device and is downloaded to your device when you visit a website; while most cookies are harmless and intended to enhance your browsing experience, some can be used without your permission to track your online activity

Multi-factor authentication: also known as two-factor authentication, this is an account log-in process that requires a user to enter two or more pieces of evidence in order to gain access

Cloud: software and services which are made available to users via the internet, rather than being run on the device itself or the organisation's own local servers

Artificial intelligence

Given the increasingly attractive benefits of artificial intelligence (AI) to society, it may be tempting to use online AI tools to automate routine data-processing tasks and increase productivity. The use of AI by organisations and businesses can potentially save time and money. However, there are still some potential risks which have not yet been robustly addressed. For example, depending on the technology, there is the potential for information to be accessible to others which might inadvertently result in a data breach, or allow competitors to access client data. There is also the potential for the technology to **hallucinate** and produce a response containing misleading or false information which looks credible. Until organisations and businesses can be assured that data input is secure and data processing outputs are trustworthy and reliable, there is a need to exercise caution when using AI and for experienced individuals to check the accuracy of the outputs.

Key term

Hallucinate: in the context of AI, this refers to when the technology misinterprets data and the resulting output is inaccurate or does not make sense; this type of misinterpretation presents risks to the user if the output is not checked for accuracy before being used

How to respond to security breaches

To reduce the risk of cyberattacks, most organisations and businesses have policies in place of not sharing or asking for sensitive or security information by email or telephone.

What to do following a security breach

All organisations and businesses should have policies and procedures in place to respond to a suspected or confirmed security or data breach. The priority should be to identify if and how the breach occurred and take immediate action to contain it and stop any further breaches. The next steps should be to:

▶ review the relevant policies and procedures and implement any actions to reduce the possibility of a similar breach happening again

▶ review security settings and check that firewalls and anti-virus protection are up to date on all devices, and to require all staff to change their passwords

▶ provide staff with updated training to recognise suspicious messages and other security threats,

for example if users receive a suspicious communication, they should not trust the contact details given in the email or text message but should contact the organisation directly

▶ check if the breach involves personal data; if it does, it may need to be reported to the ICO, which is the data protection authority (DPA) in the UK as well as the individual(s) whose data has been accessed or made available to unauthorised persons.

Where a breach is reportable to the ICO, this must be done within 72 hours of discovering it. The ICO has a self-assessment tool that organisations can use if they are not sure whether the breach is reportable, which you can find on its website.

If a breach is reportable, organisations can either complete the ICO's online form or a downloadable form if the organisation is unable to access its computer system, for example due to a cyberattack.

If the breach is the result of a significant cyber incident, it may also be appropriate to report it to the National Cyber Security Centre (NCSC). If the organisation or business is not sure whom to contact, it can use the UK government signposting service; you can search for 'where to report a cyber incident' on the UK Government website (www.gov.uk) to access it.

Preventing security breaches through fraud, theft or loss

In addition to threats of online cyberattacks, organisations and businesses should also be aware of other potential risks such as fraud. If important or sensitive documents need to be distributed, organisations should ideally do this through secure electronic means. Furthermore, the documents should be protected from unauthorised edits by saving them in a read-only format or applying restrictive settings. For example, a document might be sent as a read-only PDF file or password-protected Word file. However, if hard copies of documents need to be sent, organisations normally use a secure, traceable postal or courier service. The documents are securely packaged and clearly labelled.

Industry tip

Keeping blank copies of letterheaded paper with the organisation's logo securely locked in a cabinet to which only authorised staff have access can reduce the potential for a criminal to produce official-looking documents.

Organisations and businesses can also help to reduce the risk of information loss or theft by keeping paper copies of confidential information secure, for example in a locked cupboard or filing cabinet or in a locked room to which only certain staff have access. In extreme cases, documents may be stored in a safe. Photocopiers should be checked after use to make sure an important document has not been left inside. It should also be ensured that important documents are shredded or securely disposed of once they are no longer required.

Organisations and businesses normally invest significant resources into training their staff to make sure they understand their legal responsibilities when handling data, as well as how they should manage data to reduce the risk of security breaches. Initial training is normally included within the induction process for new employees when they start work. It is then reinforced through regular refresher training to make sure employees understand how they can contribute to good data management practice and to make them aware of potential new security risks.

Purpose of current legislation

Given the value associated with information and data and the various legal and illegal purposes for which it may be used, current legislation associated with personal information and data has a number of closely related objectives:
▶ support organisations and businesses with their lawful processing of personal data
▶ protect the personal data of individuals
▶ regulate how organisations process individuals' data
▶ prevent organisations from sharing/selling individuals' data without permission.

The aim of legislation is to support organisations and businesses to manage information and data appropriately and provide data owners with confidence that their data or property is secure. However, as there is a continuous risk of data breaches and criminal activity is becoming increasingly sophisticated, individuals, organisations and businesses within the land-based sector should take a proactive approach to data security.

Data Protection Act 2018 and the GDPR

The key legislation in the UK associated with personal data is the Data Protection Act 2018 and the UK GDPR.

These are the UK's implementation of the European Union General Data Protection Regulation (GDPR) and were intended to support the needs of an increasingly digital economy and society. Together they govern how personal data is used by the government, organisations and businesses. They are together informally referred to as the GDPR.

In the UK, the GDPR regulates either:
▶ 'the processing of personal data wholly or partly by automated means; or
▶ the processing of personal data which forms part of, or is intended to form part of, a filing system'.

Source: Information Commissioner's Office website,
What is personal information: a guide

Therefore, the GDPR is mainly focused on electronic **processing** of organised personal data, such as employment records stored by an employer in a computer system.

> **Key term**
>
> **Processing**: a variety of operations performed on raw data to transform it into a useful format; it may involve collecting, recording, storing, retrieving, organising, structuring, sharing, disclosing, adapting, altering, erasing or destroying data

There are two key roles associated with personal data processing. These are the 'controller' and the 'processor', and both have specific responsibilities:
▶ The controller makes decisions on the reason for and method of processing personal data.
▶ The processor is responsible for processing the personal data on behalf of the controller.

It is important that each role understands their own responsibilities, as well as being confident that the other is compliant with their own responsibilities.

> **Improve your English**
>
> Compliant and compliance come from the verb 'comply', meaning to follow or obey instructions or legal requirements. Think of some examples of procedures your employer might ask you to follow in order to be compliant.

Data protection principles

The GDPR sets out the data protection principles that everyone responsible for using personal data must comply with. These principles are stated at the start of the legislation and considered to be the foundations upon which good data protection practice is built. They require everyone to ensure personal data is:

▶ used fairly, lawfully and transparently (i.e. it must be clear to the individual why their personal data is being used and they can be reassured it is for a lawful purpose)

▶ used for specified, explicit purposes (i.e. the individual must be told what their personal data is being used for and this use cannot be vague or general)

▶ used in a way that is adequate, relevant and limited to only what is necessary (i.e. an individual's personal data should only be used for the purpose they were told it was to be used for)

▶ accurate and, where necessary, kept up to date (i.e. an individual's personal data should be regularly checked and, if necessary, amended as soon as possible to ensure it is correct)

▶ kept for no longer than is necessary (i.e. an individual's personal data must not be kept after it has been used for the original purpose)

▶ handled in a way that ensures appropriate security, including protection against unlawful or unauthorised processing, access, loss, destruction or damage (i.e. an individual's personal data must be securely stored so it can only be used for the intended reason).

If an individual is unhappy with how their data is being used by an organisation or business, they can make a complaint to the ICO. If the ICO determines the data protection requirements have not been complied with, it can take legal action and/or fine the organisation or business. The fines are intended to be proportionate and incentivise organisations and businesses to comply with their data protection responsibilities. The level of any fine is determined on the individual circumstances of each infringement. Currently, the standard maximum amount is either £8.7 million or 2 per cent of the total annual worldwide turnover of the organisation or business (whichever is higher). However, in serious non-compliance, the higher maximum fine is either £17.5 million or 4 per cent of the total annual worldwide turnover of the organisation or business (whichever is higher).

Test yourself

Adele needs to hire some landscaping machinery from a hire company. As part of the initial checks, she is asked to provide biometric information (a scan of her face taken using her computer's camera) and photographic identification (a scan of her driving licence). It is not clear to Adele why this personal data is needed and for how long the company will keep it.

Consider the data protection principles above and suggest how the hire company could reassure potential customers like Adele that it is compliant with data protection law.

Assessment practice

1 Identify **three** examples of special categories of personal data. (3 marks)
2 Explain why '123456' is not considered a strong password. (2 marks)
3 Describe **three** potential warning signs of a phishing email. (3 marks)
4 Explain how two-factor authentication works. (3 marks)
5 Describe **two** occasions when an employer should provide data security training for their staff. (4 marks)
6 Job applicants have certain data rights. For example, they may believe their application has not been fairly handled so might want to find out more about how their personal information was used.

Explain **two** data requests a land-based employer should ensure they are able to manage. (4 marks)
7 Bryony runs a small wildlife consultancy in southwest England. The company has been operating for 12 years and has a well-developed customer base. However, a new competitor consultancy is advertising on social media that it is expanding into the southwest. Bryony wants to ensure this competitor does not access client or other commercial data about her company.

Explain how Bryony might protect the company's commercially sensitive data from competitors. (6 marks)
8 Explain **three** reasons why a competitor might be interested in accessing a business' client and customer sales data. (6 marks)

9 Dani has chosen to work as a self-employed garden design consultant in East Anglia. To help generate new clients and customers, Dani has come up with a name for the business as well as a logo. In addition, Dani is creating leaflets and building a website which will feature example designs and information to promote the new business.

Explain how a newly established business owner like Dani might protect the copyright of their work. (6 marks)

10 Describe the possible impact of a cyberattack on a land-based business. (6 marks)

Further reading

You may find some of the following websites helpful for further information on information and data:
▶ National Cyber Security Centre
▶ *Cyber security for farmers* on the National Cyber Security Centre website
▶ Information Commissioner's Office
▶ Intellectual Property Office.

Glossary

Abatement notice: a legal enforcement notice that informs the recipient of actions they are required to take in relation to a statutory nuisance

Accident: a distinct and identifiable unintended incident, associated with an external stimulus which causes physical injury; the term includes non-consensual violence to individuals at work

Adaption strategies: actions and activities undertaken to limit the negative impacts of climate change

Adware: a type of malware that causes unwanted advertising, such as pop-ups, to be displayed on a device when the user is online

Agricultural activities: defined by the HSE as including cultivation of ground, sowing and harvesting of crops, horticulture, fruit growing, seed growing, dairy farming, livestock breeding and keeping (including the management of livestock up to the point of slaughter or export from Great Britain, so it covers livestock markets), forestry (and arboriculture), the use of land as grazing land, market gardens and nursery grounds, and the preparation of land for agricultural use

Application: also referred to as 'app', a program designed for a specific purpose

Appointed person: someone in the workplace who is responsible for looking after first-aid equipment and facilities and calling the emergency services; the role includes responsibility for maintaining and replacing the contents of any first-aid kit(s)

Audits: official inspections of an organisation's financial reports usually carried out by an independent body

Capability: a judgement made about an individual's ability to undertake the role for which they are employed; an employer may choose to have a discrete capability procedure, rather than deal with performance issues through a disciplinary procedure

Capital gains: the increase in the value of a capital asset, for example a rental property or second home, when it is sold; put simply, a capital gain occurs when an asset is sold for more than what was originally paid for it

Carbon footprint: the amount of greenhouse gases released as a result of a business' or organisation's activities; the term includes all greenhouse gases but makes explicit reference to carbon because carbon dioxide

(CO_2) is considered the main greenhouse gas and the impact of other greenhouse gases can be expressed as carbon dioxide equivalent

CE: certification marking required for certain products sold in the EU market; it shows that the product meets relevant health, safety or environmental requirements

Circular economy: system in which pollution and waste are eliminated as resources are kept in circulation through reuse or recycling, for example composting, refurbishment and remanufacture

Climate change: a long-term shift in temperature and weather patterns

Cloud: software and services which are made available to users via the internet, rather than being run on the device itself or the organisation's own local servers

Coaching: a process aimed at improving performance, where an individual learns by being helped to find the answer to their own problems; it focuses on the current position rather than what has happened in the past or what might happen in the future

Commodities: economic goods or resources that can be bought or sold, for example coffee, copper and barley

Competent person: based on the HSE definition of 'competence', this is an individual with the training, skills, experience, knowledge and ability to perform a task safely; the specific level of competence of an individual should be proportionate to their role

Conservation covenants: legally binding agreements between a landowner (such as a property developer) and a charity or public body (such as a local authority) to do (or not do) something to conserve the heritage or natural features of their land; these covenants must deliver a public good but do not have to allow public access onto the land

Continuous employment: when an employee works for an employer without a break in employment; it is calculated from the first day they started working for that employer; some breaks in employment count towards continuous employment, for example annual leave or sickness, maternity, paternity, parental or adoption leave, but other breaks do not, such as when the employee is on strike

Cookie: a text file that contains data used to identify your computer/device and is downloaded to your device when you visit a website; while most cookies are harmless and intended to enhance your browsing experience, some can be used without your permission to track your online activity

Creditors: individuals or institutions such as banks and finance companies that extend credit to a business or organisation to borrow money, usually in the form of a loan or contract, which must be paid back

Cyberattack: deliberate unauthorised attempt (successful or unsuccessful) to access a computer system or network, normally for an illegal purpose

Dangerous occurrence: an incident which has the potential to cause death or serious injury, even though no one is harmed; the types of incident are listed in RIDDOR

DBS check: a process carried out by the Disclosure and Barring Service (DBS) that provides a criminal record data check of an individual; the individual receives a certificate and it can be valid for up to three years, but this depends on the employer requirements and role being carried out by the individual

Discrimination: disadvantaging an individual by offering them less favourable treatment in comparison to others; the treatment does not have to be an intentional or deliberate action, or series of actions, to be considered unlawful

Discrimination by association: discrimination where the individual concerned does not hold the protected characteristic but is wrongly believed to hold it because they associate with someone else who holds the protected characteristic, for example an individual is wrongly believed to be trans because they regularly go out with and associate with trans people

Discrimination by perception: discrimination where the individual concerned does not hold the protected characteristic but is wrongly believed to hold it, for example an individual is wrongly believed to hold specific religious beliefs because of their name or place of birth

Dividends: how companies distribute their earnings to shareholders; when a company pays a dividend, each share of stock of the company an individual owns entitles them to a set dividend payment (which can be in the form of cash, additional shares of stock or warrants to buy stock)

Dynamic risk assessment: continuously reviewing a risk assessment throughout the period of work to respond to changing circumstances and hazards

Employee: someone who works under a fixed-term or permanent contract

Equality: providing the same opportunities to everyone by removing barriers to success and not unfairly providing an individual with less favourable treatment in comparison to others

Equitable approach: identifying existing differences and addressing these by individually adjusting resources and opportunities to allow everyone to achieve a positive outcome; in short, achieving a level playing field

Equity: justice and fairness for an individual

FAQs: frequently asked questions may be found on a company website or at the bottom of a page of instructions relating to a product or service; their location may depend on the business and not all businesses have them

Firewall: a specialist security feature that selectively manages the communication of data into, within or out of a network; it is intended to block data that is considered potentially dangerous or is not trusted

Forcings: factors that affect climate which are not normally considered to be part of the global climate system; they can include natural phenomena such as volcanic eruptions or changes in the orbit of the Earth and the Earth's crust, as well as changes in the composition of the atmosphere as a result of human activity

Fraudulent action: an intentionally deceptive and dishonest act or omission that misleads, or attempts to mislead, another, in order to obtain a financial or other benefit or to avoid an obligation or incurring an obligation; types of fraud include tax fraud, credit card fraud and bankruptcy fraud

Global warming: the increase in the average surface temperature of the Earth as a consequence of greenhouse gas emissions

Greenhouse gases: gases that absorb infrared radiation emitted from the Earth's surface, rather than letting it travel into space, and re-emit it back to the Earth, causing the surface to heat up; key greenhouse gases associated with human activity include carbon dioxide (CO_2), methane (CH_4) and nitrous oxide (N_2O)

Greenwashing: a derogatory term used to describe an approach to marketing where an organisation or business presents its activities, products or services as environmentally sound, when this might not be true; critics suggest this misleads or deceives customers and the public, eroding trust and undermining genuine efforts towards sustainable goals

Grievance: a formal complaint made by an employee about their treatment at work by their employer or someone else they work with

Hacking: a collective term used to describe the use of computer networks to gain unauthorised access to or control over data

Hallucinate: in the context of AI, this refers to when the technology misinterprets data and the resulting output is inaccurate or does not make sense; this type of misinterpretation presents risks to the user if the output is not checked for accuracy before being used

Hazard: something which has the potential to cause harm or adversely affect the health of individuals

Health surveillance: a series of repeated health checks intended to identify ill health caused by work activities; in addition to where individuals may be exposed to substances hazardous to health, health surveillance may also be required to comply with other regulations (for example where an individual's health is at risk from noise or vibration)

Holder: defined by the Environment Agency as the legal entity or individual who has control over waste at the time it is discarded

Identifier: a single piece of personal data that can be used to identify an individual

Inclusion: the creation of an environment in which all individuals feel they are respected, accommodated and welcomed

Induction: the structured process where new staff are introduced to their role (including colleagues, facilities and the workplace), given responsibilities and provided with the equipment and resources they require; the key knowledge is provided on the first day, but the whole process may take several days or weeks, depending on the role and the employer's situation (for example multiple worksites)

Integrated working platforms: they have their own controls that are linked to and isolate the controls in the lift truck so that the height and movements of the lift truck and working platform can only be controlled by the individual in the working platform; they provide a higher level of safety than non-integrated working platforms

Intellectual property (IP): creations of the mind, such as inventions, literary and artistic works, designs, symbols, names and images used in commerce; IP is protected in law by, for example, patents, copyright and trademarks, which enable people to earn recognition or financial benefit from what they invent or create; the IP system aims to create an environment in which creativity and innovation can flourish by ensuring the right balance between the interests of innovators and the wider public

Internal dynamics: the ongoing interactions between the different interconnected systems which impact the global climate system; these include the atmosphere, hydrosphere, lithosphere, cryosphere and biosphere

Interpersonal skills: abilities that relate to how an individual communicates, interacts and collaborates with others

Job specification (or person specification): a list of skills, knowledge, experience and qualities that an employer requires an individual to hold for them to successfully undertake a specific role; this is different from a job description, which sets out the tasks and responsibilities an individual is expected to undertake if appointed to a specific role; however, it is common for a job description and a person specification to be included in one document

Key performance indicators (KPIs): individual criteria that can be measured and quantified; this means that once each criterion is measured or counted, it is expressed as a numerical value, which has meaning

Land cover: the physical type of land (vegetation type, water features or construction)

Land use: the activity or purpose the land is used for (recreation, food production, housing)

Material breach: a contravention of health and safety law that an HSE inspector considers to be sufficiently serious that they need to write to the duty holder formally requiring them to take action to deal with it; the duty holder (the employer or self-employed person) is then required to pay the HSE for the time it has taken to identify the breach and support the duty holder to deal with the breach (known as the fee for intervention, FFI)

Method statements: documents that describe exactly how work tasks or activities are to be carried out and contain all the control measures identified in related risk assessments; sharing method statements with workers is an effective way to ensure they understand how they are expected to undertake an activity

Mitigation strategies: actions and activities undertaken to prevent or reduce any contribution to climate change

Modern slavery: the exploitation of individuals for personal or commercial gain; it is a serious crime that violates the human rights of victims; the term covers human trafficking, slavery, servitude and forced or compulsory labour, and its victims are defined by the Slavery and Human Trafficking (Definition of Victim) Regulations 2022

Multi-factor authentication: also known as two-factor authentication, this is an account log-in process that requires a user to enter two or more pieces of evidence in order to gain access

Nationality: the status of belonging to a particular nation; it is associated with citizenship and may not necessarily reflect where an individual was born

Net zero: achieving a balance between all greenhouse gases (including CO_2, CH_4 and N_2O) released to the atmosphere and the greenhouse gases removed from it; it differs from the term 'carbon neutral' which is narrow in scope and normally refers to achieving a balance between CO_2 released to the atmosphere and CO_2 removed from it

Non-integrated working platforms do not have separate controls so all lift truck and working platform movements are controlled by the lift truck operator, and therefore, should only be used in exceptional circumstances for 'occasional unplanned use'

Objective justification: when a proportionate and legitimate reason is used to justify applying a provision, criterion or practice in a situation when it would normally be considered direct or indirect discrimination, i.e. there is a justification to offer less favourable treatment to individuals or groups who hold a protected characteristic; for example, an employer is unable to recruit someone with a specific protected characteristic because of the occupational requirements of the job

Open-ended questions: questions requiring a detailed answer based on the respondent's knowledge, feelings and experience (qualitative data); they cannot be answered with a simple 'yes' or 'no' or with a specific piece of information (compare closed questions which are popular in questionnaires because they give a limited amount of options to choose from and collect quantitative data, which is easier to analyse)

Ordinary shares: also called common shares, these are normal shares issued by a limited company and are stocks sold on a public exchange; each share of stock generally gives its owner the right to a single vote at a company shareholders' meeting; unlike in the case of preferred shares (share issue), the owner of ordinary shares is not guaranteed a dividend

Patches: regular updates made by a software company to fix known problems with their software; some software products automatically check for patches when a device is attached to the internet and prompt the user to install them

Pollution: the release or introduction of something into the environment that causes an adverse effect; it can take a variety of forms (for example gas, solid, energy) and arises from both natural and human activities; the origin of a pollutant is commonly categorised as either:

- point source, as it originates from a specific location (for example a fuel container leaking into a stream or river)
- diffuse source (or non-point source), as it originates from multiple locations (for example pesticide or fertiliser run-off from agricultural land)

Positive action: action taken by an employer to help or support an individual with a protected characteristic, for example providing upskilling language courses to support employees whose first language is not English

Post-nominals: combinations of letters placed after a person's name to indicate achievement of an academic qualification (such as a degree) or a professional qualification (for example Chartered status), membership of an organisation or award of a national honour (for example Member of the Order of the British Empire MBE); they are often used by individuals in their email signature, on business cards and in social media profiles to summarise their achievements and provide an indication of their expertise or credibility

Processing: a variety of operations performed on raw data to transform it into a useful format; it may involve collecting, recording, storing, retrieving, organising, structuring, sharing, disclosing, adapting, altering, erasing or destroying data

Profit margins: financial ratio that measures the percentage of profit earned by a company in relation to its sales revenue

Progressive condition: a health condition which gradually gets worse over time

Protected characteristic: a trait associated with an individual which it is illegal to discriminate against

Protected period: period of time that starts when a woman becomes pregnant and continues through to the end of ordinary maternity leave (26 weeks after giving birth), or until she returns to work, whichever is sooner

Public authorities: organisations that perform a public function, which include ministerial departments and local authorities

Public bodies: publicly funded organisations that deliver a government or public service but are not ministerial departments, for example Animal and Plant Health Agency, British Wool, Environment Agency, Health and Safety Executive, Joint Nature Conservation Committee, Met Office and Veterinary Medicines Directorate; public bodies may also be partially or wholly funded through industry levies (payment demands) or customers directly paying for specific services

Qualitative data: non-numerical data, such as words, images or observations; it is generally used to gain an understanding of human behaviour, attitudes and beliefs

Quantitative data: information with a numerical value that can be quantified by being counted or measured for example length in centimetres or weight in kilograms; quantitative data tends to be structured and is suitable for statistical analysis

Racial groups: groups of people who share the same protected characteristic associated with race or ethnicity

Reasonable adjustments: changes that an employer or organisation must make to prevent an individual with a disability from being disadvantaged; what is objectively deemed reasonable will depend on factors such as the practicality of the adjustment, the cost and resources required to make the adjustment, and the size and type of organisation

Reasonably practicable: refers to employers exercising their judgement as to whether the time, money and trouble required to control workplace hazards is proportionate to the level of risk posed

Refresher training: a CPD activity that allows an individual to reinforce their existing skills and knowledge and ensure they are up to date with current industry standards

Restrictive covenant or **exclusivity clause:** a contract clause that sets out what work an employee may or may not do (such as working for someone else) during their employment or when they leave their employment

Retention rate: the accuracy of the recall of information over a given period of time

Risk: the likelihood of a hazard occurring and causing harm or adversely affecting the health of individuals

Self-employed person: someone who works independently for themselves, normally operating under either a service contract or consultancy agreement

Service level agreement (SLA): a contract between a business and a customer that states the service to be provided, the level of performance to be expected, how performance will be measured and approved, and what happens if performance levels are not met

Share issue: when a limited company offers equity in the form of shares to investors; this is an effective way for a public limited company to raise capital by selling either existing or new shares to the public, employees or a group of investors; a share issue can be either an issue in accordance with existing shareholders' pre-emptive right to subscribe or a directed share issue

Small- or medium-sized enterprises (SMEs): in the UK, a business is usually considered to be an SME if it has fewer than 250 employees and a turnover of less than £50 million

SMART: acronym standing for Specific, Measurable, Attainable, Relevant and Time-bound; a SMART objective incorporates all of these criteria to help focus efforts and increase the likelihood of achievement

Soft skills: attributes associated with an individual's awareness of, and ability to express and manage, their behaviours and emotions

Spam: unsolicited and unwanted digital communications

Spear phishing attacks: targeted phishing attacks aimed at a particular person or department within an organisation

Spyware: a type of malware that enables a cybercriminal to monitor the actions of the device user without their knowledge and to steal sensitive information

Stakeholders: any person, group or organisation that has an interest in the activities and performance of a business; they can be internal and external, from individuals to local communities to the government

Statutory nuisance: something that poses a public health risk (for example animal keeping, offensive smells, dust, noise or smoke) or substantially interferes with someone's reasonable enjoyment of their property, either regularly or for an unreasonable period of time

Stereotypes: general and oversimplified assumptions, ideas or characteristics which are used to represent a type or group of people; stereotyping a group of people does not reflect the diversity or complexity of the individuals within that group

Strong passwords: passwords that are designed to be hard for someone to guess or a programmer to work out; they usually contain at least 12 characters consisting of a mix of special characters/symbols, numbers and uppercase and lowercase letters

Sustainable development: defined by the Brundtland Report as 'development that meets the needs of the present without compromising the ability of future generations to meet their own needs'; this definition is often interpreted and adapted to meet the circumstances of the environmental, social, economic and cultural context in which it is being used

Tax deductible: expenses that are able to be deducted from taxable income or the amount of tax to be paid

Trojan: a type of malware that, once installed in a user's device, attaches itself to the device startup routine and monitors what the user does once the user connects to the internet; it allows the individual who designed it to take control of the user's device and steal, damage or perform harmful actions without the user realising

UKCA: certification marking used since 1 January 2021 that must be placed on certain products sold in the Great Britain market; it is gradually replacing the CE marking in the UK

Vicarious liability: when someone such as an employer or organisation is held responsible for unlawful acts or conduct of its employees or someone acting on its behalf

Virus: self-replicating software usually transmitted via the internet that attaches to an application inside a user's device and makes a copy of itself; it may continue to run or run every time the application is used, corrupting data and/or providing cybercriminals with access to the device

Vulnerable workers: a collective term used to refer to young workers under the age of 18 (who may need more supervision than adults), migrant workers (commonly working in agriculture and food-processing industries), new or expectant mothers and people with disabilities

Waste consignment notes: notes required every time hazardous waste (such as pesticides and oils) is moved, irrespective of whether it is passed on to someone else or not; they should be retained for at least three years

Waste transfer licence: licence normally issued by the Environment Agency which is required by any organisation that transports (carries) waste, irrespective of whether it owns or produced the waste

Waste transfer notes: legal documents which are required when non-hazardous waste is passed on to others, so that there is an audit trail from the point at which the waste is produced through to disposal; these notes should be retained for at least two years; a waste transfer note is not required for the initial collection of household waste but is required if the waste is subsequently passed on

Whistleblower: a person who discloses information about unlawful or immoral activity in the workplace; whistleblowing is also known as 'making a disclosure in the public interest'

Work: this includes time spent directly undertaking the contracted role or task, but also covers role-specific training, paid or unpaid overtime at the request of the employer, time spent at the workplace 'on call', working lunches and time spent travelling between home and the workplace if the individual does not have a fixed workplace; it does not include voluntary unpaid overtime, breaks when no work is done, holidays or travelling outside normal working hours

Worker: someone engaged under a casual contract

Working time: when a worker is required to perform work activities, duties or training at their employer's instruction; it does not include a worker's routine travel between their home and their workplace or rest breaks during the working day

Worm: a malicious program that is self-replicating but does not attach to an application and does not require a device user to execute it; it usually spreads through network connections, looking for and exploiting security vulnerabilities to install itself on other devices

Young workers: individuals who are above the statutory school leaving age but under 18 (i.e. any worker aged 15, 16 or 17); young workers must not work more than 8 hours a day and 40 hours a week and employers should be aware that if they use young workers, they must not discriminate against them because of their age

Yours sincerely: a standard sign-off for a formal email or letter when you know the recipient ('sincerely' means genuinely and is used to emphasise your honest intentions towards the person); 'sincerely' can be replaced with faithfully or truly when writing to someone whose name you do not know (for example you have addressed them as 'Sir' or 'Madam')

Index